D0984326

American Independence
The Growth of an Idea

BROWN UNIVERSITY BICENTENNIAL PUBLICATIONS
Studies in the Fields of General Scholarship

The frontispiece (reduced) in certain copies of John Dickinson's *Letters From a Farmer In Pennsylvania*, Third Edition, no. 54h, The John Carter Brown Library, Brown University.

American Independence

THE GROWTH OF AN IDEA

A Bibliographical Study of the American Political Pamphlets
Printed Between 1764 and 1776 Dealing with the Dispute
Between Great Britain and Her Colonies

BY THOMAS R. ADAMS

Librarian, The John Carter Brown Library, Brown University

BROWN UNIVERSITY PRESS
Providence, Rhode Island
1965

COPYRIGHT © 1965 BY THE COLONIAL SOCIETY OF MASSACHUSETTS
ALL RIGHTS RESERVED

LIBRARY OF CONGRESS CATALOG CARD NUMBER: 62-16995

This book first appeared in the
Publications of the Colonial Society of Massachusetts
Transactions, Vol. 43

E
189
.Z99
A4

PRINTED AT THE ANTHOENSEN PRESS, PORTLAND, MAINE
ILLUSTRATIONS BY THE MERIDEN GRAVURE COMPANY, MERIDEN, CONN.

To R. G. A.

Alma College Library
Alma, Michigan

Contents

Illustrations

Introduction

THIS is a bibliographical study of the American political pamphlets printed between the passage of the Stamp Act and the Declaration of Independence. It is confined to the pamphlets which discuss the issues and events that in a dozen years changed the British colonies in North America from loyal and even enthusiastic members of a newly enlarged empire into a nation prepared to destroy by force bonds that had bound them to the mother country for more than a century and a half. Out of the vast body of writing that has been called the literature of the American Revolution, published between 1764 and 1783, a specific class has been selected for study. First, it must be American. Second, it must concern issues or events that led directly to the Declaration of Independence. Third, it must be a political essay, and fourth, it must have appeared in the form of a pamphlet. Fifth, it must have been printed before July 4, 1776.

In this study I have used the test of publication as the basis of inclusion. By publication I mean: the pamphlets written by Americans which were printed in America; the pamphlets written by Englishmen and first printed in England which were reprinted in America; and the pamphlets written by Englishmen which, although not reprinted in America, elicited a reply written by an American and printed in America. This approach involves many problems of interpretation. At the outset, however, it has resulted in some interesting revelations.

Paine's *Common Sense* of 1776 was a runaway best seller. The twenty-five American editions recorded here only confirm that fact. However, it was something of a freak. The next ranking pamphlet went through less than half as many American editions. The following tabulation of the dozen most frequently printed pamphlets is significant.

	Number of American Editions	Number of American Cities and Towns in which editions appeared
Paine, *Common Sense*, 1776 (no. 222)	25	13
*Shipley, *Speech*, 1774 (no. 141)	12	8
**Dickinson, *Letters*, 1768 (no. 54)	7	5
Lee, *Strictures*, 1774 (no. 125)	7	6
*Rokeby, *Considerations*, 1774 (no. 134)	7	5
Allen, *Oration*, 1773 (no. 91)	7	4

Dulany, *Considerations*, 1765 (no. 11)	5	4
Franklin, *Examination*, 1766 (no. 31)	5	5
*Shipley, *Sermon*, 1773 (no. 100)	5	5
Hancock, *Oration*, 1774 (no. 117)	5	4
*Price, *Observations*, 1776 (no. 224)	5	4
Hutchinson, *Letters*, 1773 (no. 96)	5	2

* Pamphlets that appeared first in England.
** A pamphlet that was first printed in American newspapers.

The most interesting things about the above tabulation, and the bibliography as a whole, are the titles that either are not present or apparently had a limited circulation in America. The three pamphlets by James Otis appeared in a single American edition although each went through at least two London editions. Thomas Jefferson's *Summary View*, 1774, was printed only twice in America, a small Williamsburg edition and one brought out in Philadelphia. James Wilson's carefully wrought *Considerations on the Nature and extent of the Legislative authority of the British Parliament*, 1774, was printed only once, as were Alexander Hamilton's two contributions. None of the Boston radicals made the list unless one wishes to give them credit for the Hutchinson *Letters* which they published. Even the noted Tory pamphlets of Thomas Bradbury Chandler, James Galloway, and Samuel Seabury did not achieve wide circulation although in the case of the latter two threats by patriotic organizations probably provide part of the explanation. With the exception of his *Examination* of 1766 and his *Causes of the Present Distractions* of 1774, there are no works by Benjamin Franklin and in neither case did the author originally intend them to be political pamphlets. The *Examination* was an oral statement, the printed text of which Franklin always regarded as highly unsatisfactory. The *Causes of the Present Distractions* was a compilation by a Tory printer, James Rivington, from a group of writings that had originally appeared in the English press. Franklin, like Arthur Lee, devoted most of his energies to addressing the reading public in England. The two most notable writings by John Adams, *A Dissertation on the Canon and Feudal Law* of 1768 and his "Novanglus Letters" of 1775, were not issued separately in this country until after 1776, although the former was reprinted in England in 1768. The same thing is true of certain writings of Samuel Adams, William Henry Drayton, and John Joachim Zubly. There are also a number of English pamphlets frequently mentioned in the historical literature that will not be found in this study. They include Samuel Johnson's *Taxation no Tyranny* of 1775 and John Wesley's *A Calm Address to our American Colonies* of 1775. They were neither reprinted in America nor did they move any American pamphlet writer to reply to them. This is not to say that English pamphlets were not read in America. Study of booksellers' advertisements in newspapers and of the catalogues of the library of Thomas Jefferson and The Library Company of Philadelphia, or a reading of the correspondence between the thoughtful and important Americans of the period, quickly dispels any such notion. English pamphlets were sent to America in substantial numbers. Here I want to emphasize the pamphlets printed by American printers. In his *Prelude to Independence: The Newspaper War on Britain 1764-1776* (1958), Arthur M. Schlesinger demonstrates the part played by newspapers in keeping the issues alive. But printers were also businessmen. Unless there is evidence to the contrary, it can usually be assumed they did not go to the expense of printing a pamphlet unless they thought the public would buy it. This criterion of publication is not the only element to be considered in evaluating a pamphlet. All the known circumstances of publication should be taken into account, and these I tried to indicate whenever possible. However, I feel that the actual work done by colonial printers provides the fundamental standard necessary for this bibliographical study.

In restricting the study to the broad political issues that led directly up to the Declaration of Independence, all the local disputes have been omitted. A number of these, such as the proprietary struggle in Pennsylvania and the "Two Penny Act" controversy in Virginia, began well before 1764, but were fundamentally local fights. Others, such as the Regulators of North Carolina and the American Episcopate controversy, took place after 1764, but were also local or of a special nature not directly concerned with the central problem of the political relationship between Great Britain and her colonies. Incidentally the second subject has already been treated in William Nelson's *The Controversy over the Proposition for an American Episcopate, 1764-1774, A Bibliography* (1909), but it needs to be expanded to include the British side of the story. Although all events of the time played their part in building the mood for independence, it was the local events in Boston that finally touched off the larger struggle. For that reason the pamphlets growing out of the Boston events are well represented. The basic consideration for inclusion is whether or not the pamphlet dealt with the main issue: the nature of the political relationship between the colonies and Great Britain.

No poetry, plays, or satires have been included. The dramatic material has been described in Frank P. Hill's *American Plays Printed 1714-1830, A Bibliographical Record* (1934). Poetry has also been treated bibliographically in Oscar Wegelin's *Early American Poetry* (1930) for which Roger Stoddard is preparing additions toward a revision. Satires have also recently received separate treatment by Bruce I. Granger in his *Political Satire in the American Revolution 1763-1783* (1960). The official Acts and Proceedings of the state assemblies and the Continental Congress have been omitted because of the need described by J. H. Powell in his *New Books for a New Nation* (1957) for a more thorough study of the nature of government printing, and also because the publications of the Continental Congress were in general a result of the issues raised by these pamphlets. Sermons and orations have been dealt with selectively. I have chosen for inclusion those in which the issues of the day were discussed at some length or which were stimulated by a major event such as the repeal of the Stamp Act, the Boston Massacre, or the Battle of Lexington and Concord. In general, fast sermons, election sermons, and artillery sermons have been omitted when they are theological disquisitions containing only a brief reference to the political issues of the day.

In confining the study to pamphlets I have omitted the political essays that appeared in newspapers and also those that appeared as broadsides, as broadsheets, or as four-page folio publications which were more akin to broadsides than they were to the traditional pamphlet form. Moses Coit Tyler drew a distinction in his *Literary History of the American Revolution* (1897) between the political essays in newspapers and those that were published in pamphlet form. In this he was supported by a contemporary writer in the *Pennsylvania Packet* for March 25, 1776. In a piece entitled "Conversation between Cato and Plain Truth," the author contrasts two replies to Thomas Paine's *Common Sense*. Provost William Smith of the College of Philadelphia had used the pseudonym "Cato" for a series of letters he had written to the newspaper. *Plain Truth* was the title of a pamphlet (no. 208) by James Chalmers. The author of the "Conversation" has Cato say, "Our cause will never appear to advantage in a pamphlet. If you begin a series of letters in a news-paper you are at full liberty to say as much or as little as you please, to suspend your operations for a time and strike in again when occasion serves." Further on he says, "When you write a pamphlet you are expected to say the best, if not all that can be said on the subject, and if it contains a few weighty arguments the author is despised and the subject suffers. There you are obliged to come to a period, but you may write a twelve month in a news-paper and yet make the public believe that your main argument has not yet appeared." Seventeen per cent of the titles in the following bibliography also appeared in full or in part in newspapers. Ten appeared there first and were later reprinted as pamphlets and twenty-one reversed the process.

I have omitted all pamphlets that were purely English in origin and publication. To have included them would have impaired one of the purposes of the study, which is to provide a bibliography in which each pamphlet is described in terms of the American setting in which it appeared.* The number of editions, where they are printed, the approximate date of their appearance, their sale throughout the colonies, and other circumstances relating to their printing and publication all have some bearing on the significance of the individual pamphlet to its time. I have not in every case been able to provide all of this information. Through microfilm and photostats I have examined the files of at least one newspaper from every colony in which a paper was published during the years 1764-1776. In the case of South Carolina, Virginia, Pennsylvania, New York, Connecticut, and Massachusetts I have done this for two and sometimes three newspapers. I have also included a complete record of the contemporary English and continental editions of the pamphlets.

This is a bibliography for people concerned with the study of the origins of the American Revolution. I hope that others, the collector, the antiquarian bookseller, and the librarian, will also find it useful. But it is intended primarily for those men and women who feel they must examine every aspect of the many forces that caused the loyal British colonies in North America to become the first sovereign nation of the New World.

The Bibliographical Method

The study is arranged chronologically by the imprint date on the title page of the first edition. Subsequent editions are listed chronologically

---

* The other side of the story, that is, the British political pamphlets of the American Revolution, are the subject of a study I am now working on, which will cover the years 1764 to 1783. The more inclusive period has been adopted because from the British point of view American independence was still a political issue until the Treaty of Paris recognized the United States.

after the first edition. Editions bearing the same date have been listed in terms of their geographical proximity to the place of publication of the first. Thus, in the case of a Boston pamphlet all subsequent Boston editions of the same year come next, followed by the New York edition, the Philadelphia edition, and the London edition. In a few cases, when it has been possible to determine the actual date of publication from newspaper advertisements, the true chronological order of appearance has been used. An exception was made in the case of translations and the separate publication of part of the pamphlet such as an abridgment. These will be found at the end of the entry for each title.

The description:

Within each year, each title has been arranged by the author or title, or in some special cases the corporate entry. The description of the physical pamphlet is less than a full formal bibliographical analysis. Enough of the title page has been given to show the nature of the contents. The imprint is given in a separate paragraph. It too has been shortened to omit addresses of printers and booksellers. However, those parts of both the title and imprint that have been set down have followed the exact wording of the title page. Omissions have been indicated by the three dot elision symbol. The collation of each item includes the pagination, the format, and the signatures. Here a rule of bibliography has been violated, the requirement that the pagination and signatures add up to the same number of leaves. In giving the pagination only those leaves with printing on them have been included while in describing the signatures blank leaves have been included. The presence of advertising or other matter not directly related to the text has been indicated in curves following the pagination, and the presence of blank leaves has similarly been indicated following the signatures. It should be noted that blank leaves have been described only in those cases where they have been seen in a copy of the pamphlet. There are a number of cases in which a signature with an odd number of leaves strongly suggests the presence of a blank leaf, but unless a copy with the leaf has been seen no mention has been made of it. The format has been determined purely by the chain lines in the paper as set down by R. B. McKerrow in *An Introduction to Bibliography* (1927).

In the notes I have attempted to provide the basic information about the circumstances surrounding the publication of each American edition.

With certain exceptions, this has not been done for the English editions. In every case I have endeavored to give the earliest newspaper advertisement for the item. In addition I have tried to include advertisements that may have appeared in newspapers other than in the city in which the pamphlet first appeared. When I say "Advertised in" a certain issue of a newspaper, I mean that that issue contains the first announcement discovered that reads "This day published" or a similar wording indicating that the pamphlet was then being sold. Any departure from this practice is so stated. This does not mean, of course, that copies of a pamphlet were not available before the stated date. The printer may have begun sale any time during the previous week or in a few cases even earlier. I have also endeavored to give some record of the extent to which all or part of the text was reprinted in colonial newspapers. In every case where the text first appeared in a newspaper the particulars are given. However, later publication has been noted only so far as it came to light in the searches described earlier.

In pamphlets containing a large number of miscellaneous documents, I have not, in most cases, tried to provide a detailed contents note beyond what appears on the title page. However, I have noted prominent individual works, such as substantial essays or speeches or the complete reprinting of another pamphlet.

The attribution of all anonymous works, which constitute about forty per cent of the total, has been explained. In a few cases I have had simply to cite Evans or the Library of Congress Catalog as my authority, but in most cases I have been able to give further documentation. I have also noted the names of any other persons, such as editors and translators, who may have been associated with the tract, and the names of people to whom the work has been incorrectly attributed from time to time.

Editions:

The relation of one edition to another has been treated in three ways: first, those in which the same sheets or substantially the same setting of type have been used; second, where there has been a resetting with no apparent textual change; and, third, where the author has clearly made extensive textual alterations. In the case of the first two, a close word-for-word comparison may reveal minor changes which would be important to anyone preparing the text for publication. The one exception to the above is Franklin's *Examination* (no. 31) where closer study was justified because it was necessary in working out the relationship between the various printings.

This study is primarily concerned with the different editions of the pamphlets. Points that constitute states and issues have been noted when they came to my attention. There has been no systematic attempt to discover all of them. It is my belief that an exhaustive bibliographical analysis that includes a close comparison of all available copies does not belong in a work like this, designed to give the user an over-all picture of the literature. A number of the works listed here deserve such treatment, but I feel that should be reserved for individual study.

Bibliographies:

In general the only bibliographies cited are the two major ones—Sabin and Evans. The latter is particularly important because in a sense this work is a supplement to the microprint publication being carried out by Clifford K. Shipton at the American Antiquarian Society. Mr. Shipton's work has made my task much easier because he simplified the identification of ghosts; that is, nonexistent titles and editions listed by Evans. I have relied heavily on his microprint cards, and he has generously given me access to his notes for the unpublished entries. In certain cases additional specialized bibliographies, particularly author bibliographies, have been cited.

Census:

The census of copies is not intended to be complete. The libraries represented were selected in an effort to include two elements, geographical location and major collections.

The following analysis of the ten strongest collections is offered not for purposes of comparison, but to indicate the institutions where a scholar can most fruitfully pursue the study of these pamphlets. In every case the libraries listed below have near at hand substantial collections of supporting material essential in understanding the literature. These calculations are based on the 230 titles, regardless of editions, represented in the bibliography. I could have also calculated on the basis of the total number of editions or on the first editions. The results would have varied slightly, but essentially the same institutions would have been represented. The John Carter Brown Library at Brown University and the Library of Congress have between seventy and seventy-five per cent, the American Antiquarian Society and the Huntington Library have between sixty-five and sixty-nine per cent, while the following libraries have between sixty and sixty-four per cent: the Boston Athenæum, the William L. Clements Library at the University of Michigan, Harvard University Libraries, the New York Public Library, the Library Company of Philadelphia and the Historical Society of Pennsylvania, and Yale University Library. The Boston Public Library and the Massachusetts Historical Society should be included in this last group because their collections almost fall within the sixty to sixty-four per cent group. The linking of the Library Company of Philadelphia with the Historical Society of Pennsylvania is based on the proposed location of the two institutions in adjoining buildings so that the two collections will reinforce each other. However, individually they have substantial holdings. The Library Company of Philadelphia has about fifty-five per cent and the Historical Society about fifty-two per cent of the list. The library situation in Philadelphia is unusual. Its resources are spread among a large number of important libraries. For that reason all the major libraries of the city have been included in the census. Anyone planning to do work in Philadelphia should be aware of and use the Philadelphia Bibliographical Center and Union Library Catalogue. This cooperative catalogue, located at the University of Pennsylvania, is a vital factor in coordinating the library resources of the whole area.

ACKNOWLEDGMENTS

This study began in the Chapin Library at Williams College where I served as the Custodian from 1955 to 1957. On October 19, 1956, we opened an exhibition, the title of which has been used for this study. On that occasion Edmund S. Morgan delivered an address on the nature of the pamphlets that was both witty and stimulating. A number of libraries, notably The Library of Congress, The New-York Historical Society, The William L. Clements Library, The Boston Athenæum, and the University of Pennsylvania Library, loaned pamphlets on that occasion although most of the items were taken from the collection of the Chapin Library. After the exhibition was over I resolved to pursue the question of political pamphlets further, and the present study is the result.

Bibliographers are always presented with a peculiar problem when acknowledging the assistance of others. They are so completely dependent upon the legacy from bibliographers of the past, their elders, and their peers that the pages expressing their debt could easily be as long as the work itself. I shall endeavor here to mention a few of the men and women who have assisted me and who have patiently answered my many questions.

I am more indebted to Mr. John Alden than to any other single individual. He read the whole manuscript before it first went to the printer's and he then checked the galleys against copies in various Boston libraries. In the course of this work he identified the spurious edition of the Boston Massacre *Narrative* (no. 75e) and followed it up by supplying the supporting data from the records of the Boston Town Meeting. Anyone acquainted with the meticulous and thorough manner in which Mr. Alden works will understand the obligation I am under. He, of course, is in no way responsible for errors I missed, but the work is substantially better because of his kindness.

A number of other people have put me under special obligation by their willingness to answer many questions and discuss particular points. Mr. William H. Runge helped me untangle the problems of Franklin's *Examination*. The correspondence with Mr. Howard H. Peckham is one of the thickest in my file. Mr. Lyle H. Wright and Mr. Carey S. Bliss of the Huntington Library also replied to many questions. Mr. Frederick R. Goff of the Library of Congress obviously was one of my most important correspondents, as was Mr. Lewis Stark of the New York Public Library. Special mention should be made of Mr. Edwin Wolf II, who, together with the books in The Library Company of Philadelphia, provided me with some most important assistance. Mr. Lyman H. Butterfield was particularly generous in providing me with additional material for notes from his work with the Adams papers. Others who have been helpful are: Mr. H. Richard Archer, Mr. Bernard Bailyn, Mr. Whitfield J. Bell, Jr., Mr. Lloyd A. Brown, Mrs. Ruth L. Butler, Mr. C. E. N. Childs, Mr. Verner W. Crane, Mr. Donald B. Engley, Col. Richard Gimbel, Mr. Archibald Hanna, Mr. Thompson R. Harlow, Mr. Howell J. Heaney, Mr. William H. McCarthy, Miss A. Rachel Minick, Mr. B. E. Powell, Mr. William S. Powell, Mrs. Granville T. Prior, Mr. David A. Randall, Mr. Stephen T. Riley, Mr. Roger E. Stoddard, Mr. Alexander D. Wainwright, Mr. Nicholas B. Wainwright, Mrs. Neda M. Westlake, Mr. Benton W. Wilcox, Mr. John Cook Wyllie, and Miss Marjorie G. Wynne. To Mr. Lawrence C. Wroth I owe special thanks for all the help he gave after I succeeded him as the Librarian of the

John Carter Brown Library. He answered questions on several points, and
then went over the whole manuscript before it went to the printer. Finally
I want to thank the institutions which checked my short title list for loca-
tions of copies. It was a large task and beyond the call of duty for any
busy library.

I would like to express my additional thanks to four people. To Mr.
J. H. Powell I owe a debt for the origin of the idea which was contained
in an offhand comment he made many years ago. Mr. Rex D. Parady
occupies a special place because of the part he played in the initial planning of the work. Mrs. Joanne D. Prisley, my secretary, typed the whole
manuscript and in the process learned more than she ever wanted to know
about American Revolutionary pamphlets. I owe an obligation to Mr.
Walter Muir Whitehill through whose kindness arrangements were made
with the Colonial Society of Massachusetts for publication. Finally I wish
to express my thanks to Brown University for the faculty research grant
to assist in the preparation of the manuscript.

I cannot close without paying tribute to the Library and its creators who
made my task immeasurably easier than it would otherwise have been. The
John Carter Brown Library made it possible to do almost three quarters
of the work in one place. The men who built the Library, John Carter
Brown, John Russell Bartlett, John Nicholas Brown, George Parker
Winship, Worthington C. Ford, and Lawrence C. Wroth, have placed
all who work with the books of American history forever in their debt.

Providence, Rhode Island   THOMAS R. ADAMS

Bibliographies Cited

Alden   *Rhode Island Imprints 1727-1800 Edited by John Eliot Alden.* 1949.

Evans   *American Bibliography By Charles Evans.* 1903-1959, 14 vols.

Ford-*Chauncy*   *Bibliotheca Chaunciana. A List of the Writings of Charles Chauncy [by Paul Leicester Ford].* 1884.

Ford-*Franklin*   *Franklin Bibliography. A List of Books Written by, or relating to Benjamin Franklin By Paul Leicester Ford.* 1889.

Ford-*Hamilton*   *Bibliotheca Hamiltoniana; a List of Books Written by, or relating to Alexander Hamilton By Paul Leicester Ford.* 1886.

Gimbel   *Thomas Paine: A Bibliographical Check List of Common Sense With an Account of its Publication By Richard Gimbel.* 1956.

Hewlett   *James Rivington, Loyalist Printer, Publisher, and Bookseller of the American Revolution, 1742-1802; A Biographical-Bibliographical Study by Leroy Hewlett.* 1958. (A doctoral dissertation submitted to the University of Michigan.)

Holmes   *The Minor Mathers A List of their Works By Thomas James Holmes.* 1940.

Sabin   *A Dictionary of Books relating to America From its discovery to the Present Time By Joseph Sabin.* 1868-1936, 29 vols.

Wroth   *A History of Printing in Colonial Maryland 1686-1776 By Lawrence C. Wroth.* 1922.

Key to Locations

BM	The British Museum.
Bodl.*	The Bodleian Library.
CSmH	The Henry E. Huntington Library.
CtHWatk	The Watkinson Library, Trinity College.
CtHi	Connecticut Historical Society.
CtY	Yale University.
DLC	The Library of Congress.
ICN	The Newberry Library.
InU	Indiana University.
MB	The Boston Public Library.
MBAt	The Boston Athenæum.
MH	Harvard University.
MHi	The Massachusetts Historical Society.
MWA	The American Antiquarian Society.
MWiW-C	The Chapin Library, Williams College.
MiU-C	The William L. Clements Library, University of Michigan.
NHi	The New-York Historical Society.
NN	The New York Public Library.
NcD	Duke University.
NcU	The University of North Carolina.
NjP	Princeton University.
PHi	The Historical Society of Pennsylvania.
PP	The Free Library of Philadelphia.
PPAmP	The American Philosophical Society.
PPL	The Library Company of Philadelphia.
PPRos	The Philip H. and A. S. W. Rosenbach Foundation.
PU	The University of Pennsylvania.
RPB	Brown University.
RPJCB	The John Carter Brown Library, Brown University.
ScHi*	The South Carolina Historical Society.
ViU	The University of Virginia.
WHi	The State Historical Society of Wisconsin.

* Complete holdings not recorded.

The Bibliography

1764

1. [BLAND, RICHARD] 1710-1776.

The Colonel Dismounted: Or The Rector Vindicated. In a Letter addressed to His Reverence: Containing A Dissertation upon the Constitution of the Colony. By Common Sense. . . .

Williamsburg: Printed by Joseph Royle. MDCCLXIV.

1 p. l., [1]-30, i-xxvii p., 4to, [-]² [A]-G⁴.

The major part of this pamphlet deals with the Two Penny Act and the Parson's Cause, purely local issues, which had started as early as 1755 and produced between 1760 and 1765 a series of exchanges between John Camm, Langdon Carter, and Bland. Because of its local nature it would not normally have been included. However, pages 19-29 contain an argument for colonial self-government. See: *Proceedings of the American Antiquarian Society* (new series), vol. XL (1933), pp. 292-293 and Clinton Rossiter's "Richard Bland, The Whig in America," *William & Mary Quarterly* (3rd series), vol. X (1953), p. 48. Plate I.

Copies: DLC, MWA.

2. Considerations Upon The Act of Parliament, Whereby A Duty is laid of six Pence Sterling per Gallon on Molasses, and five Shillings per Hundred on Sugar of foreign Growth, imported into any of the British Colonies. Shewing Some of the many Inconveniencies necessarily resulting from the Operation of the said Act. . . .

Boston: Printed and Sold by Edes and Gill . . . MDCCLXIV.

[1]-28 p., 1 l., 8vo, [A]-D⁴ (D4 blank).

Advertised in the *Boston Gazette* for January 9, 1764. The February 6th issue of the same newspaper carried an advertisement for a "Second Edition." It may have been a reissue of this with no edition notice or it may have been a reprinting. In any case, no copy has been located that calls itself the second edition.

Evans 9625, Sabin 16030.

Copies: DLC, MB, MBAt, MWA, NHi, PHi, PPL, RPJCB.

3. [FITCH, THOMAS] ca. 1700-1774.

Reasons Why The British Colonies, In America, Should Not Be Charged With Internal Taxes, By Authority Of Parliament; Humbly Offered For Consideration, In Behalf of the Colony of Connecticut.

New-Haven: Printed by B. Mecom. MDCCLXIV.

[1]-39 p., 8vo, [A]-E⁴.

Drawn up by a committee appointed for the purpose by the Connecticut General Assembly in May of 1764. Governor Thomas Fitch was the chairman and apparently took a leading part in drafting the document. It is usually listed under his name. See: Lawrence H. Gipson's *Jared Ingersoll*, New Haven, 1920, pp. 123-125.

Evans 9658, Sabin 24588.

Copies: CSmH, CtHi, CtHWatk, CtY, DLC, InU, MB, MBAt, MH, MHi, MWA, MWiW-C, MiU-C, NHi, NN, PHi, PPAmP, PPL, PPRos, PU, RPJCB, ViU, WHi.

4a. OTIS, JAMES, 1725-1783.

The Rights of the British Colonies Asserted and proved. . . .
Boston: Printed and Sold by Edes and Gill . . . M,DCC,LXIV.

[1]-80 p., 8vo, [A]-K⁴.

Advertised in the *Boston Evening Post* for July 23, 1764.

Evans 9773, Sabin 57866.

Copies: BM, CSmH, CtHWatk, CtY, DLC, ICN, MB, MBAt, MH, MHi, MWA, MWiW-C, MiU-C, NHi, PPL, RPJCB.

4b. ———. ———.

Boston, New-England, Printed: London Reprinted, for J. Almon . . . [1764].

[1]-120 p., 8vo, B-Q⁴.

The date of publication assigned because it is listed in the *Gentleman's Magazine*, vol. XXXIII, p. 604, under December 1764. However, the RPJCB copy has "1765" added in a contemporary MS and the Monthly Catalogue of the *Monthly Review* does not list it until February of 1765. The *Boston Evening Post* for April 8, 1765 contains a reference to this edition.

Sabin 75866.

Copies: BM, CSmH, CtY, InU, MB, MiU-C, NN, PHi, PPAmP, PPL, RPB, RPJCB.

4c. ———. ———.

Boston, New-England, Printed: London Reprinted, for J. Williams . . . 1766.

Same collation.

Printed from substantially the same setting of types as no. 4b with the imprint altered. In some copies the last number of the imprint has been changed to a "5" in a contemporary hand.

Copies: CtHWatk, CtY, MBAt, MiU-C, NHi, NN, RPJCB.

4d. ———. ———. The Second Edition.

Boston, New-England, Printed: London Reprinted, for J. Almon . . . [1766?].

Same collation.

Printed from substantially the same setting of type as no. 4b.

Sabin 57866.

Copies: CSmH, CtY, DLC, MH, MHi, MiU-C, NHi, NN, RPB, RPJCB.

4e. ———. ———. The Third Edition, corrected. . . .

Boston, New-England, Printed: London Reprinted, for J. Williams . . . and J. Almon . . . 1766. . . .

Same collation.

Also issued in vol. I of *A Collection Of the most Interesting Tracts, On Subjects of Taxing the American Colonies,* London, J. Almon, 1766, and in vol. I of *A Collection of the Most Interesting Tracts Lately Published in England and America, on the Subjects of taxing the American Colonies,* London: J. Almon, 1766.

Sabin 57866.

Copies: CSmH, CtY, DLC, ICN, MBAt, MH, MWA, MiU-C, NHi, NN, PPL, RPJCB, ViU, WHi.

5a. [Pownall, Thomas] 1722-1805.

The Administration Of The Colonies.

London. Printed for J. Wilkie . . . MDCCLXIV.

2 p. l., [1]-131 p., 8vo, [A]² B-I⁸ K².

Daniel Dulany's *Considerations on the Propriety of Imposing Taxes,* Annapolis, 1765, no. 11, is, in part, a reply to this.

Sabin 64814.

Copies: BM, CtY, DLC, InU, MB, MBAt, MH, MiU-C, NHi, NjP, PPAmP, PPL, RPJCB.

5b. ———. ———. The Second Edition, Revised and Corrected, and Enlarged. . . .

London: Printed for J. Dodsley . . . and J. Walter . . . MDCCLXV.

14 p. l., [1]-202, [1]-60 p., 8vo, [-]² A⁸ a⁴ B-N⁸ O⁴ P² A-C⁸ (P2 blank).

The body of the work has been considerably enlarged and Sections I and II of an Appendix have been added.

Sabin 64815.

Copies: BM, CSmH, CtHi, CtHWatk, CtY, DLC, ICN, InU, MB, MBAt, MH, MHi, MiU-C, NHi, NN, PHi, PPAmP, PPL, RPJCB, ViU.

5c. ————. ————. The Third Edition, Revised, Corrected, and Enlarged. To which is added, An Appendix, No. III. . . .

London: Printed for J. Dodsley . . . and J. Walter . . . MDCCLXVI.

14 p. l., [1]-202, [1]-60, [1]-52 p., 8vo, [-]² A⁸ a⁴ B-N⁸ O⁴ P¹ A-C⁸ D⁶ E-G⁸ H².

Printed from substantially the same setting of type as 5b with the first two preliminary leaves reset and Section III of the Appendix added at the end, pages 1-52. This last part was also issued separately as 5f.

Sabin 64816.

Copies: BM, CSmH, CtY, ICN, InU, MB, MH, MWA, MiU-C, NHi, RPJCB, WHi.

5d. ————. ————. The Fourth Edition. . . .

London: Printed for J. Walter . . . MDCCLXVIII.

[i]-xxxi, [1]-318, [1]-73 p., 8vo, A⁸ a⁸ B-Z⁸ Aa-Bb⁸ Cc⁴ (A1 blank).

In this edition the body of the work has been enlarged and altered, Section III of 5c has been changed to the instructions sent by Pownall to Braddock and Johnson, and Sections IV and V, containing Henry VII's grant to John Cabot and the commission issued by Charles I in 1636 "erecting and establishing a board for the purpose of governing the Plantations," have been added.

Sabin 64817.

Copies: BM, CSmH, CtY, DLC, ICN, InU, MB, MBAt, MH, MHi, MWiW-C, NN, NjP, PHi, PPAmP, PPL, RPJCB, ViU, WHi.

5e. ————. ————. The Fifth Edition. In Two Volumes. . . .

London: Printed for J. Walter . . . MDCCLXXIV.

v. I: 2 p. l., i-xv, [1]-288 p., 8vo, [-]² A-T⁸; v. II: 1 p. l., [i]-xi, [1]-308 p., 8vo, [-]¹ A⁴ B-U⁸ X².

Volume I is an altered and shortened version of 5d with chapter headings added. Volume II contains the new material of Part II and an Appendix of twelve sections, including all the sections that appear in 5d. A sixth edition was printed in 1777.

Sabin 64818.

Copies: BM, CSmH, CtHWatk, CtY, ICN, InU, MB, MBAt, MH, MHi, MiU-C, NHi, NN, NjP, PHi, ViU.

5f. [————]. Considerations On The Points lately brought into question as to the Parliament's Right of Taxing the Colonies . . . Being Appendix, Section III, To The Administration of the Colonies.

London: Printed for J. Dodsley . . . and J. Walter . . . MDCCLXVI.

1 p. l., [1]-52 p., 8vo, [-]¹ E-G⁸ H².

This is Section III of the Appendix to 5c and is printed from substantially the same setting of type with a title page added. On the basis of press marks, Mr. John Alden points out that this was probably imposed at the same time as 5c rather than printed at a later time from standing type.

Sabin 62821.

Copies: CtY, DLC, ICN, InU, MiU-C, NN, RPJCB, ViU, WHi.

5g. ————. The Administration Of The British Colonies. Part The Second. Wherein A Line of Government between . . . Great Britain, and the Rights of the Colonies is drawn, And A Plan of Pacification is suggested. To which is added, A Postscript, Being Remarks on the Pensylvania [*sic*] Instructions, And The "New Essay on the Constitutional Power of the Parliament over the Colonies. . . . "

London: Printed for J. Walter . . . MDCCLXXIV.

[i]-xi, [1]-171 p., 8vo, [-]² a⁴ b-l⁸ m⁶.

The pages through 150 were printed from substantially the same setting of type as the pages of 5e, vol. II; pages 151-160, "Memorial on a line of demarcation," are a reprint of pages 259-269; and pages 161-171 contain "Additions to Section I of the Appendix to the First Volume." John Alden points out that this is a reimposition from standing type. The "Postscript" is a reply to John Dickinson's *Essay on the Constitutional Power of Great Britain*, Philadelphia, 1774, no. 110.

Sabin 64821.

Copies: CtY, DLC, MB, MiU-C, NHi, NN, RPJCB, WHi.

6. Reasons Against the Renewal Of The Sugar Act, As it will be prejudicial to the Trade, Not Only Of the Northern Colonies, But To That of Great-Britain Also.

Province of the Massachusetts-Bay. Boston: N.E. Printed for Thomas Leverett . . . MDCCLXIV.

[1]-19 p., 4to, [A]-B⁴ C².

Evans 9812, Sabin 68255.

Copies: DLC, MBAt, MHi, RPJCB, WHi.

7. [THACHER, OXENBRIDGE] 1720-1765.

The Sentiments of a British American. . . .

Boston: Printed and Sold by Edes and Gill . . . 1764. . . .

[1]-16 p., 8vo, [A]-B⁴.

Advertised in the *Boston Gazette* for September 3, 1764. For authorship see: Clifford K. Shipton's *Sibley's Harvard Graduates,* vol. X, 1958, p. 326.

Evans 9851, Sabin 95160.

Copies: DLC, ICN, MB, MBAt, MHi, MWA, MWiW-C, NN, RPJCB.

8. WOOD, WILLIAM, d. 1639.

New-England's Prospect. Being A true, lively, and experimental Description of that part of America, commonly called New-England . . . The Third Edition. . . .

London, Printed 1639. Boston, New-England, Re-printed, By Thomas and John Fleet . . . and Green and Russell . . . 1764.

1 p. l., i-xviii, 1-128 p., 8vo, [a]-b⁴ c² B-R⁴.

Advertised in the *Boston Evening Post* for July 23, 1764. To this edition has been added a new introduction by Nathaniel Rogers which surveys the political and economic relation between Great Britain and the colonies. See also: the preface of the reprint issued by the Prince Society in 1865.

Evans 9884, Sabin 105077.

Copies: CSmH, ICN, MB, MBAt, MH, MHi, MWA, MiU-C, NN, PPL, RPJCB.

1765

9a. [CHURCH, BENJAMIN] 1734-1776.

Liberty and Property vindicated, and the St—pm-n burnt. A Discourse Occasionally made, On burning the Effigy of the St—pm-n, in New-London, in the Colony of Connecticut. By a Friend to the Liberty of his Country.

Published by desire of some of the Hearers, in the Year 1765.

[1]-11 p., 4to, [A]-C².

This was printed in either Hartford or New London.

Evans 9929.

Copies: CSmH, CtHi, CtHWatk, DLC, PPL.

9b.   [————]. ————.

Boston: Reprinted and Sold [by J. Kneeland & S. Adams] at the New Printing Office in Milk-Street, 1765.

[1]-15 p., 8vo, [A]-B⁴.

Copies: DLC, MHi, MWA.

9c.   [————]. ————.

Boston: Reprinted and Sold [by J. Kneeland & S. Adams] at the New Printing Office in Milk-Street, 1766.

Same collation.

Evans 10260, Sabin 12981.

Copies: CtHWatk, DLC.

10a.   [DICKINSON, JOHN] 1732-1808.

The Late Regulations Respecting The British Colonies On The Continent Of America Considered, In a Letter from a Gentleman in Philadelphia to his Friend in London. . . .

Philadelphia: Printed and Sold by William Bradford . . . M.DCC.LXV.

[1]-38 p., 8vo, A-E⁴ (E4 blank).

Advertised in the *Pennsylvania Journal* for December 12, 1765. Two states noted: in one, page 11 ends "would generally believed without the trial"; in the other, "would be credited without the trial."

Evans 9959, Sabin 20043.

Copies: CtY, DLC, ICN, MB, MH, MHi, MiU-C, NHi, NN, PHi, PPL, RPJCB, ViU.

10b.   [————]. ————.

Philadelphia Printed: London Re-printed, for J. Almon . . . M.DCC.LXV.

[1]-62 p., 1 l. (last l. advts.), 8vo, A-H⁴.

In view of the date of the advertisement for the Philadelphia edition, this was probably not issued until 1766. This and no. 10c were printed by William Strahan on the order of Benjamin Franklin according to Verner W. Crane's *Benjamin Franklin's Letters to the Press, 1758-1775,* Chapel Hill, 1950, p. xlix. Also issued in vol. II of *A Collection of the Most Interesting Tracts, On the Subject of Taxing the American Colonies,* London, J. Almon, 1766, and in vol. I of *A Collection of the Most Interesting Tracts, Lately Published in England and America, on the Subjects of Taxing the American Colonies,* London, J. Almon, 1766.

Sabin 20043.

Copies: CSmH, CtY, DLC, MBAt, MH, MHi, MiU-C, NN, PHi, PPL, RPJCB.

10c. [————]. ————.

Philadelphia Printed: London Re-printed for J. Almon ... MDCCLXVI.
2 p., l.,[1]-39 p., 8vo, [A]² B-F⁴.

Also issued in vol. I of *A Collection of Tracts, On the Subjects of Taxing The British Colonies in America,* London, J. Almon, 1773.

Sabin 20043.

Copies: BM, CSmH, CtY, DLC, MB, MBAt, MH, MiU-C, NN, PHi, PPL, RPJCB.

11a.   [DULANY, DANIEL] 1721-1797.

Considerations On The Propriety Of Imposing Taxes In The British Colonies, For the Purpose of raising a Revenue, by Act Of Parliament.

[Annapolis] North-America: Printed by a North-American [Jonas Green] MDCCLXV.

[1]-55 p., 4to, A-G⁴.

Advertised in the *Maryland Gazette* for Thursday, October 10, 1765, to be for sale "next Monday." The advertisements in the following newspapers may have been for any of the American editions: *Pennsylvania Gazette* for December 5, 1765, *Newport Mercury* for February 17, 1766, *Pennsylvania Journal* for March 10, 1766, *Virginia Gazette* (Purdie & Dixon) March 10, 1766, (Rind) May 6, 1766, and *South Carolina Gazette* for June 2, 1766. For full statement of the authorship and circumstances of publication see Wroth. This is a reply to Thomas Pownall's *Administration of the Colonies,* London, 1764, no. 5, to William Knox's *The Claim of the Colonies to an Exemption from Internal Taxes,* London, 1765, no. 17, and to Soame Jenyns' *The Objections to the Taxation of our American Colonies,* London, 1765, no. 16Aa. See also: Aubrey C. Land's *The Dulany's of Maryland,* Baltimore, 1955, pp. 263-267.

Evans 9956, Wroth 255.

Copies: BM, CtHi, MWiW-C, MiU-C, PHi, PP, PPAmP, PPL, RPJCB, ViU.

11b.   [————]. ————. The Second Edition.

Annapolis: Printed and Sold by Jonas Green. 1765. . . .

[1]-55 p., 4to, A-G⁴.

Advertised in the *Maryland Gazette* for October 31, 1765.

Evans 9957, Sabin 21170, Wroth 256.

Copies: CSmH, CtY, DLC, MBAt, MH, MHi, MiU-C, NHi, NN, PHi, PPAmP, PPL, RPJCB.

11c. [————]. ————.

North-America: Printed by a North-American. New-York: Re-printed by John Holt . . . 1765.

[1]-55 p., 8vo, [A]-G⁴.

Advertised for sale in the *New-York Gazette* for October 31, 1765. The *Connecticut Courant* for March 10, 1766 advertises it as "Just published in New-York." Two states noted, one with page 2 line 4 ending "may be"; the other with the same line ending "for a."

Evans 9958, Sabin 21170.

Copies: CSmH, CtHi, CtY, DLC, ICN, MBAt, MH, MWA, MiU-C, NHi, NN, NcU, PHi, PPL, RPJCB, ViU, WHi.

11d. [————]. ————.

[Annapolis?] North-America: Printed by a North-American [Jonas Green?] MDCCLXV.

[1]-90 p., 8vo, A-L⁴ M¹.

This is a reprint of no. 11a, with one addition. On page 33 there is added to a footnote the following, "N.B. It may not be amiss here to observe upon another extraordinary assertion of the writer [William Knox] of *The claim of the colonies*, with regard to *Maryland*, as the excellent author of this pamphlet has left it unnoticed." Knox is quoted as saying that Maryland was the only colony that did not claim exemption from taxation by Parliament. It is then pointed out that "as soon as their [Maryland's] assembly were called, [September 23, 1765] they (only a few weeks since) by the resolutions they entered into, and by their immediate appointment [September 24] of a committee to join the [Stamp Act] congress at *New-York*, sufficiently manifested . . . their feelings. . . ." The Committee's instructions from the Assembly were approved on September 27th, and the delegates were in attendance in New York on October 7th, when the Stamp Act Congress began. It sat until October 25th. The delegates had returned by November 27th, because on that day they submitted their expenses to the Assembly. It would appear therefore that this edition was probably printed sometime during November of 1765 before the delegates had returned. None of the other reprints of the pamphlet recorded here contain the additional footnote.

The reasons for assigning the printing to Annapolis and to Green are as follows: The tone of the footnote sounds as though it were written by a Marylander; the Gothic type used for "North-America" and "North-American" in the imprint is the same as that used in 11a and as frequently employed by Green in imprints of other pamphlets; of the thirteen type ornaments found in this pamphlet six are also found in the other two Green editions, 11a and 11b, and three more are to be found in other Green publications of the same period. The above analysis is based on a microfilm and information very kindly supplied by the owner of the pamphlet. The film is now in the John Carter Brown Library.

Wroth 258.

Copies: Privately owned.

11e. [————]. ————.

[Boston] North America [printed by William McAlpine for John Mein, 1766].

1 p., l.,[i]-ii, [5]-47, [1] p., 8vo, [A]-F⁴.

Advertised in the *Massachusetts Gazette and Boston Weekly News-Letter* for January 30, 1766. For date and printing history see: John Alden's "The Boston Edition of Daniel Dulany's 'Considerations On The Propriety Of Imposing Taxes,'" *The New England Quarterly,* vol. XXI (1940), pp. 705-711.

Evans 9959, Sabin 21170, Wroth 257.

Copies: CSmH, CtY, DLC, MB, MBAt, MH, MHi, MWA, MiU-C, PHi, PU, RPJCB.

11f. [————]. ————.

North-America Printed, London, Re-printed for J. Almon . . . MDCCLXVI.

3 p. l., 1-69 [*i.e.* 81], [1] p. (last p. advts.), 8vo, A⁸ B-L⁴, M¹.

This and no. 11g printed by William Strahan on the order of Benjamin Franklin according to Verner W. Crane's *Benjamin Franklin's Letters to the Press, 1758-1775,* Chapel Hill, 1950, p. xlix.

Sabin 21170.

Copies: BM, CSmH, CtY, DLC, InU, MB, MBAt, MH, MHi, MiU-C, NHi, NN, NjP, PHi, PPAmP, PPL, RPJCB, ViU, WHi.

11g. [————]. ————. The Second Edition.

Same imprint.

3 p. l., 1-81, [1] p. (last p. advts.), 8vo, A⁸ B-L⁴ M¹.

Printed from substantially the same setting of type as no. 11f with title page altered and number on last page corrected. This was also issued in both vol. I of *A Collection of the most Interesting Tracts, On the Subjects of Taxing the American Colonies*, London, J. Almon, 1766 and in vol. I of *A Collection Of Tracts, On the Subjects Of taxing The British Colonies in America*, London, J. Almon, 1773, and in vol. I of *A Collection of the Most Interesting Tracts, Lately Published in England and America, on the Subjects of Taxing the American Colonies*, London: J. Almon, 1766.

Copies: CSmH, CtHWatk, CtY, DLC, MB, MBAt, MH, MiU-C, NHi, NN, PPAmP, PPL, RPB, RPJCB, ViU, WHi.

12a. ELIOT, ANDREW, 1719-1778.

A Sermon Preached Before His Excellency Francis Bernard . . . May 29th 1765. Being the Anniversary for the Election of His Majesty's Council. . . .

Boston: Printed By Green and Russell . . . MDCCLXV.

[1]-59 p., 8vo, [A]-G⁴ H².

Two states noted, one with "price two shillings" below the date, one without. The Council paid the printers £29 3s. 4d. in July of 1765 for about 700 copies. See: Rollo G. Silver's "Government Printing in Massachusetts: 1751-1801," *Studies in Bibliography*, vol. XVI (1963), p. 193.

Evans 9964, Sabin 22124.

Copies: BM, CSmH, CtHWatk, CtY, DLC, ICN, InU, MB, MBAt, MH, MHi, MWA, MiU-C, NHi, NN, NcD, PHi, RPJCB.

12b. ———. ———.

Boston: Printed . . . And reprinted by J. Meres . . . London. MDCCLXV.

[1]-48 p., 8vo, [-]¹ B-F⁴ G² H¹.

Copies: MB, MH, MiU-C, NN.

13. [HOPKINS, STEPHEN] 1707-1785.

A Letter To The Author Of The Halifax Letter; Occasioned by his Book, entitled, a Defence of that Letter.

[Newport] Printed [by Samuel Hall] for the Author. MDCCLXV.

[1]-8 p., 8vo, [A]⁴.

A reply to Martin Howard's *A Defense Of The Letter From A Gentleman at Halifax*, Newport, 1765, no. 15. This has not been hitherto attributed to Hopkins, but internal evidence makes it clear that he was the author. It is a defense, written in the first person, against Howard's attack on the letter Hopkins had published in the *Providence Gazette* in the issues of February 23, March 2, 9 and April 8, 1765. The pamphlet has been assigned to Hall because the type ornaments used are the same as those found in the laws of Rhode Island of the same date printed by him.

Evans 10038, Sabin 40457, Alden 332.

Copies: DLC.

14a. [HOPKINS, STEPHEN] 1707-1785.
The Rights Of Colonies Examined. . . .
Providence: Printed by William Goddard. MDCCLXV.
[1]-24 p., 4to, [A]-C⁴.
The Rhode Island Assembly ordered this to be printed on December 22, 1764. A bill for the printing is in the Rhode Island Archives, dated December 1764. The *Boston Gazette* for December 31, 1764 advertised the pamphlet for sale. Martin Howard's *A Letter from a Gentleman at Halifax*, Newport, 1765, no. 16, was a reply. Two issues noted, the first is the official edition and has "Printed by Authority" on the title page. The second has a three-line quotation in its place. For the pamphlet controversy set off by this, see: Edmund S. and Helen M. Morgan's *The Stamp Act Crisis*, Chapel Hill [1953], p. 51 and David S. Lovejoy's *Rhode Island Politics in the American Revolution*, Providence, 1958, p. 70.

Evans 10009-10010, Sabin 32966, Alden 326-7.

Copies: CSmH, CtY, DLC, ICN, InU, MBAt, MH, MHi, MWA, MiU-C, NHi, NN, PHi, PPL, RPB, RPJCB.

14b. [———]. The Grievances Of The American Colonies Candidly Examined. . . .
London: Reprinted for J. Almon . . . MDCCLXVI. . . .
[1]-48 [*i.e.* 47], [1] p. (last p. advts.), 8vo, [A]² B-F⁴, G².
Two issues noted, one with last page incorrectly numbered and one with it correctly numbered. Also issued in vol. I of *A Collection Of the most Interesting Tracts On the Subjects of Taxing the American Colonies*, London, J. Almon, 1766.

Sabin 32967.

Copies: CSmH, CtHWatk, CtY, DLC, ICN, InU, MB, MBAt, MH, MHi, MWiW-C, MiU-C, NHi, NN, NjP, PHi, PPL, RPB, RPJCB, ViU, WHi.

15. [HOWARD, MARTIN] d. 1781.

A Defense Of The Letter From A Gentleman at Halifax, To His Friend in Rhode-Island. . . .

Newport: Printed and Sold by Samuel Hall . . . M.DCC.LXV.

[1]-30 [*i.e.* 31] p., 4to, [A]-D⁴.

Advertised in *The Newport Mercury* for April 22, 1765. It is a reply to two attacks on Howard's earlier pamphlet, *A Letter From A Gentleman at Halifax*, no. 16. The first was a letter of Stephen Hopkins' that appeared in the *Providence Gazette* for February 23, March 2, 9 and April 8, 1765. The second was James Otis' *A Vindication Of The British Colonies, Against The Aspersions of the Halifax Gentleman*, Boston, 1765, no. 20. See Alden for the fact that Evans 10013 is a ghost.

Evans 10112, Sabin 19249, Alden 328.

Copies: DLC, ICN, MBAt, MH, MHi, MWA, PPL, RPB, RPJCB.

16. [HOWARD, MARTIN] d. 1781.

A Letter From A Gentleman at Halifax, To His Friend in Rhode-Island, Containing Remarks Upon A Pamphlet, Entitled, The Rights Of Colonies Examined.

Newport: Printed And Sold By S. Hall. M.DCC.LXV.

[1]-22 p., 4to, [A]-C⁴ (C4 blank).

Advertised in *The Newport Mercury* for February 11, 1765 as to be sold on the 13th. It is a reply to Stephen Hopkins' *The Rights of Colonies Examined*, Providence, 1765, no. 14.

Evans 10011, Sabin 40286, Alden 329.

Copies: DLC, ICN, MBAt, MH, MWA, PPL, RPB, RPJCB.

16aa. [JENYNS, SOAME] 1704-1787.

The Objections To The Taxation of our American Colonies, By The Legislature of Great Britain, Briefly Consider'd.

London: Printed for J. Wilkie . . . 1765. . . .

[1]-20 p., 4to, A-B⁴ C².

Reprinted in the *Newport Mercury* for May 27, 1765 and the *Massachusetts Gazette and Boston Weekly News-Letter* for June 13th. It was also reprinted in the third edition of Jenyns' *Miscellaneous Pieces in Verse and Prose*, London, 1770. Daniel Dulany's *Considerations*, Annapolis, 1765, no. 11, was in part a reply to this as was James Otis' "Considerations on Behalf of the Colonists," first printed in the *Boston Gazette* in 1765 and in the same year published twice as a pamphlet in London.

Sabin 36053.

Copies: BM, CSmH, CtY, DLC, InU, MB, MH, MiU-C, NN, NjP, PHi, PPL, RPJCB, ViU.

16ab. [————]. ————. The Second Edition.

Same imprint.

[1]-23 p., 8vo, A-C⁴.

Sabin 36053.

Copies: CSmH, CtHWatk, CtY, DLC, ICN, MBAt, MH, MiU-C, NN, PPAmP, PPL, RPJCB, WHi.

17a. [KNOX, WILLIAM] 1732-1810.

The Claim Of The Colonies To An Exemption from Internal Taxes Imposed By Authority of Parliament, Examined: In a Letter from a Gentleman in London, to his Friend in America.

London, Printed for W. Johnston . . . MDCCLXV.

1 p. l., 1-46 p., 8vo, [A]¹ B-F⁴ G³.

An extract was published in the *Georgia Gazette* for August 8, 1765. Ebenezer Devotion's *The Examiner Examined,* New London, 1766, no. 26, was a reply as was part of Daniel Dulany's *Considerations,* Annapolis, 1765, no. 11. Knox's authorship is established by a copy he had specially bound, with four other pamphlets, for presentation to Lord Walsingham. It is listed in the catalogue of the George C. F. Williams Library, Anderson Galleries Catalogue no. 2075, May 17, 18, 1926, lot no. 403. Knox continued his arguments started here in *A Letter To A Member of Parliament, Wherein the Power of the British Legislature, and the Case of the Colonists, Are briefly and impartially considered,* London, 1765.

Sabin 38180.

Copies: BM, CSmH, CtY, ICN, MB, MBAt, MH, MiU-C, NN, NjP, PHi, PP, PPAmP, PPL, RPJCB, ViU, WHi.

17b. [————]. ————.

London: MDCCLXV.

[1]-48 p., 8vo, A-F⁴.

Copies: CtHWatk, CtY, DLC, InU, MBAt, MH, MHi, MiU-C, NHi, NN.

18. MOORE, MAURICE, d. 1777.

The Justice And Policy Of Taxing The American Colonies, In Great-Britain, Considered. Wherein is shewed, That the Colonists are not a conquered People:—That they are constitutionally intituled to be taxed only by their own Consent:—And that the imposing a Stamp-Duty on the Colonists is as impolitic as it is inconsistent with their Rights. . . .

Wilmington, North-Carolina Printed by Andrew Steuart . . . MDCCLXV.

[1]-16 p., 8vo, [A]⁸.

Plate II.

Evans 10076.

Copies: NcU, RPJCB.

19. [OTIS, JAMES] 1725-1783.
Brief Remarks on the Defence of the Halifax Libel, On The British-American-Colonies. . . .

Boston: Printed and Sold by Edes and Gill . . . M,DCC,LXV.

[1]-40 p., 8vo, [A]-E⁴.

Advertised in the *Boston Gazette* for May 6, 1765. It is a reply to Martin Howard's *A Defense of the Letter from a Gentleman at Halifax*, Newport, 1765, no. 15.

Evans 10116, Sabin 7889.

Copies: BM, CtY, DLC, MB, MBAt, MHi, MWA, NN, RPB, RPJCB.

OTIS, JAMES. *The Rights of the British Colonies Asserted.* London [1765], see: 4b.

20a. [OTIS, JAMES] 1725-1783.
A Vindication Of The British Colonies, Against The Aspersions of the Halifax Gentleman, In His Letter to a Rhode-Island Friend.

Boston: Printed and Sold by Edes and Gill . . . 1765.

[1]-32 p., 8vo, [A]-D⁴.

Advertised in the *Massachusetts Gazette and Boston Weekly News-Letter* for March 21, 1765, in the *Newport Mercury* for March 25th, and in the *Providence Gazette* for April 8th. It is a reply to Martin Howard's *A Letter From a Gentleman at Halifax*, Newport, 1765, no. 16.

Evans 10117, Sabin 57868.

Copies: BM, CSmH, CtY, DLC, ICN, MB, MBAt, MH, MHi, MWA, MWiW-C, MiU-C, NHi, NN, PHi, PPL, RPB, RPJCB, ViU.

20b. ———. A Vindication Of The British Colonies. Published by Mr. Otis, at Boston. . . .

Boston, printed: London, re-printed for J. Almon . . . 1769. . . .

2 p. l., [1]-48 p., 8vo, [A]² B-G⁴.

Sabin 57868.

Copies: CSmH, CtY, ICN, MH, MHi, PPL, PU, RPJCB.

20c.   ————.   ————.   By James Otis, Esq; of Boston.

Same imprint and collation.

Signature [A] has been reset but the rest has been printed from substantially the same setting of type as no. 20b. Also issued in vol. II
   of *A Collection Of Tracts On The Subjects Of Taxing The British
   Colonies In America,* London, J. Almon, 1773.

Sabin 57868.

Copies: CtHWatk, CtY, DLC, InU, MB, MBAt, MH, MHi, MiU-C,
   NN, PHi, PPAmP, RPJCB, ViU, WHi.

POWNALL, THOMAS. *The Administration of the Colonies, The Second Edition.* London, 1765, see: 5b.

21a.   [WHATELY, THOMAS] d. 1772.

The Regulations Lately Made concerning the Colonies, And The
Taxes Imposed upon Them, considered.

London: Printed for J. Wilkie . . . 1765.

2 p. l., 3-114 p., 8vo, [A]² B-P⁴.

An extract of this appeared in the *Massachusetts Gazette and Boston
   Weekly News-Letter* for April 11, 1765 and in the *Newport Mercury*
   for April 22, 1765. Richard Bland's *An Inquiry Into the Rights of the
   British Colonies,* Williamsburg, 1766, no. 22Aa, was a reply as was, in
   part, Daniel Dulany's *Considerations,* no. 11. Despite the attribution
   to Grenville on the title page of the "Third Edition," no. 21b, we
   now know that Whately was the author. See: *Collections of the Massachusetts Historical Society* (6th series), vol. IX, p. 77.

Copies: CSmH, CtHWatk, DLC, ICN, InU, MB, MBAt, MH, MHi,
   MWA, MiU-C, NHi, NN, NjP, PHi, PP, PPL, RPJCB.

21b.   [————].   ————.   By The Late Right Hon. George Grenville. The Third Edition.

London: Printed for J. Wilkie . . . 1775. . . .

[1]-64, 67-114 p., 8vo, B-P⁴.

Logically, there should be a "Second Edition," but no copy has been
   found. In reprinting this ten years after the original edition, the

THE
Colonel Dismounted:

OR THE

Rector Vindicated.

In a Letter addressed to His REVERENCE:

CONTAINING

A Dissertation upon the CONSTITUTION
of the COLONY.

By COMMON SENSE.

Quodcunque ostendis mihi sic, incredulus odi.

HOR.

WILLIAMSBURG:
Printed by JOSEPH ROYLE, MDCCLXIV.

I. Richard Bland's *The Colonel Dismounted*, no. 1, the American Antiquarian Society.

THE

JUSTICE AND POLICY

OF TAXING

THE AMERICAN COLONIES,

IN GREAT-BRITAIN, CONSIDERED;

Wherein is shewed,

That the Colonists are not a conquered People :—— That they are constitutionally intituled to be taxed only by their own Consent :—— And that the imposing a Stamp-Duty on the Colonists is as impolitic as it is inconsistant with their Rights.

NON SIBI SED PATRIÆ.

By MAURICE MOORE, Esquire.

WILMINGTON, [NORTH-CAROLINA]

Printed by ANDREW STEUART, and sold at his Office, near the Exchange. M,DCC,LXV.

II. Maurice Moore's *The Justice And Policy Of Taxing The American Colonies*, no. 18
The John Carter Brown Library, Brown University.

publisher may have mistakenly thought he had issued a second edition.

Sabin 28771.

Copies: MH, RPJCB.

1766

22. APPLETON, NATHANIEL, 1693-1784.

A Thanksgiving Sermon On The Total Repeal Of The Stamp-Act. Preached In Cambridge, New-England, May 20th. . . .

Boston: Printed and Sold by Edes and Gill . . . 1766.

[1]-32 p., 8vo, [A]-D⁴.

Advertised in the *Massachusetts Gazette and Boston Weekly News-Letter* for May 29, 1766.

Evans 10230, Sabin 1840.

Copies: BM, CSmH, CtHi, CtY, DLC, ICN, InU, MB, MBAt, MH, MHi, MWA, MWiW-C, NHi, NN, NcD, PPAmP, RPJCB.

22Aa. [BLAND, RICHARD] 1710-1776.

An Inquiry Into The Rights of the British Colonies, Intended as an Answer to The Regulations lately made concerning the Colonies, and the Taxes imposed upon them considered. . . .

Williamsburg: Printed by Alexander Purdie, & Co. M.DCC.LXVI.

[1]-31 p., 8vo, [A]-D⁴.

Advertised in the *Virginia Gazette* (Purdie & Dixon) for March 14, 1766, where it is stated that Bland is the author. It is a reply to Thomas Whately's *The Regulations Lately Made*, London, 1765, no. 21. See also: Clinton Rossiter's "Richard Bland: The Whig in America," *William & Mary Quarterly* (3rd series), vol. X (1953), p. 50-53.

Evans 10244, Sabin 5859.

Copies: CSmH, DLC, NHi, RPJCB.

22Ab. [————]. An Enquiry [&c.]. . . .

Williamsburg, Printed . . . London, Re-printed for J. Almon . . . MDCCLXIX.

[5]-20, 17-19 p., 8vo, B-C⁴ D².

Caption-title, imprint on last page.

Also issued in vol. I of *A Collection of Tracts, On The Subjects of Taxing The British Colonies In America*, London, J. Almon, 1773.

Sabin 5859.

Copies: BM, CSmH, CtY, DLC, ICN, InU, MB, MH, MWA, MiU-C, NN, NcD, PHi, PPAmP, PPL, PU, RPJCB, ViU.

23. Candid Observations On Two Pamphlets lately published, Viz. "An Address to the Committee of Correspondence in Barbados. . . ." And "An Essay towards the Vindication of the Committee of Correspondence. . . . By a Native of Barbados. . . .

Barbados: Printed by George Esmand and Comp. MDCCLXVI.

[1]-37 p., 8vo, A-D⁴ E³.

Extracts appeared in the *Pennsylvania Gazette* for September 15 and 22, 1768, the *Pennsylvania Chronicle* for September 12 and October 3, 1768, and the *Pennsylvania Journal* for September 15, and 27, 1768. It is a reply to John Dickinson's *An Address to the Committee,* Philadelphia, 1766, no. 27, and to Kenneth Morrison's *An Essay Towards the Vindication,* Barbados, 1766, no. 36.

Sabin 3262.

Copies: PPL, RPJCB.

24. CHAUNCY, CHARLES, 1705-1787.

A Discourse On "the good News from a far Country." Deliver'd July 24th. A Day of Thanks-giving . . . on Occasion of the Repeal of the Stamp-Act. . . .

Boston: N. E. Printed by Kneeland and Adams . . . for Thomas Leverett . . . MDCCLXVI.

[1]-32 p., 8vo, [A]-D⁴.

Evans 10255, Sabin 12315, Ford-*Chauncy* 40.

Copies: BM, CSmH, CtHi, CtY, DLC, ICN, InU, MB, MBAt, MH, MHi, MWA, MWiW-C, MiU-C, NHi, NN, PHi, PPL, RPJCB, ViU, WHi.

25. Considerations Upon The Rights of the Colonists To The Privileges Of British Subjects, Introduced by a brief Review of the Rise and Progress of English Liberty, and concluded with some Remarks upon our present Alarming Situation. . . .

New-York: Printed and sold by John Holt . . . 1766.

1 p. l., [i]-ii, [1]-4, 9-27 p., 8vo, [A]-C⁴ [D]².

Advertised for sale in the *Newport Mercury* for March 31, 1766. Dedication dated December 16, 1765.

Evans 10273, Sabin 16034.

Copies: CSmH, CtY, DLC, ICN, InU, MB, MBAt, MH, MWA, NHi, PHi, PPL, RPJCB.

26a. [DEVOTION, EBENEZER] 1714-1771.

The Examiner Examined. A Letter From a Gentleman in Connecticut, To his Friend in London. In Answer to a Letter from a Gentleman in London, to his Friend in America: Intitled, The Claim of the Colonies to an Exemption from Internal Taxes imposed by Authority of Parliament, examined.

New-London: Printed and Sold by Timothy Green. MDCCLXVI.

[1]-24 p., 4to, [A]-B² C⁴ D².

Advertised in the *Connecticut Courant* for May 12, 1766. A reply to William Knox's *The Claim of the Colonies*, London, 1765, no. 17. Attribution from Evans.

Evans 10280, Sabin 23375.

Copies: CSmH, CtHi, CtHWatk, CtY, DLC, MB, MBAt, MHi, MiU-C, NHi, PPAmP, PPL, RPJCB.

26b. [———]. ———.

New-London, Printed: New-Haven, Re-printed, and sold by Samuel Green ... MDCCLXVI.

Same collation.

Printed from same setting of type as no. 26a with altered imprint.

Evans 10281.

Copies: CtHWatk, DLC, NHi.

27. [DICKINSON, JOHN] 1732-1808.

An Address To The Committee of Correspondence In Barbados. Occasioned by a late letter from them To Their Agent in London. By A North-American. . . .

Philadelphia. Printed and Sold by William Bradford . . . M,DCC,LXVI.

1 p. l., [i]-vi, [1]-18 p., 8vo, [A]-C⁴ D¹.

Advertised in the *Pennsylvania Journal* for May 29, 1766, as "Tomorrow" will be published. The letter of the Committee was printed in the *Pennsylvania Gazette* for May 1, 1766 and an extract of it appeared in the *Georgia Gazette* for June 11, 1766. This pamphlet was reprinted in the *South Carolina Gazette* for July 8, 1766.

Evans 10283, Sabin 20036.

Copies: BM, CSmH, CtY, DLC, MB, MH, MHi, MWA, MiU-C, NHi, NN, PHi, PPAmP, PPL, PU, RPJCB.

[DICKINSON, JOHN]. *The Late Regulations Respecting the British Colonies.* London, 1766, see: 10c.

28. A Discourse, Address To The Sons of Liberty, At a Solemn Assembly, near Liberty-Tree, in Providence, February 14, 1766.

Providence, in New-England: Printed and sold by Sarah and William Goddard . . . [1766].

[1]-8 p., 8vo, [A]⁴.

Signed at the end "Pro Patria." Alden notes three variants. In addition to the above issue there is one with "Newport" and another with "Boston" in place of "Providence" in the title. George P. Winship suggests John Alpin as a possible author in his *Rhode Island Imprints*, Providence, 1914, p. 21.

Evans 10286, Sabin 20237, Alden 348.

Copies: ("Providence") PHi, PPL, ("Newport") RPJCB, ("Boston") NN.

[DULANY, DANIEL]. *Considerations On the Propriety of Imposing Taxes In the British Colonies.* Boston, 1766, see: 11e.

[———]. ———. London, 1766, see: 11f, 11g.

29. EMERSON, JOSEPH, 1724-1775.

A Thanksgiving-Sermon Preach'd at Pepperrell, July 24th. 1766. A Day set apart by public Authority As a Day of Thanksgiving On the Account of the Repeal Of The Stamp-Act. . . .

Boston: Printed and Sold by Edes and Gill . . . MDCCLXVI.

[1]-37 p., 8vo, [A]-E⁴ (E4 blank).

Evans 10293, Sabin 22446.

Copies: CSmH, DLC, MB, MBAt, MH, MHi, MWA, MWiW-C, NN, RPJCB.

30. [FITCH, THOMAS] ca. 1700?-1774.

Some Reasons That Influenced The Governor To Take, And The Councillors To Administer The Oath, Required by the Act of Parliament; commonly called the Stamp Act. Humbly submitted to the Consideration of the Publick MDCCLXVI.

Hartford: Printed and sold by Thomas Green [1766].

[1]-14 p., 8vo, A-B⁴ (B4 blank).

Advertised in the *Connecticut Courant* for March 24, 1766. This defense of Governor Fitch's actions is attributed to him in the article on him in the *Dictionary of American Biography*.

Evans 10297, Sabin 24589, 86728.

Copies: CSmH, CtHi, CtY, DLC, InU, MB, MH, MHi, MWA, MiU-C, NHi, NN, PHi, PPL, RPJCB.

31a. GREAT BRITAIN. PARLIAMENT. HOUSE OF COMMONS.

The Examination of Doctor Benjamin Franklin, before an August Assembly, relating to the Repeal of the Stamp-Act, &c.

[Philadelphia: Hall and Sellers, 1766].

1-16 p., 8vo, A⁸.

Caption-title.

Advertised in the *Pennsylvania Gazette* for September 18, 1766. In assigning imprints to the first three American editions (nos. 31a to c) Ford has been followed. The absence of type ornaments or other distinguishing features in all three printings and our present state of ignorance about the types used by American printers make it impossible to make an absolute assignment. Therefore, it was thought best to leave Ford's order undisturbed. However, one tentative conclusion is offered about no. 31b. *The Examination* was also reprinted in various colonial newspapers; see note under no. 113. In addition to the collation this printing can be distinguished by the two thin rules at the head of the title.

    This rather than the London edition listed by Ford as no. 287 is the first printing. For status of London printings see no. 31e. The first clue about this printing is to be found in a letter from William Strahan, the London printer and friend of Franklin, to the Philadelphia printer David Hall, *Pennsylvania Magazine of History and Biography*, vol. X (1886). On April 7, 1766, almost two months after the day of the examination, February 13th, Strahan promised to send Hall a copy as soon as he received it from the Clerk of the House. From the way in which he expressed himself, it is clear that he had not seen the text. On May 10th he wrote Hall, "Herewith I send you, what I promised in my last, Dr. Franklin's *Examination* before the House of Commons, which I have at last procured with great Difficulty, and with some Expense. . . . If you determine to print it either in a Pamphlet by itself, or in your Paper (the former I think the best way) do not say *as taken by the Clerk of the House;* that would be highly improper, and might bring my Friend, who favoured me with it, into an ugly Scrape. You need only call it, *An Examination before a Great Assembly,* or by some such *General Title.* . . . If you do print it, however, in any Shape, pray send me a Dozen Copies of it, directed to Dr. F. to save Postage."

Evans 10300, Sabin 25501, Ford *Franklin* 290.

Copies: CSmH, CtHWatk, CtY, DLC, MB, MiU-C, NHi, NN, PHi, PPAmP, PPL, RPJCB.

31b. ———. ———.

[New York: James Parker, 1766].

1-16 p., 8vo, A-B⁴.

Caption-title.

Advertised in the *New-York Mercury* for September 29, 1766. This may have been set from no. 31a. It is almost a line-for-line copy. However, most of the hyphenations have been eliminated by what appears to be a more careful spacing of the type. In addition to the collation this printing can be distinguished by the thick and the thin rule at the top of the title.

Evans 10301, Ford *Franklin* 291.

Copies: CtY, DLC, ICN, MH, MiU-C, NN, RPJCB.

31c. ———. ———.

[Boston: T. & J. Fleet, 1766].

1-23 p., 8vo, A-C⁴.

Caption-title.

Advertised in the *Massachusetts Gazette and Boston Weekly News-Letter* for October 2, 1766 and in the *Newport Mercury* for October 13th. In addition to the collation this printing can be distinguished by the thin and the thick rule at the top of the title.

Ford no. 294 also lists another Boston edition of 1766 with 108 pages. He copied it from Haven's "Catalogue of Publications In what is now the United States Prior to the Revolution," in Isaiah Thomas' *The History of Printing in America, The Second Edition,* Albany, 1874, vol. II, p. 588. No copy has been located. This fact together with the large number of pages makes it likely that the entry is a ghost.

Evans 10302, Sabin 25501 note, Ford *Franklin* 292.

Copies: CtY, MB, MH, MHi, MWA, MiU-C, NHi, PPAmP, PPL, RPJCB.

31d. ———. ———.

Williamsburg: Printed and Sold by William Rind . . . [1766].

[1]-33 p. ?, 4to, A-I²? (I2 blank?).

Advertised in the *Virginia Gazette* (Rind) for December 4, 1766. The collation is hypothesized from the incomplete copy in MBAt which has only 32 pages. Only the last three questions addressed to Franklin are missing and it is not likely that they would have occupied more than a single page. Plate III.

Evans 10303, Ford *Franklin* 293.

Copies: MBAt.

31e. ————. The Examination of Dr. Benjamin Franklin before an Honourable Assembly, relative to the Repeal of the American Stamp Act, in MDCCLXVI.

[London: J. Almon] MDCCLXVII. . . .

1 p. l., 1-50 p., 8vo, [A]¹ B-G⁴ H¹.

Verner Crane, in his *Benjamin Franklin's Letters to the Press 1758-1775,* Chapel Hill, 1950, pp. 73-75, gives a summary account of the publication of the London editions. According to Ford no. 287 the first edition of the *Examination* was printed in London in 1766, without imprint, fifty pages long and with a caption-title reading: The | Examination | of | Doctor Benjamin Franklin, &c. |. He says that Almon issued the pamphlet in this form because he feared prosecution for publishing Parliamentary proceedings, and that in the following year the printer grew bolder and added the title pages described above and in the next item, no. 31f. Ford by the arrangement of his editions implies that the American printings were copied from the title pageless London edition. It is now clear that this latter assumption is not true because we know that the Philadelphia edition was printed from a manuscript supplied by the Clerk of the House.

There is good reason to believe that all the London editions were taken from one of the American ones, perhaps from one of the Philadelphia copies requested from Hall by Strahan, mentioned in the note to 31a. All London editions, even the known copies without a title page, were printed from the same setting of type. A textual comparison between them and the Philadelphia printing shows only six changes, five of which were clearly conscious improvements of the text.

Philadelphia	*London*
p. 10 line 58 there are, but	p. 31 line 19 there are three, but
p. 11 line 36 to any internal	p. 33 lines 21 & 22 to an internal
p. 13 line 15 send troops	p. 39 line 6 sends troops

Philadelphia	*London*
p. 14 line 18	p. 41 line 21
has occurred	has accrued
p. 15 line 51	p. 47 line 16
hold neither	lay neither

The sixth change is found on page 17, line 18 of the London edition. The word "internal" is changed to "external" thus making the sentence completely meaningless, and was in all probability a typesetter's mistake. It is reasonable to assume, therefore, that someone in London, perhaps Franklin himself, made the improvements for the English edition. We know that he had a hand in its publication because on the 8th of August, 1767, he wrote Joseph Galloway "Our friends here have thought that a Publication of my *Examination* here might answer some of the above Purposes, by removing Prejudices, refuting Falsehoods, and demonstrating our Merits with regard to this Country. It is accordingly printed and has a great Run." Crane points out that the earliest appearance of a reprint of the text in a London magazine was in July of 1767. The text of all the magazine appearances follows the London edition. On the basis of this it is reasonable to assert that there was no English edition of the pamphlet until the middle of 1767.

Ford's hypothesis that Almon issued the pamphlet first without a title page cannot be absolutely disposed of although we can be sure that he was wrong in assigning it to the year 1766. It is possible that the known copies (CSmH, CtY, MiU-C, PPAmP, PU) are simply imperfect copies of either this edition or no. 31f. The two copies that Ford records (PPL, NN) are not reported to be in those two libraries today. Even if the above existing copies were stitched and uncut as originally issued, it would be impossible to tell whether a title page had been removed at a later date because the rest of the pamphlet is identical to the two other London issues.

There is, however, a more indirect way of discounting this part of Ford's theory. The wording of this, no. 31e, title page is as innocuous as the one requested by Strahan for the American edition. Indeed the titles are almost the same except that the word "August" has been changed to "Honourable," a more proper term to use for the House of Commons. In the second version of the title, no. 31f, the printer, if anything, becomes more cautious for there he omits even the indirect reference to Parliament. Indeed it could be argued that if Almon did issue the pamphlet with only the caption-title, which also omits a reference to the Stamp Act, he did so last because he became even more cautious. This would be pure conjecture, but the argument is no less compelling than the one Ford uses for putting the version first.

Ford *Franklin* 289 & errata on p. xi.

Copies: MH, PPL, WHi.

31f. ————. The Examination Of Doctor Benjamin Franklin, Relative to the Repeal Of The American Stamp Act, In MDCCLXVI.

[London: J. Almon] MDCCLXVII. . . .

Same collation.

The same sheets as no. 31e with a variant title page. Inspection of two stitched and uncut copies makes it clear that the title page and the last page were never conjugate. It is this version of the title that is used in the reprint of the *Examination* in the *Gentleman's Magazine* and the *London Magazine* for July 1767 and in Benjamin Vaughan's edition of Franklin's *Political, Miscellaneous, Philosophical Pieces,* London, 1779. It is also the wording used in vol. III of *A Collection of the Most Interesting Tracts, Lately Published in England and America, On the Subjects of Taxing the American Colonies,* London, J. Almon, 1767. Smyth in his reprint in *The Writings of Benjamin Franklin,* 1906, vol. IV, pp. 413-448 gives, in footnotes, ten changed readings which he says are from the "second edition." None of these appear in any of the editions described here or in the reprints mentioned above. I have been unable to determine where Smyth found this version.

Sabin 25502, Ford *Franklin* 288.

Copies: CtY, DLC, ICN, InU, MB, MBAt, MiU-C, NHi, NN, PHi, PPAmP, RPJCB, ViU.

31g. ————. Die Verhörung Doctor Benjamin Franklins vor der Hohen Versammlung der Hauses der Gemeinen vor Grossbrittannien, die Stämpel-Act, &c.

Philadelphia, Gedruckt und zu finden bey H. Miller . . . 1766.

[1]-43 p., 8vo, A-E⁴ F².

The undated French translation, *Interrogatoire De Mr. Franklin,* with a Strasbourg imprint tentatively assigned to 1767 by Ford 296 and Sabin 25504, was not printed until 1777 according to an unpublished letter in the American Philosophical Society from the translator Charles De Hirschberg to Franklin, dated October 23, 1777.

Evans 10304, Sabin 25503, Ford *Franklin* 297.

Copies: CtY, PHi, PPL.

[HOPKINS, STEPHEN]. *The Grievances of the American Colonies Candidly Examined.* London, 1766, see: 14b.

32. INGERSOLL, JARED, 1722-1781.

Mr. Ingersoll's Letters Relating To The Stamp-Act.

New-Haven: Printed and sold by Samuel Green . . . M,DCC,LXVI.

1 p. l., [i]-iv, [1]-68 p., 4to, [-]¹ A-S².

Advertised in the *Connecticut Courant* for October 13, 1766, and reprinted in the *Boston Evening Post* between October 27 and November 24, 1766. See also: Lawrence H. Gipson's *Jared Ingersoll*, New Haven, 1920, p. 380.

Evans 10342, Sabin 34744.

Copies: CtHi, CtHWatk, CtY, DLC, MBAt, MH, MHi, MWA, MiU-C, NN, PPL, RPJCB, WHi.

OTIS, JAMES. *The Rights of the British Colonies Asserted.* London, 1766, see: 4c, 4d, 4e.

33. [JOHNSON, STEPHEN] 1724-1786.

Some Important Observations, Occasioned by, and adapted to, The Publick Fast, Ordered by Authority, December 18th, A.D. 1765. On Account of the Peculiar Circumstances of the present Day. . . .

Newport: Printed and sold by Samuel Hall. 1766.

1 p. l., [1]-61 p., 4to, [-]² A-G⁴ H².

Advertised in the *Newport Mercury* for March 31, 1766. Attributed to Johnson by Evans. Evans 10434 is a ghost entry for this.

Evans 10346, Sabin 36323, Alden 351.

Copies: MH, MHi, MWA, NHi, NN, PPAmP, RPB, RPJCB.

34. A Letter To The North American, On Occasion of his Address To The Committee of Correspondence In Barbados. By a Native of the Island.

Barbados: Printed by George Esmand and Comp. M.DCC.LXVI.

1 p. l., [1]-47 p., 8vo, [-]² A-F⁴ (F4 blank).

A reply to John Dickinson's *An Address to the Committee of Correspondence in Barbados,* Philadelphia, 1766, no. 27.

Sabin 20038.

Copies: DLC, MH, NN, PHi, PPL, RPJCB.

35a. MAYHEW, JONATHAN, 1720-1766.

The Snare broken. A Thanksgiving-Discourse, Preached . . . May 23, 1766. Occasioned By The Repeal Of The Stamp-Act. . . .

Boston: Printed and Sold by R. & S. Draper . . . Edes & Gill . . . and T. & J. Fleet . . . 1766.

[i]-viii, 1-44 p., 8vo, [A]-F⁴ G².

Advertised in the *Massachusetts Gazette and Boston Weekly News-Letter* for May 29, 1766.

Evans 10388, Sabin 47148.

Copies: CSmH, CtHi, CtY, DLC, InU, MBAt, MH, MHi, MWA, MWiW-C, MiU-C, NHi, NN, PHi, PPL, RPJCB, ViU.

35b. ———. ———. The Second Edition.

Boston: Re-Printed and Sold by R. & S. Draper . . . Edes & Gill . . . and T. & J. Fleet . . . 1766.

[i]-viii, 9-52 p., 8vo, [A]-F⁴ G².

Evans 10389, Sabin 47148.

Copies: CtHi, CtY, DLC, ICN, MB, MH, MHi, MWA, MiU-C, NHi, PPL, RPJCB.

35c. ———. ———.

Boston Printed, and London reprinted, for G. Kearsly . . . [1766?].

[i]-vi, [1]-41 p., 8vo, A³ B-C⁸ D⁵.

Sabin 47148.

Copies: BM, CtY, DLC, MH, MiU-C, RPJCB.

36. [MORRISON, KENNETH] d. 1780.

An Essay Towards the Vindication Of The Committee of Correspondence In Barbados, From the Aspersions and Calumnies thrown upon them in an anonymous Piece, Printed in Philadelphia, under the Title of an Address to them, occasioned by their Letter to their Agent in London . . . By a Barbadian. . . .

Barbados: Printed by George Esmand and Comp. M,DCC,LXVI.

[1]-26 p., 8vo, A-C⁴ D¹.

A reply to John Dickinson's *An Address to the Committee of Correspondence*, Philadelphia, 1766, no. 27. In a contemporary hand on the RPJCB copy is the notation that this is by "The Rev. Mr. Morison." For discussion of this pamphlet and Morrison see: the John Carter Brown Library *Annual Report*, 1957-58, pp. 22-26 and William Dickson's *Letters on Slavery*, London, 1789, p. 45.

Sabin 3267.

Copies: PHi, RPJCB.

37. Mühlenberg, Heinrich Melchior, 1711-1782.

[Ein Zeugniss von der Güte und Ernst (*sic*) Gottes gegen sein Bundesvolk in Alten und neuen Zeiten und des Volkes Undankbarkeit, gelegentlich des Dankfestes wegen Aufhebung der Stempel-Acte 1. August 1766. . . .]

[Philadelphia: Gedruckt by Henrich Miller, 1766].

From Evans, a copy is said to be in NN but it cannot be located. However, it is known that Mühlenberg was concerned about the Stamp Act. In his *Journals*, translated by Tappert and Doberstein, 1942-1945, vol. II, p. 318, there is an entry for March 30, 1767, in which he says that in a letter of that date to William Pasche he "Mentioned that since June of last year I wrote letters dated September 18, 19, and 20 and sent them together with a small box of tracts pertaining to the Repeal of the Stamp Act, to Messrs. Mildred and Roberts, merchants in London."

Evans 10401.

38a. The Necessity Of Repealing The American Stamp-Act Demonstrated: Or, A Proof that Great-Britain must be injured by that Act. In a Letter to a Member of the British House of Commons. . . .

London: Printed for J. Almon . . . MDCCLXVI. . . .

[1]-46 p., 1 l. (last l. advts.), 8vo, A-F⁴.

Also issued in vol. II of *A Collection of the Most Interesting Tracts On the Subjects of Taxing the American Colonies*, London, J. Almon, 1766.

Sabin 52213.

Copies: CSmH, CtHWatk, CtY, DLC, ICN, InU, MB, MH, MHi, MWiW-C, MiU-C, NHi, NN, NjP, PHi, PPAmP, PPL, RPJCB, ViU.

38b. ———.

London; Printed. Boston Re-Printed, and Sold by Edes and Gill . . . 1766.

[1]-31 p., 8vo, [A]-D⁴.

Advertised in the *Boston Gazette* for February 24, 1766 and in the *Connecticut Courant* for March 10, 1766 as "just published in Boston."

Evans 10402, Sabin 52213.

Copies: DLC, MBAt, MHi, MWA, MiU-C, NN, PPL, RPJCB.

39. PATTEN, WILLIAM, 1738-1775.

A Discourse Delivered at Hallifax [*sic*] In the County of Plymouth, July 24th 1766. On the Day of Thanks-giving . . . for the Repeal of the Stamp-Act. . . .

Boston: N. E. Printed by D. Kneeland . . . for Thomas Leverett . . . MDCCLXVI.

[1]-22 p., 8vo, [A]-C^4 (C4 blank).

Evans 10440, Sabin 59121.

Copies: CtY, DLC, ICN, InU, MB, MH, MHi, MWA, NN, RPB, RPJCB.

40a. PENNSYLVANIA. UNIVERSITY.

Four Dissertations, On The Reciprocal Advantages Of A Perpetual Union Between Great-Britain And Her American Colonies. Written For Mr. Sargent's Prize Medal. To which (by Desire) is prefixed, An Eulogium, Spoken on the Delivery of the Medal at the Public Commencement in the College of Philadelphia, May 20th, 1766.

Philadelphia: Printed by William and Thomas Bradford . . . M,DCC,LXVI.

[i]-x, [i]-viii, 1-12, [1-2], [1]-112 p., 8vo, A^4 a-c^4 A-O^4.

Although the *Pennsylvania Journal* of June 5, 1766 describes this as "In press and to be published by subscription," the first announcement of its actual publication appears in the *Journal* for October 23, 1766. Also advertised in the *South Carolina and American General Gazette* for November 28, 1766. The dissertations are by John Morgan, Stephen Watts, Joseph Reed, and Francis Hopkinson. The Eulogium is by Provost William Smith. Mr. Sargent was a Bristol merchant who had given the money for the medal instead of making a contribution to the support of the college when asked by Smith during a fund-raising trip to England. Sargent specified that union with Great Britain was to be the topic of the dissertation.

Evans 10400, Sabin 84611.

Copies: BM, CSmH, CtY, DLC, MB, MH, MHi, MWA, MiU-C, NN, NjP, PHi, PPRos, PPL, PU, RPJCB, ViU.

40b. ———. ———.

Philadelphia Printed. London Re-printed, For T. Payne . . . and D. Wilson . . . [1766?].

1 p. l., [i]-viii, 1-12, [1-2], [1]-112 p., 8vo, a-c^4 A-O^4.

Sabin 84612.

Copies: BM, CtY, ICN, InU, MB, MBAt, MH, MiU-C, RPJCB.

41a. [Pitt, William, 1st Earl of Chatham] 1708-1788.
Political Debates.

A Paris [*i.e.* London], Chez J. W. Imprimeur . . . MDCCLXVI. . . .
1 p. l., [1]-18 p., 8vo, [A]¹ B-C⁴ [D]¹.

William Hick's *The Nature and Extent of Parliamentary Power*, Philadelphia, 1768, is a reply to this speech on the repeal of the Stamp-
Act. For a discussion of the unreliability of the reporting of this and
other Parliamentary debates see: Basil Williams' *The Life of William
Pitt*, 1913, vol. II, p. 337. These remarks were also frequently re-
printed with other speeches of the period, but only separately printed editions have been included here. The original circulation of the
libraries for the census of copies did not distinguish between this and
no. 41b. Therefore, some of the copies listed thereunder may actually be this edition.

Sabin 63761.

Copies: MB, MiU-C.

41b. [————]. ———— [with a four-line quotation from "The Great
Commoner"].

Same imprint.

2 p. l., [1]-18 p., 8vo, [A]² B-C⁴ [D]² ([D]2 blank).

This edition was entirely reset. Other distinguishing features are the
following different catch words. The ones for no. 41a are given
first: p. 6—Ber!, Number!; p. 8—confirmed, firmed; p. 12—ed,
and.

Sabin 63761.

Copies: BM, CtY, DLC, ICN, MB, MBAt, MH, MiU-C, NN, NcD,
PHi, PPL, PU, RPJCB.

41c. [————]. The Celebrated Speech of A Celebrated Commoner.
. . .

London: Printed for Stephen Austin, in Ludgate Street. MDCCLXVI.

1 p. l., [1]-18 p., 8vo, [A]¹ B-C⁴ [D]¹.

The body of this was printed from substantially the same setting of type
as no. 41b. However, the title page, the first two pages, and the
last two pages were reset.

Sabin 63066.

Copies: BM, CSmH, CtHWatk, CtY, DLC, MBAt, MH, MiU-C, NHi,
PPL, RPJCB, ViU.

41d. [————]. ————. A New Edition, Corrected.
Same imprint.
[1]-17 p., 8vo, B-C⁴.
Sabin 63066.
Copies: BM, CSmH, CtY, ICN, InU, MB, MH, MWA, MiU-C, RPJCB.

41e. [————]. ————. A New Edition.
London: Printed for J. Bew ... MDCCLXXV.
[1]-22 p., 8vo, [A]-C⁴ (C4 blank).
Copies: BM, MiU-C, PPAmP, PPL, RPJCB.

POWNALL, THOMAS. *The Administration of the Colonies. The Third Edition.* London, 1766, see: 5c.

————. *Considerations On the Points Lately Brought into Question as to the Parliament's Right of Taxing the Colonies.* London, 1766, see: 5g.

42a. [RAY, NICHOLAS].
The Importance Of The Colonies of North America, And the Interest of Great Britain with regard to them, Considered. Together with Remarks on the Stamp-Duty. . . .
London: Printed for T. Peat ... 1766.
2 p. l., [1]-16 p., 4to, [A]-E².
Sabin 68030.
Copies: CSmH, CtY, MH, MHi, MiU-C, RPJCB.

42b. ————. ————. By Nicholas Ray.
Same imprint and collation.
Printed from substantially the same setting of type as no. 42a.
Copies: MBAt, MH, MiU-C.

42c. ————. ————. By Nicholas Ray, now of London; a Native, and formerly a Citizen of New-York.
London, printed: New-York, re-printed, 1766. By John Holt . . . At the Cost of the Author . . . for the Benefit of the Society for the Encouragement of Arts, Manufactures and Agriculture, in New-York.
2 p. l., [1]-16 p., 4to, [A]-E².
Advertised in the *Boston Evening Post* for February 17, 1766, the *Penn-*

sylvania Journal for March 10, 1766 and the *Virginia Gazette* (Purdie & Dixon) for April 18, 1766.

Evans 10471, Sabin 68031.

Copies: CSmH, CtY, DLC, InU, MB, MBAt, MiU-C, NHi, NN, PHi, PP, PPAmP, PPL, RPJCB.

43. ROWLAND, DAVID SHERMAN, 1719-1794.

Divine Providence Illustrated and Improved. A Thanksgiving-Discourse, Preached . . . June 4, 1766 Being His Majesty's Birth Day, and Day of Rejoicing, Occasioned By The Repeal Of The Stamp-Act. . . .

Providence, (New-England) Printed by Sarah Goddard, and Company. [1766].

2 p. l., [i]-viii, [1]-31 p., 8vo, [-]² [A]-E⁴.

Evans 10483, Sabin 73557, Alden 359.

Copies: CSmH, CtY, DLC, InU, MH, MHi, MWA, MiU-C, NHi, PPL, RPB, RPJCB.

43Aa. STAMP ACT CONGRESS, New York, 1765.

Proceedings Of The Congress At New-York.

Annapolis: Printed by Jonas Green, Printer to the Province. MDCCLXVI.

[1]-28 p., fol., A-G⁶.

Caption-title, imprint on p. 28.

Advertised in the *Maryland Gazette* for September 11, 1766. This is the report of the Maryland delegates to the Congress delivered to the Maryland House of Representatives on November 27, 1766. See also: Lawrence C. Wroth's "The Bibliographical Way," *The Colophon, New Series*, vol. III (Spring, 1938), pp. 228-229.

Evans 10424, Sabin 65831, Wroth 273.

Copies: DLC, RPJCB.

43Ab. ————. Authentic Account Of The Proceedings Of The Congress Held At New-York, In MDCCLXV, On the Subject of the American Stamp Act.

[London: J. Almon] MDCCLXVII. . . .

1 p. l., 1-37 p., 8vo, B-F⁴.

A reprint of no. 43Aa with the instructions to each of the delegations omitted. Also issued in vol. III of *A Collection of the Most Interesting Tracts, Lately Published in England and America, On the Subjects of Taxing the American Colonies,* London, J. Almon, 1767.

Yr. Mr. 5 8

322

THE

EXAMINATION

OF

Dr. BENJAMIN FRANKLIN,

BEFORE AN

AUGUST ASSEMBLY,

House of Commons 1776.

Relating to the REPEAL of the STAMP-ACT, &c.

WILLIAMSBURG:

Printed and Sold by WILLIAM RIND, opposite the CAPITOL.

III. The Williamsburg edition of Franklin's *Examination*, George Washington's copy, no. 31d, The Boston Athenæum.

The STAMP-ACT REPEALED;

A

SERMON,

Preached in the MEETING at SAVANNAH in
GEORGIA, June 25th, 1766.

By J. J. ZUBLY, V. D. M.

𝔓ublished at the 𝕽equest and 𝕰xpence of the 𝕳earers.

Brethren, ye have been called unto liberty; only
use not liberty as an occasion to the flesh.
But if ye bite and devour one another, take heed
that ye be not consumed one of another. GALAT.
v. 13, 15.

SAVANNAH: Printed by JAMES JOHNSTON.

M,DCC,LXVI,

IV. John Joachim Zubly's *The Stamp-Act Repealed*, no. 46a,
the Houghton Library, Harvard University.

Sabin 53537.

Copies: BM, CSmH, CtY, DLC, ICN, InU, MB, MBAt, MH, MHi, MWA, MWiW-C, MiU-C, NN, NcU, PHi, PPAmP, PPL, RPJCB, ViU.

44. STILLMAN, SAMUEL, 1737-1803.

Good News from a far Country. A Sermon Preached at Boston, May 17. 1766. Upon the Arrival of the important News Of The Repeal of the Stamp-Act. . . .

Boston: Printed by Kneeland and Adams . . . for Philip Freeman . . . MDCCLXVI.

[1]-34 p., 4to, [A]-D⁴ E² (E2 blank).

Advertised in the *Boston Gazette* for June 16, 1766.

Evans 10503, Sabin 91796.

Copies: CSmH, CtY, DLC, ICN, MB, MBAt, MH, MHi, MWA, MiU-C, NN, RPJCB, ViU, WHi.

45. THROOP, BENJAMIN, 1712-1785.

A Thanksgiving Sermon, Upon the Occasion, of the glorious Newes of the repeal of the Stamp Act; Preached in New-Concord, in Norwich, June 26, 1766. . . .

New-London: Printed by Timothy Green, MDCCLXVI.

[1]-16 p., 4to, [A]-B⁴.

Evans 10506, Sabin 95761.

Copies: DLC, MWA, NN.

46a. ZUBLY, JOHN JOACHIM, 1724-1781.

The Stamp-Act Repealed; A Sermon, Preached in the Meeting at Savannah in Georgia, June 25th, 1766. . . .

Savannah: Printed by James Johnston. M,DCC,LXVI.

1 p. l., [1]-30 p., 4to, [-]¹ A-C⁴ D³.

Half-title reads: Mr. Zubly's Sermon On the Repeal Of The Stamp-Act. Plate IV.

Evans 10529, Sabin 106392.

Copies: MH.

46b. ———. ———. The Second Edition.

Same imprint and collation.

Advertised in the *Georgia Gazette* for August 27, 1766.

Evans 10530, Sabin 106393.
Copies: DLC, MWA, NHi.

46c. ———. ———.

Georgia printed, South-Carolina, Re-Printed by Peter Timothy. M,DCC,LXVI, and to be sold at Mr. John Edwards, and Mr. Edward Jones's Store, in Charles-Town.

[1]-24 p., 4to, A-C⁴.

Advertised in the *South Carolina Gazette* for August 11, 1766. Evans
    10532 lists a Philadelphia edition printed by Henry Miller without
    collation or location. No copy has been located. It is probably a ghost.
    Perhaps Evans confused it with no. 204a.

Evans 10531, Sabin 106393.
Copies: MBAt.

1767

47. CHARLESTON, S. C., MERCHANTS.

A Representation Of Facts, Relative to the Conduct of Daniel Moore, Esquire; Collector of His Majesty's Customs at Charles-Town, In South Carolina . . . Transmitted By the Merchants of Charles-Town, To Charles Garth . . . Agent for the Province of South-Carolina; And Recommended in a Letter from the Honourable The Committee of Correspondence.

Charles-Town, South-Carolina: Printed by Charles Crouch . . . 1767.
[i]-vii, [1], [3]-38 p., fol., [a-b]² [A]-I².

This was the opening publication in the series dealing with the actions
    of the Charleston, S. C. customs-house officers that led to the charges
    of fraud and the exchange between Henry Laurens and Sir Egerton
    Leigh, nos. 57 and 66. For a partial discussion see: Oliver M. Dicker-
    son's *The Navigation Acts And the American Revolution*, Philadelphia,
    1951, pp. 224-231; Leila Sellers' *Charleston Business on the Eve of
    the Revolution*, Chapel Hill, 1934, pp. 49-50; and Carl Ubbelohde's
    The Vice-Admiralty Courts and the American Revolution, Chapel Hill,
    1960. All of these studies, however, omit this pamphlet although it
    is clearly a part of the incident.

Evans 10748, Sabin 50342.
Copies: BM, MiU-C, RPJCB.

48a. [COLDEN, CADWALLADER] 1688-1776.

The Conduct Of Cadwallader Colden, Esquire, Late Lieutenant-

Governor Of New York: Relating To The Judges Commissions, Appeals To The King, And The Stamp-Duty.

[London] Printed In the Year MDCCLXVII.

1 p. l., [1]-66 p., 8vo, [-]¹ A-H⁴ [I]¹.

For discussion of authorship and printing, see *Collections of the New York Historical Society*, vol. X (1877), pp. 132-176. In the RPJCB copy in the handwriting of Lawrence C. Wroth is the following statement: "Wilberforce Eames says this is the London edition."

Sabin 14276.

Copies: CSmH, CtY, ICN, InU, MH, MWA, MiU-C, PHi, RPJCB.

48b. [————]. ————.

[New York] Printed in the Year MDCCLXVII.

2 p. l., [2]-56 p., 8vo, [-]² A² B-G⁴ H².

In the RPJCB copy in the handwriting of Lawrence C. Wroth is the following statement: "Wilberforce Eames says this is the New York edition."

Evans 10582.

Copies: DLC, NHi, PPL, RPJCB.

49. The Commercial Conduct Of the Province of New-York Considered, And The True Interest of that Colony attempted to be shewn. In a Letter to The Society of Arts, Agriculture, and Oeconomy.

Printed for the Benefit of the Society of Arts, Agriculture, and Oeconomy, of New-York. 1767.

[i]-iv, 5-20 p., 4to, [A]-E².

An abstract appeared in the *Massachusetts Gazette and Boston Weekly News-Letter* for December 4, 1767 and in the *Newport Mercury* for December 28, 1767.

Evans 10584, Sabin 14971.

Copies: CtHWatk, CtY, DLC, MBAt, MH, MWiW-C, MiU-C, NHi, NN, PPL.

50. CUMINGS, HENRY, 1737-1823.

A Thanksgiving Sermon Preached at Billerica, November 27. 1766.
. . .

Boston: N. E. Printed by Kneeland and Adams . . . for Thomas Leverett . . . MDCCLXVII.

[1]-32 p., 8vo, [A]-D⁴.

On the repeal of the Stamp Act.

Evans 10596, Sabin 17901.

Copies: BM, ICN, MB, MBAt, MH, MHi, MWA, NHi, NN, RPJCB.

51. FISH, ELISHA, 1719-1795.

Joy and Gladness: A Thanksgiving Discourse, Preached in Upton, Wednesday, May 28, 1766; Occasioned By The Repeal Of The Stamp-Act. . . .

Providence, in New-England: Printed and sold by Sarah Goddard, and Company . . . M,DCC,LXVII.

1 p. l., [1]-17 p., 8vo, [-]¹ A-B⁴ [C]¹.

Evans 10612, Sabin 24428, Alden 362.

Copies: CtY, MWA, PPL, RPJCB.

GT. BRIT. PARLIAMENT. HOUSE OF COMMONS. *The Examination of Dr. Benjamin Franklin . . . Relative to the Repeal of the American Stamp Act.* [London] 1767, see: 31e, 31f.

52a. [LLOYD, CHARLES] 1735-1773.

The Conduct Of The Late Administration Examined. With An Appendix, Containing Original and Authentic Documents. . . .

London; Printed for J. Almon . . . MDCCLXVII.

[1]-160 p., 1 l., i-liv, [2] p. (last 2 p. advts.), 8vo, [A]² B-U⁴ X² [-]¹ a-g⁴.

The first portion of this is said to have been dictated by George Grenville to Lloyd who was his secretary. See the article on Lloyd in the *Dictionary of National Biography.*

Sabin 22624.

Copies: BM, CSmH, CtHWatk, CtY, DLC, ICN, InU, MB, MBAt, MH, MWiW-C, MiU-C, NHi, NN, NjP, PPL, RPJCB, ViU, WHi.

52b. [———]. ———. The Second Edition.

London; Printed for J. Almon . . . MDCCLXVII. . . .

1 p. l., [5]-160 p., 1 l., i-liv, [2] p. (last 2 p. advts.), 8vo, [A]¹ B-U⁴ X² [-]¹ a-g⁴.

Printed from substantially the same setting of type as no. 52a. To the title page has been added a statement that this is "Relative to the American Stamp-Act" and the half title is omitted. Also issued in vol. III of *A Collection of the most interesting Tracts, Lately Published in*

England and America, on the Subjects of Taxing the American Colonies, London, J. Almon, 1767 and in vol. II of *A Collection of Tracts on the Subjects of Taxing The British Colonies in America,* London, J. Almon, 1773.

Sabin 15203.

Copies: BM, CSmH, CtHWatk, CtY, DLC, InU, MH, MHi, MiU-C, NHi, NN, PHi, PPAmP, PPL, PU, RPJCB, WHi.

52c. [————]. ————.

London: Printed. 1767. Boston: Re-printed and sold by Edes and Gill . . . 1767.

[1]-107 p., 4to, [A]-N⁴ O².

Advertised in the *Boston Evening Post* for May 18, 1767.

Evans 10663, Sabin 15202.

Copies: CtHi, CtY, DLC, MB, MBAt, MH, MHi, MWA, MiU-C, NHi, NN, PHi, PPL, RPJCB.

STAMP ACT CONGRESS, 1765. *Authentic Account of the Proceedings of the Congress.* London, 1767, see: 43ab.

1768

53. The Constitutional Right of The Legislature Of Great Britain To Tax the British Colonies In America Impartially Stated. . . .

London: Printed for J. Ridley . . . MDCCLXVIII.

2 p. l., [i]-xi, [1]-60 p. (1st p. l. adv.), 8vo, [A]⁴ a⁴ B-H⁴ I².

A reply to this is to be found in the Appendix to *A Letter To the Right Honourable Earl of Hilsborough,* first printed in London in 1769 and Boston reprinted the same year, no. 67.

Sabin 16138.

Copies: BM, CSmH, CtY, DLC, ICN, InU, MB, MiU-C, NHi, NN, PPAmP, RPJCB.

54a. [DICKINSON, JOHN] 1732-1808.

Letters From A Farmer In Pennsylvania, To The Inhabitants Of The British Colonies.

Philadelphia: Printed by David Hall, and William Sellers. MDCCLXVIII.

[1]-71 p., 8vo, A-I⁴.

Advertised in the *Pennsylvania Gazette* for March 17, 1768. These twelve letters appeared first in the *Pennsylvania Chronicle* between

November 30, 1767, and February 8, 1768. Before the end of 1767 almost every colonial newspaper began to reprint the series. Some printed only a few of the letters, but others printed all twelve. For an account of the newspaper appearance see: Arthur M. Schlesinger's *Prelude to Independence*, New York, 1958, pp. 88-91.

Evans 10875.

Copies: BM, CSmH, DLC, MB, MH, MWiW-C, MiU-C, NHi, NN, PHi, PPAmP, PPL, RPJCB.

54b. [————]. ————. The Second Edition.

Same imprint and collation.

Advertised in the *Pennsylvania Gazette* for June 16, 1768.

Evans 10879, Sabin 20044.

Copies: CtY, ICN, InU, MWA, NN, PHi, PPAmP, PPL, RPJCB.

54c. [————]. ————.

Boston: Printed By Mein and Fleeming, And To Be Sold By John Mein . . . MDCCLXVIII.

[1]-146, [2] p. (last 2 p. advts.), 8vo, [A]-S⁴ T².

Advertised in the *Boston Evening Post* for April 4, 1768, and the *Newport Mercury* for April 25th. There are two states noted, the first with six lines of text on page 55 and T2 blank, the second with seven lines on p. 55 and on T2 "To the ingenious Author of certain patriotic Letters, subscribed A Farmer"—a letter ordered to be printed by the town of Boston, March 22, 1768. For the omission of a significant passage in this edition see: William W. Crosskey's *Politics and Government*, Chicago, 1953, pp. 1289-1291.

Evans 10876, Sabin 20044.

Copies: BM, CSmH, CtHi, CtHWatk, DLC, InU, MB, MBAt, MH, MHi, MWA, MiU-C, NHi, NN, PPL, RPJCB, ViU, WHi.

54d. [————]. ————.

Boston: Printed and Sold by Edes & Gill . . . MDCCLXVIII.

[1]-80 p., 4to, A-K⁴.

Advertised in the *Massachusetts Gazette and Boston Weekly News-Letter* for May 26, 1768. The *Connecticut Courant* for June 13th advertised either this or no. 54e.

Evans 10877, Sabin 20044.

Copies: CtHWatk, CtY, ICN, MB, MBAt, MH, MHi, MWA, MiU-C, NHi, PHi, PPL, RPJCB, ViU, WHi.

54e. [————]. ————.

New-York: re-printed by John Holt . . . 1768.

[1]-118 p., 12mo, [-]² A⁴ B² C⁴ D² E⁴ F² G⁴ H² I⁴ K⁴ L² M⁴ N²
O⁴ P⁴ Q² R² S⁴ T² (T2 blank).

Advertised in the *New-York Journal* for April 22, 1768.

Evans 10878, Sabin 20044.

Copies: CtHi, CtY, DLC, MBAt, MH, MWA, NHi, NN, PHi, RPJCB,
ViU, WHi.

54f. [————]. ————.

London. Printed for J. Almon . . . MDCCLXVIII.

2 p. l., [i]-iii, [1]-118 p., 8vo, [A]⁴ B-H⁸ I³.

Pages i-iii contain the preface "The British Editor to the Reader" which
is by Benjamin Franklin. See Verner W. Crane's *Benjamin Franklin's
Letters to the Press 1758-1775,* Chapel Hill, 1950, pp. 121-122.

Sabin 20044.

Copies: BM, CSmH, CtY, DLC, ICN, InU, MBAt, MH, MWiW-C,
MiU-C, NHi, NN, PHi, PPAmP, PPL, RPJCB.

54g. [————]. ————. To which are Added, as an Appendix, The
Speeches of Lord Chatham, and Lord Camden, The one upon the Stamp
Act, the other on the Declaratary Bill, With A Preface by the Dublin
Editor.

[Dublin] Printed for J. Sheppard . . . MDCCLXVIII.

[i]-vii, [8]-119, [1], [1]-29 p., 8vo, A-P⁴ A-C⁴ D³.

The "Preface" is the one by Franklin in no. 54f.

Sabin 20044.

Copies: DLC, MiU-C.

54h. [————]. ————. The Third Edition.

Philadelphia: Printed by William and Thomas Bradford . . .
M,DCC,LXIX.

1 p. l., [1]-104 p., 8vo, [-]¹ A-N⁴.

Some copies were issued with the engraved portrait of Dickinson that
had been advertised in the *Pennsylvania Chronicle* for October 17,
1768. See: *The Annual Report of the John Carter Brown Library 1953-
54,* pp. 34-37 and R. T. H. Halsey's edition of *Letters from a Farmer
in Pennsylvania,* New York, 1903, pp. xxxviii-xlii. Two issues noted,
one with x's on the outside corners of the ornaments around the
initial I on p. 1 and one with rosettes.

Evans 11238, Sabin 20044.

Copies: BM, CSmH, DLC, MH, MWA, MiU-C, NHi, NN, PHi, PPAmP, PPL, PU, RPJCB, ViU.

54i. [————]. The Farmer's and Monitor's Letters. To The Inhabitants of The British Colonies.

Williamsburg: Printed by William Rind, MDCCLXIX.

1 p. l., [i]-iii, [1]-36, 33-97, [1] p., 4to, [-]¹ A-K² K-O² P³ Q-Z² Aa-Bb².

Advertised in the *Virginia Gazette* (Rind) for June 29, 1769. The *Maryland Gazette* for April 20, 1769, carried an advertisement of Rind's proposal for the publication of this. The ten "Monitor's Letters," which were written by Arthur Lee, first appeared in Rind's newspaper between February 23 and April 28, 1769. See: Richard Henry Lee's *Life of Arthur Lee*, Boston, 1829, pp. 18-19. The unnumbered page at the end contains Dickinson's "Song of Liberty."

Evans 11239, Sabin 20044.

Copies: CSmH, DLC, MBAt, MWA, RPJCB.

54j. [————]. Letters From A Farmer [&c.]....

Philadelphia Printed; And London Re-Printed For J. Almon . . . MDCCLXXIV.

[1]-136 p., 8vo, [A]-R⁴.

This may be the edition that was being offered for sale in the *Pennsylvania Journal* for December 21, 1774. Sabin lists a Philadelphia edition of this date with this collation in the Library of Congress. They do not own any such copy and the entry is probably a ghost resulting from a misreading of the imprint of this edition.

Sabin 20044.

Copies: BM, CSmH, CtY, DLC, ICN, MB, MH, MHi, MiU-C, NHi, NN, NcD, PPL, RPJCB.

54k. [————]. Lettres D'Un Fermier De Pensylvanie, Aux Habitans De L'Amérique Septentrionale, Traduites de l'Anglois.

A Amsterdam, [*i.e.* Paris?] Aux Dépens De La Compagnie. M.DCC.LXIX.

[i]-xxviij, [1]-258 p., 8vo, a⁸ b⁶ A-Q⁸ R¹.

Contains on pages iii-xxviij "Préface Du Traducteur" and "Avis De L'Editeur de Londres." The latter is a translation by Jacques Borbeu-Dubourg of Benjamin Franklin's preface to Almon's London edition of 1768, no. 54f. Also on pages 215-258 extracts from the *Pennsylvania Chronicle* and the *London Chronicle*, "Notice de la Pensyl-vanie," "Observations . . . sur l'accroissement de l'espece humaine, la population pays, &c. par Benjamin Francklin . . ." and "Epilogue Du Traducteur."

Sabin 20045.

Copies: CtY, DLC, MB, MH, MiU-C, PHi, PPAmP, PPL, PU, RPJCB.

55. [DOWNER, SILAS].

A Discourse Delivered in Providence, In The Colony of Rhode-Island, upon the 25th. Day of July, 1768. At The Dedication of the Tree of Liberty . . . By a Son of Liberty.

Providence: Printed and Sold By John Waterman . . . MDCCLXVIII.

[1]-16 p., 8vo, [A]-B⁴.

Author attribution from Alden.

Evans 10886, Sabin 20767, Alden 383.

Copies: CSmH, CtY, DLC, ICN, MH, MHi, MWA, MiU-C, NHi, NN, PHi, RPB, RPJCB.

56a. [HICKS, WILLIAM] 1735-1772.

The Nature and Extent of Parliamentary Power Considered; In some Remarks upon Mr. Pitt's Speech in the House of Commons, previous to the Repeal of the Stamp-Act. With an Introduction Applicable to the present situation of the Colonies. . . .

Philadelphia, Printed [by William and Thomas Bradford?] Anno MDCCLXVIII.

[i]-xvi, [1]-32 p., 8vo, [A]⁴ B-C² D-F⁴ [G]⁴.

Originally appeared in the *Pennsylvania Journal* in six installments be-tween January 21 and February 25, 1768. Also reprinted in the *Boston Evening Post* from February 15 to March 21, 1768, and in the *South Carolina Gazette* from March 28 to April 11, 1768. The au-thorship is based on an attribution in a contemporary hand on the DLC copy. Printing credited to the Bradfords because as the print-ers of the *Journal* it would have been reasonable for them to have re-printed it. A reply to Pitt's speech on the repeal of the Stamp Act, first published as *Political Debates*, London, 1766, no. 41.

Evans 10985.

Copies: DLC, NN, PHi.

56b. [————]. ————.

New-York, reprinted from the Pennsylvania Journal by John Holt . . . 1768.

[1]-40 p., 12mo, A-C⁶ D².

Advertised in the *New-York Journal* for July 7, 1768.

Evans 10986, Sabin 52052.

Copies: DLC, NHi, NN, PPL.

57a. [LAURENS, HENRY] 1723-1797.

Extracts From The Proceedings Of The Court Of Vice-Admiralty In Charles-Town, South-Carolina; In the Cause, George Roupell, Esq; v. the Ship Ann and Goods: With A Few Explanatory Remarks. To which is subjoined, some General Observations On American Custom-House Officers, And Courts Of Vice-Admiralty. . . .

[Philadelphia] America: Printed, [sold by William and Thomas Bradford] Anno Domini, M,DCC,LXVIII.

[i]-iv, [1]-20 p., 4to, A-C⁴.

> The documents printed here were sent by Laurens to William Fisher of Philadelphia, part owner of the ship *Ann*, in the fall of 1768. They continue the dispute begun in the *Representation of Facts*, no. 47. Fisher had them printed late in 1768, and at first apparently intended them for private distribution. However, in the *Pennsylvania Journal* for February 16, 1769, the Bradfords offered them for public sale probably because of the Charleston publication of the same month, no. 51b. For discussion see: Oliver M. Dickerson's *The Navigation Acts and The American Revolution*, Philadelphia, 1951, pp. 224-231; David S. Lovejoy's "Rights Imply Equality, The Case Against Admiralty Jurisdiction in America: 1764-1776," *William and Mary Quarterly* (3rd series), vol. XVI (1959), pp. 459-484; and Carl Ubbelohde's *The Vice-Admiralty Courts and the American Revolution*, Chapel Hill, 1960, pp. 104-114.

Evans 10945, Sabin 23532, 39925.

Copies: MBAt, MWA, NN, PPAmP, PPL.

57b. [————]. Extracts From The Proceedings Of The High Court Of Vice-Admiralty, In Charlestown, South-Carolina, Upon Six Several Informations, Adjudged By The Honourable Egerton Leigh, Esq; Sole Judge of that Court . . . With explanatory Remarks, &c. And Copies of two extraordinary Oaths. To Which Are Subjoined, Recapitulation, Reflections Arising From A Retrospect Of A Late Case, And Some General Observations On American Custom-House Officers, and Courts of Vice-Admiralty. . . .

Charlestown: Printed by David Bruce. MDCCLXIX.

[i]-iv, 1-42, 1-5, 1-4 p., fol., [A]-L² M¹ A² [B]¹ [C]².

According to Ubbelohde, this was published in February of 1769. It is an enlarged version of no. 57a with all the material after page 36 and pages 1-5 at the end added.

Copies: CSmH, MHi, MWA, NN, PPAmP, RPJCB.

57c. [————]. ————. The Second Edition, With An Appendix. . . .

Same imprint.

2 p. l., 1-49, [1]-4 p., 1 l., [1]-64 p., fol., [A]-M² [N]² [O]¹ [P]² [-]¹ A-Q².

Advertised in the *South Carolina Gazette and Country Journal* for April 4, 1769, as to be published "sometime in the month of June" and in the issue of July 25, 1769, as to be published on August 3rd. *An Appendix To The Extracts From The Proceedings of the High Court of Vice-Admiralty . . . Containing Strictures upon, and proper Answers to, A Pamphlet Entitled The Man Unmasked Published by Egerton Leigh. Together With A full Refutation of Mr. Leigh's Attempts to vindicate his Judicial Proceedings* . . . has separate paging (1-64 at end) and title page with the same imprint as the main body of the pamphlet. It is a reply to Leigh's *The Man Unmasked,* Charleston, 1769, no. 66. For further bibliographical notes see: A. S. Salley's "The First Presses of South Carolina," *Papers of the Bibliographical Society of America,* vol. II (1907-1908), pp. 68-69 and "Bibliographical Note" by V. H. Paltsits, *ibid.,* vol. XXXV (1941), pp. 294-297.

Evans 11307.

Copies: ScHi.

58a. The Power And Grandeur Of Great-Britain, Founded On The Liberty Of The Colonies, And The Mischiefs attending the Taxing them by Act of Parliament Demonstrated. . . .

New-York: Printed and Sold by James Parker . . . M,DCC,LXVIII.

[1]-24 p., 8vo, [A]-C⁴.

Advertised in the *New-York Journal* for July 28, 1768, the *Pennsylvania Chronicle* for August 8th, the *Pennsylvania Gazette* for August 18th as "Lately Published at New-York and to be sold by David Hall" and the *Providence Gazette* for August 27th.

Evans 11049, Sabin 64781.

Copies: CSmH, CtY, InU, MB, MH, MWA.

58b. ———.

Philadelphia: Printed and Sold by William Goddard . . . M,DCC,LXVIII.
[1]-22 p., 8vo, [A]-C⁴ (C4 blank).
Evans 11050, Sabin 64781.
Copies: MWA, NN, PHi, PPAmP, PPL, PU, RPJCB.

POWNALL, THOMAS. *The Administration of the Colonies. The Fourth Edition.* London, 1768, see: 5d.

59a. [SAYRE, STEPHEN] 1736-1818.

The Englishman Deceived; A Political Piece: Wherein Some very important Secrets of State are briefly recited, And offered to the Consideration of the Public. . . .

London: Printed for G. Kearsly . . . 1768. . . .

1 p. l., i-ii, 1-53 p., 8vo, [A]² B-D⁴ E³ F-H⁴.

An extract appeared in the *Newport Mercury* for August 8, 1768. Attributed to Sayre by the Library of Congress Catalog.

Sabin 22623.

Copies: CSmH, CtY, DLC, InU, MB, MH, MWA, MiU-C, NHi, NjP, PPL, PU, RPJCB.

59b. [———]. ———.

London: Printed, New-York reprinted by John Holt . . . MDCCLXVIII.
1 p. l., [i]-ii, [1]-40 p., 8vo, [B]-F⁴ G².
Advertised in the *New-York Journal* for October 20, 1768.
Evans 11065, Sabin 22623.
Copies: CSmH, CtHi, DLC, NHi, NN, PPL.

59c. [———]. ———.

London, Printed, 1768. Salem: Re-printed and sold by Samuel Hall . . . 1768.

[1]-38 p., 4to, [A]-E⁴ (E4 blank).

Evans 11066, Sabin 22623.

Copies: CSmH, CtY, DLC, ICN, MB, MBAt, MH, MHi, MWA, NN, NjP, PPL, RPJCB.

60. Some Observations Of Consequence, In Three Parts. Occasioned by the Stamp-Tax, Lately imposed on the British Colonies.

[Philadelphia?] Printed [By Hall and Sellers?] for the Author, MDCCLXVIII.

[i]-x, 11-80 p., 8vo, [A]-K⁴.

The Preface is signed "Loyal Patriot." The assignment of the printing of this to Hall and Sellers in Philadelphia is taken from Charles
R. Hildeburn's *A Century of Printing, The Issues of the Press in Pennsylvania,* Philadelphia, 1885, item no. 2399.

Evans 11073, Sabin 86680.

Copies: DLC, MH, PPL.

1769

61a. [BANCROFT, EDWARD] 1744-1821.

Remarks On The Review of the Controversy Between Great Britain
and her Colonies. In Which The Errors of its Author are exposed. . . .

London, Printed for T. Becket and P. A. De Hondt . . . MDCCLXIX.

2 p. l., [1]-126 p., 1 l. (last l. advts.), [A]² B-I⁸.

A reply to William Knox's *The Controversy Between Great Britain and
her Colonies Reviewed,* London, 1769, no. 65. For assignment of
author see no. 61b.

Sabin 3111.

Copies: BM, CSmH, CtY, DLC, InU, MH, MHi, MiU-C, NN, PHi,
PP, PPAmP.

61b. ———. ———. By Edward Bancroft.

London: Printed in the Year 1769. New-London, in New-England:
Re-printed and Sold by T. Green. M,DCC,LXXI.

[1]-130 p., 8vo, [A]-Q⁴ R² (R2 blank).

Evans 11976, Sabin 3111 note.

Copies: BM, CSmH, CtHi, CtHWatk, CtY, DLC, ICN, MB, MBAt, MH,
MHi, MWA, MWiW-C, MiU-C, NHi, NN, RPJCB, WHi.

[BLAND, RICHARD] *An Enquiry into the Rights of the British Colonies.* London, 1769, see: 22ab.

62a. BOSTON.

An Appeal To The World; Or A Vindication Of The Town of Boston, From Many false and malicious Aspersions Contain'd In certain Letters and Memorials, written by Governor Bernard, General Gage, Commodore Hood, the Commissioners of the American Board of Customs,
and others . . . Published By Order Of The Town.

Printed And Sold By Edes and Gill . . . Boston, 1769.

[1]-37 p., 8vo, [A]¹ B-E⁴ [F]³ ([F]3 blank).

Advertised in the *Massachusetts Gazette and Boston Weekly News-Letter* for October 26, 1769. Two states noted, one with the correction as called for in the errata on page 18 corrected and one with it not corrected. Issued in reply to the letters of Bernard and others published in Boston that same year, nos. 68 and 69. This was the work of a committee, but apparently much of the actual writing was done by Samuel Adams although a surviving manuscript draft in his hand differs in some particulars from the printed version. See: *The Writings of Samuel Adams*, edited by Harry A. Cushing, New York, 1904, vol. I, p. 416.

Evans 11133, Sabin 6478.

Copies: CSmH, CtY, DLC, MB, MBAt, MH, MHi, MWA, MWiW-C, MiU-C, NHi, NN, PPL, RPJCB, ViU.

62b. ⸻. Appendix To The American Gazette; Containing An Appeal to the World [&c.]. . . .

Boston, Printed . . . Reprinted, in London, by G. Kearsly. M.DCC.LXIX. 1 p. l., 1-34 p., 8vo, [A]¹ B-E⁴ [F]¹.

Normally found at the end of *The American Gazette*, London, G. Kearsly, 1770. Evans 11134 is probably a ghost entry for this.

Copies: BM, RPJCB.

62c. ⸻. An Appeal To The World [&c.]. . . .

Published by Order of the Town of Boston, And Reprinted in London, By the Direction of Dennys De Berdt, Esq; M.DCC.LXIX.

1 p. l., 1-34 p., 8vo, [A]¹ B-E⁴ [F]¹.

A reissue of no. 62b with a cancel title page and a cancel slip reading "An Appeal &c." pasted over the head-title. "Appendix &c." on page 1.

Copies: BM, CSmH, CtY, MWiW-C, MiU-C, RPJCB.

62d. ⸻. ⸻.

Boston, Printed . . . London, Reprinted for J. Almon . . . 1770. . . .

1 p. l., [1]-58 p., 8vo, [A]² B-H⁴.

Also issued in vol. IV of *A Collection of Tracts, On The Subjects Of Taxing The British Colonies In America*, London, J. Almon, 1773.

Sabin 6478.

Copies: BM, CSmH, CtY, DLC, ICN, InU, MB, MBAt, MH, MiU-C, NN, PHi, PPAmP, PPL, RPJCB, ViU.

63a.   BOSTON, MERCHANTS.

Observations On Several Acts of Parliament, Passed In the 4th, 6th and 7th Years of his present Majesty's Reign: And Also, On The Conduct of the Officers of the Customs, Since Those Acts were passed, And The Board of Commissioners appointed To Reside in America. Published by the Merchants of Boston.

[Boston] Printed by Edes & Gill, M,DCC,LXIX.

1 p. l., [1]-24 p., 4to, [A]¹ B⁴ B-C⁴.

Evans 11393 lists an edition with the following imprint and collation: "Boston: Printed by Edes & Gill, 1769, pp. 24, 8vo." No copy has been located with Boston in the imprint and it is probably a ghost based on a confusion of this and no. 63b.

Evans 11392, Sabin 6536.

Copies: BM, CSmH, CtHi, CtY, DLC, InU, MB, MBAt, MH, MHi, MWA, MiU-C, NHi, NN, PHi, PPL, RPJCB, WHi.

63b. ———. ———.

Boston: Printed . . . London: Reprinted for G. Kearsly . . . and J. Almon . . . M.DCC.LXX. . . .

1 p. l., 1-37 p., 8vo, [A]¹ B-F⁴ (F4 blank).

Sabin 6536.

Copies: BM, CSmH, CtHi, CtY, DLC, ICN, MHi, MiU-C, NN, RPJCB.

63c. ———. Observations Of The Merchants At Boston in New-England, Upon Several Acts of Parliament. . . .

[London, J. Almon] MDCCLXX.

2 p. l., 1-37 p., 8vo, [A]² B-E⁴ F³.

Printed from substantially the same setting of type as no. 63b with new title and half title added. Also issued in vol. IV of *A Collection of Tracts On the Subjects of Taxing The British Colonies in America,* London, J. Almon, 1773.

Copies: CSmH, CtY, DLC, InU, MH, NN, RPJCB.

64a.   The Case Of Great Britain And America, Addressed To The King, And Both Houses of Parliament.

London: Printed for T. Becket and P. A. De Hondt . . . MDCCLXIX.

2 p. l., [1]-35 p., 8vo, [A]² B-E⁴ F².

Reprinted in the *Maryland Gazette* for March 9 and 16, 1769, in the *Pennsylvania Chronicle* for April 3 and 10, 1769, and in the *Virginia Gazette* (Purdie & Dixon) for April 3, 13 and 20, 1769, (Rind)

April 13, 20 and 27, 1769. The British Museum and Bodleian catalogues attribute this to Gervase Parker Bushe while Cushing and Halkett and Laing attribute it to George B. Butler.

Sabin 9637.

Copies: CSmH, CtHi, CtY, NN, PPL, RPJCB.

64b. ———. The Second Edition.

Same imprint.

2 p. l., [1]-43 p., 8vo, [A]² B-F⁴ G².

Note on the second leaf reads "In this edition, the author has endeavoured to remedy some of the greatest defects of the preceding one ... he wishes that the first edition of this pamphlet be forgotten."

Sabin 9637.

Copies: BM, CtHWatk, CtY, DLC, InU, MBAt, MH, MiU-C, NHi, NN, PPAmP, PPL, RPJCB, ViU.

64c. ———. The Third Edition.

Dublin: Printed for James Williams ... MDCCLXIX.

2 p. l., [1]-43 p., 8vo, [A]-F⁴.

A reprint of no. 64a.

Sabin 9637.

Copies: CSmH, CtY, DLC, ICN, MB, MH, MiU-C, PPL, RPJCB.

64d. ———.

London: Printed, Philadelphia, Re-Printed by William and Thomas Bradford ... MDCCLXIX.

1 p. l., [1]-16 p., 8vo, A-B⁴ C² (C2 blank).

Advertised in the *Pennsylvania Journal* for April 13, 1769. A reprint of no. 64a. Two states noted, one with page 7 correctly numbered and one with it numbered 6.

Evans 11193, Sabin 9637.

Copies: CSmH, CtHWatk, CtY, DLC, ICN, MHi, MiU-C, NHi, NN, NcD, NjP, PHi, PPAmP, PPL, PU, RPJCB.

64e. ———. The Third Edition.

London, Printed. Boston, Re-printed, and Sold by Edes & Gill ... And by T. & J. Fleet ... [1769].

[1]-15 p., 4to, [A]-B⁴.

Advertised in the *Boston Evening Post* for May 22, 1769. A reprint of no. 64b.

Evans 11194.

Copies: CtHi, CtY, DLC, MB, MBAt, MH, MHi, MWiW-C, PPL, RPJCB.

[DICKINSON, JOHN]. *Letters from a Farmer in Pennsylvania. The Third Edition.* Philadelphia, 1769, see: 54h.

[————]. *The Farmers and Monitor's Letters.* Williamsburg, 1769, see: 54i.

[————]. *Lettres D'un Fermier De Pennsylvanie.* Amsterdam, 1769, see: 54k.

65a.   [KNOX, WILLIAM] 1732-1810.

The Controversy Between Great Britain and her Colonies Reviewed; The Several Pleas Of The Colonies, In Support of their Right to all the Liberties and Privileges of British Subjects, and to Exemption from the Legislative Authority of Parliament, Stated And Considered. . . .

London: Printed for J. Almon . . . MDCCLXIX.

2 p. l., [1]-207, [i]-lv p., 8vo, [A]² B-I⁸ K⁴ L-O⁸ P⁴ a-c⁸ d⁴.

Knox's authorship established on the same basis as no. 17. See also: *Historical Manuscripts Commission Report on Manuscripts in Various Collections,* vol. VI, p. 104. Also issued as vol. III of *A Collection of Tracts On the Subjects of Taxing The British Colonies in America,* London, J. Almon, 1773 in which the title page has been reset, the half-title converted into an errata leaf following the title page, and "A New Catalogue of Books and Pamphlets, printed for J. Almon . . ." dated November, 1770, added on 16 pages at the end. The catalogue of the Houghton Library, at Harvard, records at least four other states of this pamphlet. Edward Bancroft's *Remarks on the Review of the Controversy,* London, 1769, New London reprinted, 1771, no. 61b, is a reply.

Sabin 38180.

Copies: BM, CSmH, CtHWatk, CtY, DLC, ICN, InU, MB, MBAt, MH, MHi, MiU-C, NHi, NN, NcD, NjP, PHi, PPAmP, PPL, RPJCB, ViU, WHi.

65b.   [————]. ————.

Dublin: Printed for W. Watson . . . MDCCLXIX.

1 p. l., [1]-207, [i]-lv p., 1 l. (last l. advts.), 8vo, [A]¹ B-I⁸ K⁴ L-O⁸ P⁴ a-c⁸ d⁴.

Sabin 38180.
Copies: CSmH, CtY, DLC.

65c. [————]. ————.
Boston: Printed By Mein and Fleeming . . . MDCCLXIX.
[1]-100 p., 4to, [A]-M⁴, N².
Evans 11305, Sabin 38180.
Copies: CSmH, CtY, DLC, MB, MBAt, MH, MHi, MWA, MiU-C, NN,
PHi, PPAmP, PPL, RPJCB, ViU.

[LAURENS, HENRY]. *Extracts from the Proceedings of the High Court of
Vice-Admiralty.* Charlestown, 1769, see: 57b, 57c.

66.   LEIGH, SIR EGERTON, 1733-1788.
The Man Unmasked: Or, The World Undeceived, In The Author
Of A Late Pamphlet, Intitled, "Extracts From The Proceedings Of
The High Court Of Vice-Admiralty In Charlestown. . . .
Charles-Town: Printed By Peter Timothy, M,DCC,LXIX.
[1]-154, 1-44, 1-16 p., 1 l. (last l. errata), 4to, A-Z⁴ Aa-Dd⁴.
Advertised in the *South Carolina Gazette & Country Journal* for April
4, 1769. A reply to Henry Laurens' *Extracts From The Proceedings,*
Charleston, 1769, no. 57b.
Evans 11308, Sabin 39927.
Copies: DLC, MBAt, MHi, MWA, NN, NcD, PPL.

67a. A Letter To The Right Honourable The Earl of Hilsborough [*sic*],
On The Present Situation Of Affairs In America . . . Also An Appendix
in Answer to a Pamphlet intituled, The Constitutional Right of Great-
Britain to tax the Colonies. . . .
London, Printed for George Kearsly . . . MDCCLXIX.
1 p. l., [1]-117 p., 8vo, [A]¹ B-P⁴ Q³.
The Appendix is a reply to an anonymous pamphlet, *The Constitutional
Right of Great Britain,* London, 1768, no. 53.
Sabin 31912.
Copies: CSmH, DLC, ICN, InU, MH, NN, ViU.

67b. ————.
London: Printed, Boston: Re-Printed, and Sold by Edes and Gill . . .
1769.

[1]-55 p., 8vo, [A]-G⁴.

Advertised in the *Boston Gazette* for November 27, 1769.

Evans 11310, Sabin 1792a, 31912.

Copies: CtY, DLC, MB, MBAt, MH, MHi, MWA, MiU-C, NHi, NN, PHi, PPL, RPJCB.

68a. MASSACHUSETTS. GOVERNOR, 1760-1770 (FRANCIS BERNARD).

Copies of Letters from Governor Bernard, &c. to the Earl of Hills-borough.

[Boston: Edes and Gill, 1769].

[1-4] p., fol., [A]².

Caption-title.

These are the "Bernard Letters" written in October, November, and December of 1768. In a letter to Lord Barrington dated April 12, 1769, *Barrington-Bernard Correspondence*, Cambridge, 1912, p. 200, Bernard said "There are just now arrived 6 of my Letters & 1 of General Gage's attested by the Clerk of the Papers; & Mr. Bollan who has sent them hither promises the rest as soon as they can be copied. The Councellors to whom they were sent immediately met, ordered these Papers to be printed; but the Publication of them, is deferred until Observations can be finished to accompany them, which a Gentleman has been hard at Work upon & will have completed in a Day or two. They are then to be sent about the Province in order to inflame the People against the Election in May next, which they will effectually do. In the Mean time they have been read by the whole town at the Printers." An announcement of the existence of the letters appears in the *Boston Gazette* for April 17, 1769. They were reprinted in a number of newspapers among which were a Supplement to the *Pennsylvania Journal* for May 11, 1769, the *Maryland Gazette* for May 18th through the 25th, and the *South Carolina Gazette* for June 1st.

This printing and nos. 68b and 68c have been assigned to Edes and Gill because they were the printers for the House of Representatives and the printers of later editions of the letters, nos. 68d and 68e. They may have printed nos. 68a-c to be circulated surreptitiously prior to the official publication.

Copies: MBAt, MHi, RPJCB.

68b. ———. ———.

Same imprint.

[1]-16 p., 4to, A-B⁴.

Caption-title.

A comparison of this and no. 68a shows that they were printed from the same setting of type. The folio was printed first and then the standing type was rearranged for this quarto edition, resulting in some unusual spacings in this printing.

Evans 11178.

Copies: CSmH, CtHi, CtY, MBAt, MWA, PPL, RPJCB.

68c. ———. ———.

Same imprint.

[1]-28 p., 8vo, A-C⁴ D².

Caption-title.

This is an entirely new setting and may have been issued to go with no. 69a.

Evans 11179.

Copies: MHi.

68d. ———. Letters To The Right Honorable The Earl of Hillsborough, From Governor Bernard, General Gage, And The Honorable His Majesty's Council For the Province of Massachusetts-Bay. With An Appendix Containing Divers Proceedings referred to in the said Letters.

Boston: New-England. Printed by Edes and Gill . . . 1769.

[1]-83 p., fol., [a]-e² f¹ g-x² [y]¹.

This is the official publication of the "Letters" with the "Observations" referred to by Bernard in the note to no. 68a. The *Boston News-Letter* for July 27, 1769 advertises "A few setts are to be dispos'd of." Evans lists this as having been issued with the *Journals of the Honourable House of Representatives* for 1769-1770; however, the note mentioned above indicates that they were also available separately. Sabin 4924 lists a Salem edition which has not been located. It is probably a ghost for no. 69b.

Evans 11332, Sabin 4924.

Copies: BM, CSmH, CtY, DLC, ICN, MB, MBAt, MH, MWA, MWiW-C, MiU-C, NN, PHi, RPJCB, ViU.

68e. ———. ———.

Boston: New-England. Printed . . . London: Re-printed for J. Almon . . . [1769?].

[1]-122, 123*-124*, 123-165 p., 8vo, [A]¹ B-Q⁴ *R¹ R-X⁴ Y².

Also issued in vol. IV of *A Collection of Tracts, On The Subjects of Taxing the British Colonies in America*, London, J. Almon, 1773.

Sabin 4924.

Copies: CSmH, CtHWatk, DLC, ICN, InU, MB, MBAt, MH, MWiW-C, MiU-C, NN, PPAmP, PPL, RPJCB, WHi.

69a. MASSACHUSETTS. GOVERNOR, 1760-1770 (FRANCIS BERNARD).

Letters To The Ministry From Governor Bernard, General Gage, and Commodore Hood. And Also Memorials to the Lords of the Treasury, From The Commissioners of the Customs. With Sundry Letters and Papers annexed to the said Memorials.

Boston: Printed By Edes & Gill . . . 1769.

[1]-108 p., 8vo, [A]-N⁴ O².

Advertised in the *Massachusetts Gazette and Boston Weekly News-Letter* for September 7, 1769. These were the additional letters Bernard referred to in the letter of April 12, 1769, quoted in the note under no. 68a, when he said that William Bollan, the agent of Massachusetts in London, would send the "rest as soon as they can be copied." By the time these had appeared Bernard had left Boston.

Evans 11176, Sabin 4923.

Copies: CSmH, CtHWatk, CtY, DLC, ICN, MB, MBAt, MH, MHi, MWA, MWiW-C, MiU-C, NHi, NN, PHi, PPL, RPJCB, ViU.

69b. ———. ———.

Salem: Reprinted and sold by Samuel Hall . . . 1769.

[1]-24 p., 4to, [A]-B [*i.e.* C]⁴.

This consists of the first third of the letters only. The note at the end indicates that the rest were to appear, but no copies of them have been located.

Copies: CtY, MH, MWA, NHi, RPJCB.

69c. ———. ———.

Boston: New-England. Printed . . . London: Re-printed for J. Wilkie . . . [1769?].

[1]-146 p., 8vo, A-I⁸ K¹.

Sabin 4923.

Copies: CSmH, CtY, DLC, ICN, InU, MB, MBAt, MH, MiU-C, NHi, NN, PPL, RPJCB, WHi.

70. MASSACHUSETTS. GOVERNOR, 1760-1770 (FRANCIS BERNARD).

A third extraordinary Budget of Epistles and Memorials between Sir Francis Bernard . . . some Natives of Boston . . . and the present Ministry. . . .

[Boston: Printed by Edes & Gill, 1769].

[1]-8 p., 4to, [A]⁴.

Caption-title.

Advertised in the *Massachusetts Gazette and Boston Weekly News-Letter* for December 14, 1769. A continuation of nos. 68 and 69.

Evans 11177, Sabin 4927.

Copies: ICN, MH, MHi, MWA, PPL, RPJCB.

71. [MEIN, JOHN].

A State Of The Importations From Great-Britain Into the Port of Boston, From the beginning of Jan. 1769, to Aug. 17th 1769. With the Advertisements of a Set of Men . . . Who entered into a Solemn Agreement, (as they called it) Not to import Goods from Britain . . . The whole taken from the Boston Chronicle, in which the following Papers were first published.

Boston: Printed by Mein and Fleeming, 1769.

2 p. l., 1-130 p., 4to, [-]² A-Z² Aa-Mm² (Mm2 blank).

For a discussion see: C. M. Andrews, "Boston Merchants and the Non-Importation Movement," *Publications of the Colonial Society of Massachusetts*, vol. XIX (1916-1917), pp. 226-230; A. M. Schlesinger, "Propaganda and the Boston Newspaper Press," *Ibid.*, vol. XXXII (1933-1937), pp. 411-416; and J. E. Alden, "John Mein: Scourge of Patriots," *Ibid.*, vol. XXXIII (1937-1942), pp. 571-599. For a continuation in 1770 see no. 83.

Evans 11336, Sabin 47406.

Copies: CSmH, CtY, DLC, MBAt, MH, MHi, MWA, NHi, RPJCB.

OTIS, JAMES. *A Vindication of the British Colonies.* London, 1769, see: 20b, 20c.

72a. [POWNALL, THOMAS] 1722-1805.

The C——— having gone through the examination of the Facts contained in the North American Papers, and the discussion of the opinions and resolutions formed and originated in another place. . . .

[London? 1769?].

1-12 p., fol., A⁶.

This has no caption-title, but begins with Pownall's speech as above. It was reprinted in the *Pennsylvania Chronicle* for May 8, 15, 22, 29, 1769.

Copies: NN.

72b. [————]. The Speech Of Th-m-s P-wn-ll, Esq; Late G-v-rn-r of this Province, in the H————se of C————m————ns, in Favor of America.

[Boston: Sold by T. & J. Fleet and Edes and Gill, 1769].

1-16 p., 4to, A-B⁴.

Caption-title.

Advertised in the *Boston Evening Post* for Monday, April 24, 1769, as to be published "next Thursday." Evans 11424-6 lists a second, a third, and a fourth edition all printed in 1769. None have been found that are so labeled. A comparison of the various copies of this pamphlet may show variations in type suggesting that there was more than one printing. Sabin 64831 lists a Boston, 1770 edition which has not been found either.

Evans 11423.

Copies: BM, CtHWatk, CtY, DLC, ICN, InU, MB, MBAt, MH, MHi, MWA, MiU-C, NHi, NN, RPJCB, WHi.

73. [State of the Embarrassments (*sic*) and Difficulties the Trade labors under by means of the late Regulations and Revenue Acts. Drawn up by Messrs. Wells, Inches, Dennie, Molineaux and Smith.]

[Boston, 1769].

[24 p., 4to].

No copy of this has been located and it appears to be based upon Haven's "Catalogue of Publications in What is Now the United States, Prior To The Revolution," in Isaiah Thomas' *The History of Printing in America, Second Edition,* Albany, 1874, vol. II, pp. 309-664.

Evans 11478, Sabin 90612.

74a. [ZUBLY, JOHN JOACHIM] 1724-1781.

An Humble Enquiry Into The Nature of the Dependency of the American Colonies upon the Parliament of Great-Britain, And The Right of Parliament to lay Taxes on the said Colonies. . . .

[Charleston, S. C.] Printed in The Year M,DCC,LXIX. . . .

1 p. l., [1]-26 p., 4to, [-]¹ A-F² G¹.

Advertised in the *South Carolina Gazette* for June 5, 1769 and the *Geor-*

gia Gazette for June 7, 1769. An extract also appeared in the *Georgia Gazette* for June 28 to July 9, 1769. The attribution to Zubly is based on a statement by Henry Miller in his *Pennsylvanischer Staatsbote* for October 20, 1775, cited by Hildeburn in his *A Century of Printing: the Issues of the Press in Pennsylvania* (1886) no. 3310, where he refers to no. 74b.

Sabin 106387.

Copies: CSmH, MWA, MH, PHi, PPL, RPJCB.

74b. ———. Great Britain's Right To Tax Her Colonies. Placed in the clearest Light, By a Swiss. . . .

[London? 1774?]

[1]-55 p., 8vo, B-H⁴.

A reprint of 74a. *A Catalogue of the Books belonging to The Library Company of Philadelphia,* Philadelphia, 1789, pp. 189 and 196, lists copies of the pamphlet and gives Philadelphia 1775 as the imprint. Charles Hildeburn in his *A Century of Printing, The Issues of the Press in Pennsylvania 1685-1784,* no. 3310, apparently copied. Perhaps he did so because the librarian who compiled the 1789 *Catalogue* was Zachariah Poulson, the printer who began his apprenticeship in Philadelphia only two or three years after the pamphlet was printed. Ordinarily this evidence that is almost contemporary would lend weight to Poulson's listing. However, there is an unusual semicircular type ornament on the title page. Mr. Alden Johnson of Barre, Massachusetts, who is currently at work on a study of American type ornaments, very kindly checked the matter for me and could not find that the ornament had ever been used by an American printer. This, together with searches in Philadelphia libraries by Mr. Wilman Spawn and my own searches in the John Carter Brown Library, both of which produced negative results, has led me to list the place of printing as London with a query.

Sabin 28437, vol. 29, p. 292.

Copies: CSmH, CtY, DLC, MiU-C, NN, PPL, RPJCB.

74c. [———]. ———.

London: Printed by J. Delegal . . . and Sold by W. Davenhill . . . and G. Kearsley . . . MDCCLXXIV.

1 p. l., [1]-55 p., 8vo, B⁴ (Bl+[-]¹), C-H⁴.

This is no. 74b with a full title page inserted between the half-title and the first page of text. The inserted page does not have the stab holes found through the rest of the pamphlet, thus indicating that it was probably added after folding and sewing.

Sabin 28437, vol. 29, p. 292.
Copies: ICN, MiU-C, PPAmP, PPL, RPJCB.

1770

BOSTON. *An Appeal to the World*. London, 1770, see: 62d.

75a. BOSTON.

A Short Narrative Of The horrid Massacre in Boston, Perpetrated In the Evening of the Fifth Day of March, 1770. By Soldiers of the XXIXth Regiment . . . With Some Observations On The State Of Things Prior To That Catastrophe.

Printed by Order of the Town of Boston, And Sold by Edes and Gill. . . . And T. & J. Fleet . . . 1770.

[1]-35, [1]-80, 79-81 p., 8vo, [A]-P⁴.

This report was drawn up by a committee consisting of James Bow-doin, Joseph Warren, and Samuel Pemberton appointed by the Town Meeting, March 12, 1770. C. K. Shipton, in his sketch of Bowdoin in *Sibley's Harvard Graduates*, vol. XI, p. 528, says it was primarily Bowdoin's work. The report, which occupies pages 1-35, first count, was presented and accepted at the meeting on March 19th, at which time it was ordered to be printed. Apparently it was decided later to add the ninety-six depositions at the end because some are dated as late as March 24th. The printing could not have been completed until after March 30th, because that is the date of the certifications of various Justices of the Peace and of the Governor on pages 79-80. The frontispieces sometimes described as belonging to this and other Boston editions belong to the London editions. See: Clarence S. Brigham's *Paul Revere's Engravings*, Worcester, 1954, pp. 47-48. Evans 11582 records a Philadelphia edition but no copy has been found and it is probably a ghost. Although the pamphlet was ordered to be printed by the Town of Boston, Rollo G. Silver in "Government Printing in Massachusetts: 1751-1801," *Studies in Bibliography*, vol. XVI (1963), p. 178, points out that the General Court reimbursed the Town £49 6d. in June of 1771 to discharge their bill with the printers.

Copies: MBAt.

75b. ———. ———.

Same imprint.

[1]-38, [1]-80, 79-81 p., 8vo, [A]-D⁴, E1-2, [-]1, E3-4, F-P⁴.

Same as no. 75a except that pages 37-38, first count, have been added containing a justification of the final paragraph of the report. According to the minutes of the Town Meeting of March 22nd, it was voted to send copies to England. It was this issue that was sent because all British reprints contain the added justification found here. It was voted in the meeting of March 26th not to distribute any copies in this country because it "may be supposed by the unhappy Persons now in custody for tryal as tending to give undue Byass to the mind of the Jury."

Evans 11581, Sabin 6739.

Copies: CSmH, DLC, ICN, MB, MBAt, MH, MiU-C, RPJCB.

75c. ———. ———.

Same imprint.

[1]-48, [1]-80, 79-81, 85-88 p., 8vo, [A]-D⁴, E1-2, o⁴, [-]², E3-4, F-P⁴ [Q]².

Printed from substantially the same setting of type as no. 75b except for the two following additions which contain statements that indicate that this printing was intended for American distribution: 1) pages 39-48, first count, contain an account of the Commissioners of the Customs; 2) pages 85-88, at the end, contain a list of the people in Great Britain to whom copies of no. 75b of the pamphlet were sent and a letter addressed to the Duke of Richmond. The second is sometimes found inserted before the incorrectly paged index which occupies pages 79-81. This additional material is probably what is referred to in the following extract from the minutes of the Town Meeting for May 8, 1770. "The Committee who drew . . . a narrative of the late horrid Massacre . . . presented an Appendix to said Narrative, which have been read and considered, Voted, that the same be accepted." The prohibition against distribution was still in effect at this time.

Copies: CtY, DLC, PHi, PPL.

75d. ———. ———.

Same imprint.

[1]-48, [1]-88 p., 8vo, [A]-E⁴ (E2 + o⁴ +[-]²) F-P⁴ [Q]².

Printed from the same setting of type as no. 75c except that the errors in page numbering have been corrected. Like no. 75c, pages 85-88 are sometimes found inserted before the index which here occupies pages 81-83.

Copies: BM, CSmH, CtHWatk, CtY, DLC, InU, MB, MWiW-C, MiU-C, NHi, NjP, PPL.

75e. ———. ———. To which is added an Appendix containing the several Depositions. . . .

Boston, Printed, by Order of The Town, by Messirs. [*sic*] Edes and Gill; And Re-printed for W. Bingley . . . London. MDCCLXX. [and Boston again reprinted by Edes and Gill? 1770.]

3 p. l., [5]-48, [1]-83 p., 8vo, [-]² [A]³ B-D⁴, E1-2, o⁴, [-]², E3-4, F-P⁴.

This was printed from substantially the same setting of type as no. 75d, but with the following very significant changes. The title page of 75d was discarded and in its place was printed a half-title and title that closely copies the Bingley, London, no. 75f below. Pages 43-44, second count, and 77-78 are reset, the former in accordance with the Erratum on page 79 of no. 75d. The explanation for this Boston imitation of Bingley's London edition while there were still undistributed copies of the earlier edition in Boston may be found in the minutes of the Town Meeting of July 10th. At that time an attempt to release the earlier Boston printing for distribution was voted down. The Bingley London edition was first advertised in the *London Chronicle* two months earlier on May 5th. By July copies were undoubtedly being brought back from England, for in that same Town Meeting of July 10th, letters from England concerning the "horrid Massacre" were read to the meeting. Edes and Gill, after printing copies for the Town Meeting two months before, had probably kept the type standing in anticipation of a substantial sale once the pamphlet was released. They now found copies of the London edition being circulated with the ban on their copies still enforced, probably because the trial of the soldiers was not to be held until the following November. Apparently their solution was to bring out a surreptitious edition and market it through another bookseller, because the *Boston Evening Post* for July 16th carries the following advertisement: "Next Wednesday will be published (from the London edition) and to be sold at the Printing Office in Milk Street [*i.e.,* Kneeland and Adams] A Narrative . . . To which is added an Appendix . . .". It is also possible, of course, that the type forms were actually taken to Kneeland and Adams' shop and the printing was done there.

Copies: CSmH, CtY, DLC, MB, MBAt, MH.

75f. ———. ———. To which is added an Appendix. . . .

Boston, Printed, by Order of the Town . . . And Re-printed for W. Bingley . . . London. MDCCLXX.

3 p. l., [5]-38, 1-83 p., folding frontispiece, 8vo, [-]² A-P⁴.

A reprint of no. 75b. Advertised in the *London Chronicle* for May 5, 1770. See: Brigham cited in no. 75a.

Sabin 6740.

Copies: BM, CSmH, DLC, InU, MB, MBAt, MH, MHi, MWiW-C, MiU-C, RPJCB, ViU.

75g. ———. ———.

Printed by Order of the Town of Boston: London, Re-printed for E. and C. Dilly . . . and J. Almon . . . M.DCC.LXX.

[1]-166 p., frontispiece, 8vo, [A]-X⁴ (X4 blank).

A reprint of no. 75a. See: Brigham cited in no. 75a. Also issued in vol. IV of *A Collection of Tracts on the Subjects of Taxing the British Colonies in America*, London: J. Almon, 1773.

Sabin 6740.

Copies: BM, CSmH, DLC, InU, MB, MH, MHi, MWiW-C, MiU-C, NN, PPAmP, RPJCB.

75h. ———. A Letter From The Town Of Boston, To C. Lucas, Esq . . . Inclosing A Short Narrative Of The Massacre Perpetrated There [&c.]. . . .

Printed By Order Of The Town Of Boston, And Dublin: Reprinted By Tho. Ewing . . . [1770?].

[1]-56 p., 8vo, [A]-C⁸ D⁴.

Charles Lucas, a Member of Parliament from Dublin, was one of the people on the list, mentioned in the note to no. 75b, to whom copies of the Boston edition were sent. This is an abridgment of no. 75a. Twelve of the eighty depositions were omitted and others shortened. A copy was received by the Boston town meeting March 10, 1771.

Sabin 6741 & 11583.

Copies: DLC, MH, MiU-C, RPJCB.

75i. ———. Additional Observations To A Short Narrative Of The Horrid Massacre in Boston. . . .

Printed by Order of the Town of Boston. MDCCLXX [London: Re-printed for E. and C. Dilly, 1770].

[1]-12 p., 8vo, [A]⁶.

Although issued separately, this is also found bound at the end of no. 75f. Evans incorrectly lists this as having been printed in Boston. Actually it contains the material omitted from nos. 75a and b but included in no. 75c.

Evans 11583, Sabin 6741.

Copies: BM, CtY, DLC, ICN, InU, MB, MH, MHi, MWiW-C, NN, PPAmP, PPL, RPJCB.

BOSTON. MERCHANTS. *Observations On Several Acts of Parliament.* London, 1770, see: 63b, 63c.

76. CHAUNCY, CHARLES, 1705-1787.

Trust in God, the Duty of a People in a Day of Trouble. A Sermon Preached, May 30th. 1770. At the request of a great number of Gentlemen, friends to the Liberties of North America, who were desirous, notwithstanding the removal of the Massachusetts General-Court (unconstitutionally as they judged) to Cambridge, that God might be acknowledged in that house of worship at Boston. . . .

Boston: Printed by Daniel Kneeland, for Thomas Leverett . . . 1770.
[1]-38 p., 8vo, [A]-E⁴ (E4 blank).
Advertised in the *Massachusetts Gazette and Boston Weekly News-Letter* for June 7, 1770.
Evans 11599, Sabin 12330, Ford-*Chauncy* 48.
Copies: BM, CSmH, CtHWatk, CtY, ICN, InU, MB, MBAt, MH, MHi, MWA, MWiW-C, MiU-C, NN, NcD, PPL, RPJCB.

77. A Fair Account Of The Late Unhappy Disturbance At Boston in New England; Extracted From the Depositions that have been made concerning it by Persons of all Parties. With An Appendix, Containing Some Affidavits and other Evidences relating to this Affair, not mentioned in the Narrative of it that has been published at Boston.

London, Printed for B. White . . . MDCCLXX.
[1]-28, 1-31 p., 8vo, [B]-H⁴ I².
In part this was a reply to *A Short Narrative Of The Horrid Massacre in Boston,* Boston, 1770, no. 75. It contains 28 numbered affidavits at the end. They begin with number 97 and run through 125. The last one was made by Andrew Oliver and describes the actions that resulted in the removal of the troops from Boston after the Boston Massacre together with the Council's part in the affair. The Council took exception to Oliver's statements in *Proceedings Of His Majesty's Council . . . Relative to The Deposition of Andrew Oliver,* Boston, 1770, no. 80.
Sabin 6735.
Copies: BM, CtY, DLC, MB, MBAt, MH, MWiW-C, MiU-C, RPJCB.

78. JOHNSON, STEPHEN, 1724-1786.

Integrity and Piety the best Principles of a good Administration of Government. . . . A Sermon Preached Before The General Assembly Of The Colony of Connecticut, at Hartford, On The Day Of Their Anniversary Election, May 10, 1770. . . .

New-London, Printed by Timothy Green . . . M,DCC,LXX.

[1]-39 p., 4to, [A]⁴ B-G² H⁴.

Evans 11691, Sabin 36322.

Copies: CSmH, CtHi, CtY, DLC, ICN, MH, MHi, MWA, NHi, NN, RPJCB.

79a. LATHROP, JOHN, 1740-1816.

Innocent Blood Crying To God From The Streets Of Boston. A Sermon Occasioned By The Horrid Murder . . . by a Party of Troops . . . On The Fifth Of March, 1770. . . .

London: Printed for E. and C. Dilly . . . and J. Almon . . . MDCCLXX.

[i]-iv, 5-22 p., 4to, 4⁴ B⁴ C³.

Sabin 39184.

Copies: CSmH, MBAt, MH, NN.

79b. ———. ———.

London, Printed. Boston: Re-Printed and Sold by Edes and Gill . . . M,DCC,LXXI.

[i]-iv, 5-21 p., 8vo, [A]-C⁴ (C4 blank).

Advertised in the *Boston Evening Post* for April 29, 1771.

Evans 12094, Sabin 39184.

Copies: CtY, DLC, InU, MB, MBAt, MH, MWA, NHi, NN, NjP, RPJCB, ViU.

80. MASSACHUSETTS. COUNCIL.

Proceedings Of His Majesty's Council Of The Province Of Massachusetts-Bay, Relative To The Deposition of Andrew Oliver, Esq; Secretary of the said Province, Concerning what passed in Council in Consequence of the unhappy Affair of the 5th of March 1770.

Boston, New-England: Printed by Edes and Gill . . . MDCCLXX.

1 p. l., 1-33 p., fol., [-]¹ a-h² i¹.

This is a reply to deposition no. 125 by Andrew Oliver in *A Fair Account of the Late Unhappy Disturbance At Boston*, London, 1770, no. 77. This was ordered to be printed as an appendix to the *Journal* of the House of Representatives, Evans nos. 11734-36.

Evans 11737, Sabin 45940.

Copies: CSmH, CtY, DLC, MB, MBAt, MH, MHi, MWA, MiU-C, NN, RPJCB.

81a. MASSACHUSETTS. GENERAL COURT. HOUSE OF REPRESENTA-TIVES.

Copy of the Complaint of the House of Representatives of Massachu-set's-Bay [*sic*] against Sir Francis Bernard: With Sir Francis Bernard's Answer. Now depending before His Majesty in Council.

[London, 1770].

[1]-6 p., 1 l., fol., [A]-B².

Docket-title on verso last leaf.

Copies: CtY.

81b. ———. ———.

[Boston, 1770].

1-15 p., 4to, A-B⁴.

Caption-title.

Advertised in the *Massachusetts Gazette and Boston Weekly News-Letter* for May 10, 1770. Reprinted in the *Newport Mercury* for May 14 and 21, 1770. Also issued as a broadside, Evans 11731.

Evans 11730, Sabin 4922.

Copies: DLC, MB, MH, MHi, MWA, NN, PPL.

81c. ———. ———.

Same imprint.

1-16 p., 4to, A-B⁴.

Printed from substantially the same setting of type as no. 81b with "Report of the Lords of the Committee relative to Foregoing the Complaint, &c. March 7. 1770" added on page 16.

Copies: DLC, MBAt.

82. [A Short but Serious Address to the Inhabitants of Pennsylvania, by a Well Wisher to his King and Country].

[Philadelphia: William Goddard, 1770].

No copy has been located, but this title was advertised in the *Pennsylvania Chronicle* for October 8, 1770.

Evans 11854, Sabin 80610.

83a. A State of Importations From Great-Britain, Into The Port of Boston, From the beginning of January, 1770: Taken from the Cockets and Manifests, sworn to by the Masters of the several Vessels.

Boston: Printed [by John Fleming?] in the Year, MDCCLXX.

[1]-51 p., 4to & 8vo, A-D⁴ E-I².

A continuation of John Mein's *A State of the Importations,* issued in 1769, no. 71. By 1770 he had left the country so he could not have had a hand in this publication, but it was probably compiled by his partner John Fleeming. The types used are the same as no. 71. It includes an account of the period from January 8 to May 15, 1770. The collations of this and no. 83b are conjectured from the known copies, which are imperfect, on the basis of the wording of their title pages.

Copies: MH (pp. 49-51 wanting).

83b. A State of Importations [&c.] . . . From the beginning of January 1770. To which is added, An Account of such of these goods have been re-shipt for Great Britain. The Whole taken from the Custom House of the port of Boston.

Boston, Printed [by John Fleeming?] in the year 1770.

[1]-59 p., 4to & 8vo, A-D⁴ E-L².

Consists of the sheets of no. 83a with an altered title page and the "Account of Goods reshipt to Great Britain" added on pages 53-59.

Copies: PHi (pp. 53-59 wanting).

83c. A State of Importations [&c.] . . . From the beginning of January, 1770. To which is added, An Account of all the Goods that have been re-shipt From the above Port for Great-Britain, since January 1769. The whole taken from the Custom house of the Port of Boston.

Same imprint.

[1]-78, 78-87 p., 4to & 8vo, A-D⁴ E-M² O¹ P-Q² R¹ S-T².

This consists of the sheets of no. 83b with "State of the Importations for 1770 (Continued)" covering the period May 24th to June 29th on pages 61-78.

Evans 11744.

Copies: DLC, MHi, MWA, PPL.

84a. WEMMS, WILLIAM, defendant.

The Trial of William Wemms, James Hartegan, William M'Cauley, Hugh White, Matthew Killroy, William Warren, John Carrol, and Hugh Montgomery, Soldiers in his Majesty's 29th Regiment of Foot, For

The Murder of Crispus Attucks, Samuel Gray, Samuel Maverick, James Caldwell, and Patrick Carr, On Monday-Evening, the 5th of March 1770 ... Taken in Short-Hand by John Hodgson.

Boston: Printed by J. Fleeming ... M,DCC,LXX.

[1]-217 p., 4to, [A]-Z⁴ Aa-Dd⁴, [Ee]¹.

Although advertised in the *Massachusetts Gazette and Boston Weekly News-Letter* for December 27, 1770 as "in press," the earliest announcement of actual sale found was in the *Boston Evening Post* for January 21, 1771.

Evans 11683, Sabin 96951.

Copies: CSmH, CtY, DLC, MB, MBAt, MH, MHi, MWA, NN, PHi, PPAmP, PPL, RPB, RPJCB.

84b. ———. ———.

Boston Printed, London reprinted for T. Evans ... [1771?].

[1]-216 p., 8vo, [A]-Z⁴ Aa-Dd⁴.

Copies: MH, MiU-C.

1771

BANCROFT, EDWARD. *Remarks on the Review of the Controversy.* New-London, 1771, see: 61b.

LATHROP, JOHN. *Innocent Blood Crying to God From the Streets of Boston.* London, 1771, see: 79b.

85. LOVELL, JAMES, 1738-1814.

An Oration Delivered April 2d, 1771 . . . To Commemorate the bloody Tragedy Of The Fifth of March, 1770. . . .

Boston: Printed by Edes and Gill, by Order of the Town of Boston. 1771.

[1]-19 p., 4to, [A]-B⁴ C².

The earliest advertisement found was in the *Massachusetts Gazette and Boston Weekly News-Letter* for April 9, 1772, where in a notice for Warren's *Oration* for 1772, no. 88, there is the statement that a few of these are still left.

Evans 12099, Sabin 42374.

Copies: CSmH, CtHi, CtY, DLC, ICN, InU, MB, MBAt, MH, MWiW-C, MiU-C, NHi, NN, PHi, PPL, PPRos, RPJCB, ViU.

86. TUCKER, JOHN, 1719-1792.

A Sermon Preached At Cambridge, Before His Excellency Thomas Hutchinson, Esq; . . . His Honor Andrew Oliver, Esq; . . . And The Honorable His Majesty's Council, And The Honorable House of Representatives, Of The Province Of The Massachusetts-Bay in New-England, May 29th. 1771. Being the Anniversary for the Election of His Majesty's Council for said Province. . . .

Boston: New-England: Printed by Richard Draper . . . MDCCLXXI.

[1]-63 p., 8vo, A-D⁸.

Evans 12256, Sabin 97325.

Copies: BM, CSmH, CtHi, CtHWatk, CtY, DLC, ICN, InU, MB, MBAt, MH, MHi, MWA, MiU-C, NHi, NN, PPL, RPJCB, ViU.

1772

87a. BOSTON. COMMITTEE OF CORRESPONDENCE.

The Votes and Proceedings Of The Freeholders and other Inhabitants Of The Town of Boston, In Town Meeting assembled . . . To which is prefixed, as Introductory, An attested Copy of a Vote of the Town at a preceeding Meeting.

Boston: Printed By Edes And Gill . . . And T. and J. Fleet . . . [1772?].

[i]-iv, [1]-43 p., 8vo, [A]² B-F⁴ G².

This consists of the report submitted November 20th at a "Meeting of the Freeholders and other Inhabitants of the Town of Boston" by a Committee appointed at the meeting of November 2nd "to state the Rights of the Colonists and of this Province in particular, as Men, as Christians, and as Subjects . . . with the infringments and violations thereof. . . . " Although the report was presented as the work of the Committee, it was largely written by Samuel Adams. A manuscript of it exists in his handwriting. See: H. A. Cushing's *Writings of Samuel Adams,* New York, 1906, vol. II, p. 350. Evans 12331 lists also a *Report of A Committee of the Inhabitants of Boston On the Rights of the Colonists* . . . Boston [1772] which is clearly a ghost entry for this pamphlet. Probably Evans had an incomplete copy but did not recognize it as such and copied the caption-title. Two states noted, one with the last three lines of the title reading | *To which is prefixed,* | *As Introductory, an attested Copy of a Vote* | *of the Town at a preceeding Meeting.* | The other reads | *To which is prefixed, as Introductory,* | *An Attested Copy of a Vote of the Town* | *at a preceeding Meeting.* | "A Letter of Correspondence to the other Towns," pages 30-35, was also issued as a broadside. See: W. C. Ford's *Broadsides, Ballads &c. Printed in Massachusetts,* no. 1608.

Evans 12332, Sabin 6568.

Copies: BM, CSmH, CtHWatk, CtY, DLC, ICN, InU, MB, MBAt, MH, MHi, MWA, MWiW-C, MiU-C, NHi, NN, NcD, PHi, PPL, RPJCB, ViU.

87b. ———. ———.

Boston, Printed: London, reprinted; and sold by J. Wilkie . . . MDCCLXXIII.

   1 p. l., [i]-viii, [1]-43 p., 8vo, [-]¹A-F⁴ G².

The "Preface of The British Editor" is by Benjamin Franklin. See: Verner W. Crane's *Benjamin Franklin's Letters to the Press 1758-1775*, Chapel Hill, 1950, pp. 225-226.

Sabin 6569.

Copies: CSmH, CtY, DLC, MB, MiU-C, NN, RPJCB, WHi.

87c. ———. ———.

Dublin: Printed by George Faulkner . . . MDCCLXXIII.

[i]-viii, [1]-32 p., 8vo, A-E⁴.

A reprint of no. 87b.

Copies: MH.

88a. WARREN, JOSEPH, 1740-1775.

An Oration Delivered March 5th, 1772. At The Request Of The Inhabitants Of The Town Of Boston; To Commemorate The Bloody Tragedy Of The Fifth Of March, 1770. . . .

Boston: Printed by Edes and Gill . . . 1772.

[1]-18 p., 4to, [A]-B⁴ C² (C2 blank).

Advertised in the *Massachusetts Gazette and Boston Weekly News-Letter* for March 26, 1772.

Evans 12600, Sabin 101477.

Copies: BM, CtY, DLC, MB, MBAt, MH, MHi, MWA, NN, PHi, PPRos, RPB, RPJCB, ViU.

88b. ———. ———.

Same imprint and collation.

"⟨Second Edition⟩" printed at the bottom of the title page below the mourning border. Advertised in the *Massachusetts Gazette and Boston Weekly News-Letter* for April 9, 1772. Printed from substantially the same setting of type as no. 88a.

Evans 12601, Sabin 101477.

Copies: CSmH, CtY, DLC, MB, MHi, MiU-C, RPJCB, ViU, WHi.

89. [ZUBLY, JOHN JOACHIM] 1724-1781.

Calm and Respectful Thoughts on the Negative of the Crown on a Speaker chosen and presented by the Representatives of the People: Occasioned by some Publications in the Georgia Gazette, of May and June 1772, wherein the late Assembly of that Province is charged with encroaching on the Rights of the Crown. By a Freeman. . . .

[Savannah, J. Johnston, 1772].

[1]-24 p., 8vo, A-C⁴.

Caption-title.

Sabin 106383.

Copies: DLC, MWiW-C, NjP.

1773

90. [ALLEN, JOHN] fl. 1764.

The American Alarm, Or The Bostonian Plea, For the Rights, and Liberties, of the People . . . By The British Bostonian.

Boston: Printed and Sold by D. Kneeland, and N. Davis . . . M,DCC,LXXIII.

[1]-35, [1]-8, [1]-9, [1]-16, [i]-iii p., 4to, [A]-I⁴.

Advertised in the *Massachusetts Gazette and Boston Weekly News-Letter* for April 8, 1773. The same newspaper for December 10, 1772 identifies John Allen as "The British Bostonian" who wrote *An Oration Upon the Beauties of Liberty,* no. 91. The title page of *The Watchman's Alarm,* no. 103, lists the "British Bostonian" as the author of both this and the *Oration.* At one time attributed to Isaac Skillman.

Evans 13014, Sabin 1037, 81585.

Copies: CSmH, DLC, ICN, MB, MBAt, MH, MHi, MWA, MiU-C, RPJCB.

91a. [ALLEN, JOHN] fl. 1764.

An Oration, Upon the Beauties of Liberty, Or the Essential Rights of the Americans. Delivered At the Second Baptist-Church in Boston. . . .

Boston: Printed and Sold by D. Kneeland, and N. Davis . . . M,DCC,LXXIII.

[i]-xiv, [15]-31 p., 12mo, [A]-B⁴ C⁶ D².

Advertised in the *Massachusetts Gazette and Boston Weekly News-Letter* for January 7, 1773. For authorship see no. 90. The Dedication is signed "A British Bostonian." At one time attributed to Isaac Skillman.

Evans 13015, Sabin 81586.

Copies: DLC, MBAt, MH, MHi, MWA, MiU-C, NHi, NN, PHi, PPL.

91b. [————]. ————.

Same imprint.

[i]-xiv, [15]-31 p., 8vo, [A]-D⁴.

"The Second Edition Corrected" on half-title. Advertised in the *Massachusetts Gazette and Boston Weekly News-Letter* for January 21, 1773.

Evans 13016, Sabin 81586.

Copies: DLC, InU, MHi, MWA, MiU-C, NcD, RPJCB, WHi.

91c. [————]. ————. The Third Edition, carefully corrected by the Author, in which are many Additions . . . By a British Bostonian.

Boston: N. E. Printed and Sold by E. Russell . . . M,DCC,LXXIII.

[i]-xxix, [30]-80 p., 4to, [A]-K⁴.

Advertised in the *Boston Evening Post* for May 17, 1773. This edition revised and enlarged.

Copies: MBAt, MH, MWA, RPJCB.

91d. [————]. ————. The Fourth Edition, [&c.]. . . .

Same imprint and collation.

Printed from substantially the same setting of type as no. 91c.

Evans 13018, Sabin 81587.

Copies: CtHi, DLC, ICN, MB, MHi, MWA, NHi, NN, PPL, RPB, RPJCB.

91e. [————]. ————. ⟨The Third Edition corrected.⟩

New-London: Printed by T. Green, for Joseph Knight . . . M.DCC.LXXIII.

[1]-23 p., 4to, [A]-C⁴.

A reprint of no. 91b.

Evans 13017, Sabin 81586.

Copies: CSmH, CtHi, CtHWatk, DLC, MB, MBAt, MHi, MWA, NN, RPJCB.

91f. [————]. ————. The Fifth Edition.
  Hartford: Reprinted by Ebenezer Watson, 1774.
  [1]-40 p., 8vo, [A-B]⁸ C⁴.
  A reprint of no. 91c.
  Evans 13627.
  Copies: CtHi, WHi.

91g. [————]. ————.
  Wilmington, Printed and Sold by James Adams . . . M,DCC,LXXV.
  [i]-xi, 12-21 p., 8vo, [A]-C⁴ (C4 blank).
  A reprint of no. 91b.
  Evans 14457.
  Copies: NN, RPJCB.

BOSTON. *Votes and Proceedings of the Freeholders and other Inhabitants of the
  Town of Boston . . . to which is Prefixed as Introductory an Attested Copy of
  a Vote of the Town.* London, 1773, see: 87b.

————. ————. Dublin, 1773, see: 87c.

92. BOSTON.
  The Votes and Proceedings Of The Freeholders and other Inhabit-
ants Of the Town of Boston, In Town Meeting Assembled, Accord-
ing to Law, The 5th and 18th days of November. 1773. . . .
  Boston: Printed for Joseph Greenleaf . . . M,DCC,LXXIII.
  [1]-15 p., 4to, [A]-B⁴.
  Concerning "The petition of a large number of the inhabitants, setting
    forth—— 'That they are justly alarmed at the report that the *East-
    India* company in *London* are about shipping a cargo, or cargoes of
    tea into this and other colonies. . . .' "
  Evans 12692, Sabin 6567.
  Copies: CSmH, CtY, DLC, InU, MB, MHi, MWA, MiU-C, NN, PPL,
    RPJCB.

93. CHAPLIN, EBENEZER, 1773-1822.
  Civil State compared to Rivers, all under God's controul [*sic*], and
what People have to do when Administration is grievous. In A Discourse
Delivered in Sutton, 2d Parish, January 17, 1773. Being the Day preceeding the Town Meeting, Which then stood Adjourned To consider
and act upon the Letter, &c. From Boston. . . .

Boston: Printed and Sold by John Boyles . . . MDCCLXXIII.

[1]-24 p., 4to, [A]-C⁴.

Evans 12712, Sabin 11966.

Copies: MB, MBAt, MHi, MWA, NcD.

94a.   CHURCH, BENJAMIN, 1734-1776.

An Oration, Delivered March Fifth, 1773 . . . To Commemorate the Bloody Tragedy Of The Fifth Of March, 1770. . . .

Boston: Printed and Sold at the New Printing-Office [J. Greenleaf] . . . M,DCC,LXXIII.

[1]-20 p., 4to, [A]-B⁴ C².

Evans 12722 lists a Boston, 1773 "Second Edition" in MHi. Only an imperfect copy of this is there. No other copy of a second edition has been located, and it is probably a ghost.

Evans 12721, Sabin 12983.

Copies: BM, CSmH, CtHi, CtY, MB, MBAt, MH, MHi, MWA, MiU-C, NN, PHi, ViU.

94b. ——. ——. ⟨The Third Edition, Corrected By the Author.⟩

Boston: Printed by Edes and Gill . . . M,DCC,LXXIII.

[1]-18 p., 4to, [A]-B⁴ C² (C2 blank).

Advertised in the *Massachusetts Gazette and Boston Weekly News-Letter* for March 18, 1773.

Evans 12723, Sabin 12983.

Copies: CSmH, CtHi, CtY, DLC, ICN, InU, MB, MBAt, MH, MHi, MWA, MWiW-C, MiU-C, NN, NcD, PPL, PPRos, RPJCB.

94c. ——. ——. The Fourth Edition.

Boston: Printed by J. Greenleaf . . . 1773.

[1]-20 p., 4to, [A]-B⁴ C².

Printed from substantially the same setting of type as no. 94a.

Evans 12724, Sabin 12983.

Copies: CtHi, CtY, MHi, MWA, RPJCB.

94d. ——. ——. The Fourth Edition.

Salem: Re-printed by Samuel and Ebenezer Hall . . . 1773.

[1]-16 p., 4to, [A]-B⁴.

Copies: NHi, ViU.

95. HOWARD, SIMEON, 1733-1804.

A Sermon Preached To The Ancient And Honorable Artillery-Company, In Boston, New-England, June 7th, 1773. . . .

Boston: Printed and Sold by John Boyles . . . 1773.

[1]-43 p., 8vo, [A]-E⁴.

Advertised in the *Massachusetts Gazette and Boston Weekly News-Letter* for June 17, 1773.

Evans 12813, Sabin 33278.

Copies: BM, CSmH, CtY, DLC, MB, MBAt, MH, MHi, MWA, MiU-C, NN, PHi.

96a. HUTCHINSON, THOMAS, 1711-1780.

Copy Of Letters Sent to Great-Britain, by his Excellency Thomas Hutchinson, the Hon. Andrew Oliver, and several other Persons, Born and Educated Among Us. . . .

Boston: Printed by Edes and Gill . . . 1773.

[1]-40 p., 4to, [A]¹ B-F⁴ (F4 blank).

The *Massachusetts Spy* for June 3, 1773, carried a public announcement of the existence of these letters, but they were not issued until sometime after June 9th and before June 17th. The *Massachusetts Gazette and Boston Weekly News-Letter* for June 10th published a letter of Hutchinson's dated the 9th in which he says that the letters have not yet been made public. The June 17th issue of the same newspaper contains the announcement that they "have been printed and are to be sold by Edes & Gill." Apparently the Committee of Correspondence began sending out copies of the pamphlet to different parts of the country soon thereafter. The printed letter of transmittal (Evans 12690) is dated June 22, 1773. The letters were reprinted extensively in newspapers throughout the colonies during 1773. The following are some of their appearances: *Pennsylvania Journal*, June 30th to July 14th; *Pennsylvania Gazette*, July 5th to 19th; *New-York Journal*, July 8th to August 19th; *South Carolina Gazette*, August 9th to 23rd; and *South Carolina Gazette and Country Journal*, August 24th to September 7th. The various Boston printings of this pamphlet are complicated by the existence of mixed issues. However, the distinctions given in these entries probably constitute the basic pattern of the book. Two states of this particular issue have been noted. One has an errata on page 40 and the other has it removed and the corrections made. The New York Public Library owns an interesting copy. It lacks the title page, but is otherwise in good condition and in original stitching. It is not impossible that a few copies were issued in this form. In his *Prelude To Inde-*

pendence, New York, 1958, pp. 150-152, Arthur M. Schlesinger tells of the manner in which the Assembly withheld the letters while throwing out hints to arouse public interest. Edes and Gill must have received the text of the pamphlet to be set in type well before the date intended for release and they could easily have circulated a few copies surreptitiously without the title page. The fact that the title was printed on a separate leaf rather than on the blank leaf at the end and then placed at the front of the pamphlet suggests that there might have been a time lag between the printing of the body of the pamphlet and the title page.

Sabin 34071.

Copies: CSmH, CtY, DLC, ICN, MB, MBAt, MH, MHi, MWA, MWiW-C, MiU-C, NHi, NN, NcD, PHi, PPL, PU, RPJCB, ViU.

96b. ———. ———.

Same imprint.

[1]-40, [1]-8 p., 4to, [A]^1 B-E^4 F^3 [G]^4.

This is made up of either one of the two states described in no. 96a plus an eight-page addition which contains the resolves of the House of Representatives on the Letters. These eight pages have been noted in three states which may have been issued both separately and with the pamphlet. The *Massachusetts Gazette and Boston Weekly News-Letter* notes on June 17th that the text of the Resolves have not been received by the printer and the issue of June 24th prints their text. All three states have caption titles. The first reads: "The Committee appointed to consider certain Letters laid before the House of Representatives, reported the following Resolves. Tuesday, June 15, 1773. Resolved, that the Letters. . . ." The second reads "On Tuesday June 16, 1773, the House of Representatives by a very large Majority came into the following Resolves, upon the Letters that had been laid before them on Wednesday the second of the same Month, viz. Resolved, that the Letters. . . ." The third reads "On Wednesday June 16, 1773, the House of Representatives . . . [&c. the same as the second]." This last state has the correct day of the week and thus determines the order of the issues.

Sabin 34071.

Copies: CSmH, NN, RPJCB.

96c. ———. ———.

Same imprint.

[1]-51 p., 4to, [A]^1 B-E^4 [F]^3 G^4.

This is no. 96a to which has been added pages 41-51 that contain

"Copy of a letter returned with those signed Thomas Hutchinson, Andrew Oliver, &c. from England," which is signed "G. Rome." Evans says that this last part was printed in Philadelphia by Thomas Bradford. However, this is highly unlikely. The Rome Letter appeared in the *Boston Evening Post* for June 28, 1773. Bradford did not print the Hutchinson Letters in his *Pennsylvania Journal* until June 30th. The Letter was also printed as a broadside. See: W. C. Ford's *Broadsides, Ballads &c. Printed in Massachusetts*, no. 1423, where it is incorrectly entered under 1767, the original date of Rome's letter.

Evans 12818.

Copies: DLC.

96d. ———. ———.

Boston: Printed. Salem: Re-printed, and sold by S. & E. Hall. 1773.

[1]-30 p., 4to, [A]-D⁴.

A reprint of no. 96a.

Evans 12819, Sabin 34071.

Copies: CtY, MB, MH, MHi, MWA, MWiW-C, NHi, NN.

96e. ———. The Representations Of Governor Hutchinson and others, Contained In Certain Letters Transmitted to England, And afterwards returned from thence, And laid before the General-Assembly of the Massachusetts-Bay. Together With The Resolves Of the Two Houses thereon.

Boston: N. E. Printed and Sold by Edes and Gill . . . 1773.

1 p. l., [i]-ii, [3]-94 p., 4to, [A]² B-M⁴ N².

A reprint of no. 96c with the proceedings of the House of Representatives added on pages 50-94.

Evans 12820, Sabin 34085.

Copies: CSmH, CtHi, CtY, DLC, MB, MBAt, MHi, MWA, MiU-C, PHi, PPL, RPJCB.

96f. ———. The Letters Of Governor Hutchinson, And Lieut. Governor Oliver, &c. Printed at Boston. And Remarks Thereon. With The Assembly's Address, And the Proceedings Of the Lords Committee Of Council. Together with The Substance of Mr. Wedderburn's Speech Relating To Those Letters.

London: Printed for J. Wilkie . . . MDCCLXXIV.

2 p. l., [1]-73, [74-76], *77-*80 p., 1 l., 77-126 p., 8vo, [A]² B-L⁴ (L1 + [-]¹ *L²) M-Q⁴ R³.

This collection was edited by Israel Mauduit.
Copies: BM, CtY, PHi, RPJCB.

96g. ———. ———.
Same imprint.
1 p. l., [1]-73, [74-76], *77-*80 p., 1 l., 77-78, *79-*80, 79-126 p., 8vo, [A]¹ B-L⁴ (L1 + [-]¹ *L², L3 + [-]¹) M-Q⁴ R³.
Differs from no. 96f by the insertion of pages *79-*80, second count, in Wedderburn's speech.
Copies: DLC, MBAt, MiU-C, PPAmP, RPJCB.

96h. ———. ———.
Same imprint.
1 p. l., [1]-73, [74-76], *77-*80 p., 1 l., 77-78, *79-*80, 79-134 p., 8vo, [A]¹ B-L⁴ (L1 + [-]¹ *L², L3 + [-]¹) M-Q⁴ R³ S⁴.
Same as no. 96g with the Report of the Committee of the Council for Plantation Affairs added in pages 127-134.
Sabin 34072.
Copies: CtY, PPL, RPJCB.

96i. ———. ———. And the Report of the Lords Committee to his Majesty in Council. The Second Edition.
Same imprint.
2 p. l., [1]-142 p., 8vo, [A]² B-I⁸ K⁷.
A reprint of no. 96h. In the RPJCB copy G2 is a cancel and in MB copy it is not.
Sabin 34072.
Copies: BM, CtY, DLC, ICN, MB, MBAt, MH, MHi, NN, NjP, PPAmP, PPL, RPJCB, ViU.

96j. ———. ———.
Dublin: Printed for W. Gilbert . . . MDCCLXXIV.
[1]-97 p., 8vo, A-M⁴ N¹.
A reprint of no. 96g.
Copies: DLC, MH, RPB, RPJCB.

97. MASSACHUSETTS. GOVERNOR, 1770-1774 (THOMAS HUTCHIN-SON).
The Speeches Of His Excellency Governor Hutchinson, To The Gen-

eral Assembly Of The Massachusetts-Bay. At a Session begun and held
on the Sixth of January, 1773. With The Answers Of His Majesty's
Council And The House Of Representatives Respectively. . . .

Boston; New-England: Printed by Edes And Gill . . . M,DCC,LXXIII.
[1]-126 p., 4to, [A]-Q⁴ (Q4 blank).

These speeches were printed in the *Massachusetts Gazette and Boston
Weekly News-Letter* between January and March of 1773. The
House ordered 700 copies printed for itself and 100 for the Council on March 6, 1773. See: Rollo G. Silver's "Government Printing
in Massachusetts: 1751-1801," *Studies in Bibliography*, vol. 16
(1963), p. 178.

Evans 12856, Sabin 34086.

Copies: BM, CSmH, CtHWatk, CtY, DLC, ICN, InU, MB, MBAt, MH,
MHi, MWA, MWiW-C, MiU-C, NHi, NN, PHi, PPAmP, PPL,
RPJCB, ViU.

98. [MATHER, SAMUEL] 1706-1785.

An Attempt To Shew, That America Must Be Known To The
Ancients; Made At The Request, And To Gratify The Curiosity, Of
An Inquisitive Gentleman: To Which Is Added An Appendix, Concern-
ing The American Colonies, And Some Modern Managements Against
Them. . . .

Boston New-England: Printed by J. Kneeland . . . for T. Leverett,
and H. Knox . . . MDCCLXXIII.

[1]-35 p., 8vo, [A]-D⁴, E².

Advertised in the *Massachusetts Gazette and Boston Weekly News-Letter*
for March 11, 1773. The preface is signed "Samuel Mather."

Evans 12861, Sabin 46792, Holmes 61.

Copies: BM, CSmH, CtHi, CtHWatk, CtY, DLC, ICN, MB, MBAt, MH,
MHi, MWA, MiU-C, NHi, NN, NcD, NjP, PPL, RPB, RPJCB, ViU,
WHi.

99a. [PROUT, TIMOTHY].

Diana's Shrines Turned Into Ready Money, By Priestly Magic; Or,
Virtue Given Up. Being Remarks on Remarks on the Northern Priest's
Pamphlet, entitled, A————a known to the A————ts. In a Letter to
the Author. ⟨Numb. I.⟩ . . .

New-York: Printed [by Hugh Gaine] in the Year MDCC,LXXIII.

[1]-23 p., 8vo, [A]-C⁴.

The introduction to this is a letter dated June 24, 1773, from Hugh
Gaine in New York to Ezkeiel Russell in Boston. Apparently Rus-

sell had sent the manuscript of this reply to Samuel Mather's *Attempt to Shew that America Must be known to the Ancients*, Boston, 1773, no. 98, to Gaine in New York to be printed because of the opposition to such a pamphlet in Boston. Gaine says that he is sending five hundred copies of the pamphlet to Russell and will be happy to print other things for him that might be needed. Apparently this caused Sabin to list an edition with the imprint, "Printed by H. G. in New York for E. Russell in Boston." No such copy has been found. For authorship and circumstances of composition see: C. K. Shipton's sketch of Prout in *Sibley's Harvard Graduates*, vol. XI, p. 56. The only copy of this edition located has the "Appendix" mentioned on the title page of 99b. It begins on page 16. Copies may also have been issued without it.

Copies: MBAt.

99b. [————]. ————. In a Letter to the Author. In which is contained an impartial Appendix, setting forth the Right of the British Parliament, as well as the real Advantages that would arise to the honest Merchant, by the Prevention of the iniquitous Practice of Smuggling . . .

Same imprint and collation.

The alteration in the title page made in standing type. Signature B reset but signatures A and C printed from the same setting as 99a.

Evans 12965, Sabin 66232.

Copies: CtY, MH, MHi, MWA, PPL, RPJCB.

100a. SHIPLEY, JONATHAN, Bp. of St. Asaph, 1714-1788.

A Sermon Preached before the Incorporated Society For The Propagation of the Gospel in Foreign Parts . . . February 19, 1773.

London: Printed by T. Harrison and S. Brooke . . . MDCCLXXIII.

[i]-xxiv, 1-62 p., 1 l., 8vo, a-c⁴ A-H⁴.

An extract of this appeared in the *Virginia Gazette* (Purdie & Dixon) for February 17, 1774. This sermon, pleading for a more moderate policy in dealing with the colonies, occupies pages i-xxiv. The last part of the pamphlet is devoted to the administration of the Society. Only the Sermon is reprinted in the editions listed below.

Sabin 80504.

Copies: BM, CSmH, CtHi, CtHWatk, CtY, DLC, ICN, MH, MHi, NHi, NN, NcU, PHi, PPL, RPJCB.

100b. ———. ———.

London Printed: Boston, New-England, Re-Printed: And to be Sold by Thomas and John Fleet . . . 1773.

[1]-17 p., 8vo, A-B⁴ [C]¹.

Advertised in the *Massachusetts Gazette and Boston Weekly News-Letter* for June 10, 1773.

Evans 13009, Sabin 80505.

Copies: CSmH, CtHi, CtY, DLC, MB, MBAt, MHi, MWA, MiU-C, NHi, NN, RPJCB.

100c. ———. ———.

London, Printed: Newport, Rhode-Island, Reprinted and Sold by Solomon Southwick . . . M,DCC,LXXIII.

[1]-16 p., 8vo, [A]-B⁴.

Advertised in the *Newport Mercury* for June 21, 1773.

Evans 13011, Sabin 80507, Alden 527.

Copies: CtHi, CtY, DLC, MB, MH, MHi, MWA, NHi, NcU, PPAmP, RPJCB.

100d. ———. ———.

London, Printed: Norwich, Re-printed by Green & Spooner. [1773?].

[1]-19 p., 4to, [A]-B⁴ C².

Evans 13012, Sabin 80506.

Copies: CSmH, CtHi, MBAt, RPJCB.

100e. ———. ———.

New-York: Printed by Hodge And Shober, For Noel And Hazard. M.DCC.LXXIII.

[1]-16 p., 8vo, [A]-B⁴.

Evans 13010, Sabin 80508.

Copies: CtY, NN, NjP, PHi, PPAmP, PPL, RPJCB.

100f. ———. ———.

Philadelphia: Printed by Robert Bell . . . And Sold by William Wood-house . . . MDCCLXXIII.

1 p. l., [1]-20 p., 8vo, [A]² B-C⁴ D¹.

Advertised in the *Pennsylvania Chronicle* for July 5, 1773. Both Evans 13008 and Sabin 80509 list a 1773 edition printed by Robert Aitken.

It is probably a ghost based on an advertisement of Aitken's describing it as "just published" that appeared in three Philadelphia newspapers, the *Pennsylvania Packet* for July 12th, the *Pennsylvania Gazette* for July 14th, and the *Pennsylvania Chronicle* for July 26th. A search of Aitken's Day Books in The Library Company of Philadelphia from July to September 1773 shows that he did handle copies of the pamphlet, but the sale of only three is recorded. This suggests that he may have been selling one of the other American editions, probably the New York one.

Evans 13007, Sabin 80509.

Copies: CSmH, MWA, PHi, PPAmP, PPL, RPJCB.

100g. ———. ———. A New Edition.
  London, Printed for J. Whiston ... MDCCLXXIV.
  [1]-15 p., 12mo, [A]¹ B⁶ [C]¹.
  Sabin 80510.
  Copies: BM, InU, MBAt, MH, MiU-C, MHi, NN, PPAmP.

101. TRUMBULL, BENJAMIN, 1735-1820.
  A Discourse, Delivered At The Anniversary Meeting Of The Freemen Of The Town Of New-Haven, April 12, 1773. . . .
    New-Haven: Printed By Thomas and Samuel Green. M,DCC,LXXIII.
    [1]-38 p., 8vo, [A]-E⁴ (E4 blank).
    Evans 13049, Sabin 97184.
    Copies: CtHi, CtY, DLC, MB, MBAt, MH, MHi, MWA, NHi, NN, NjP, RPJCB.

1774

[ALLEN, JOHN]. *An Oration, upon the Beauties of Liberty.* Hartford, 1774, see: 91f.

102. ALLEN, JOHN.
  [The Patriotic Whisper In the Ears of the King; Or The Grand request Of The People of America made manifest . . . Being a Political Oration. . . .]
    [Boston: Printed by T. and J. Fleet, 1774.]
    A proposal to print this by subscription appeared in the *Boston Evening Post* for August 8, 1774. No copy has been located and it is unlikely that the publication was ever carried out. General Gage was in com-

mand at Boston with a large number of troops. The Fleets, who at this time were trying to maintain a neutral position, might well have felt that such a pamphlet would not be a wise publication.

Evans 13103.

103. [ALLEN, JOHN].

The Watchman's Alarm To Lord N---H; Or, The British Parliamentary Boston Port-Bill unwraped. Being An Oration On The Meridian of Liberty . . . By the British Bostonian. Author of the Oration on the Beauties of Liberty, the American Alarm, &c. . . .

Salem: N. E. Printed by E. Russell . . . M,DCC,LXXIV.

[1]-32 p., 4to, [A]-D⁴, frontispiece.

For note on authorship see no. 90. Evans gives Samuel and Ebenezer Hall as the printer. No copy with their names in the imprint has been located. He probably intended to record this printing. The frontispiece is a cartoon: *The able Doctor or America Swallowing the Bitter Draught*, 3⅝ x 5¾″, a re-engraving of a cartoon that first appeared in the *London Magazine* for April, 1774. See: C. S. Brigham's *Paul Revere's Engravings*, Worcester, 1954, pp. 85-86 and plate 35. The cartoon in this pamphlet was probably copied from the London impression and not from Revere's copy. See also: the British Museum's *Catalogue of Political and Personal Satires*, vol. V [London], 1935, no. 5226.

Evans 13757, Sabin 102051.

Copies: NHi, RPJCB.

104a.   A Brief Review Of The Rise And Progress, Services and Sufferings, Of New England, Especially The Province of Massachuset's-Bay. [*sic*] Humbly submitted to the Consideration of both Houses of Parliament.

London: Printed for J. Buckland . . . MDCCLXXIV. . . .

[1]-32 p., 8vo, A-D⁴.

Reprinted in the *Pennsylvania Packet* for May 30, 1774.

Sabin 7896.

Copies: BM, CtY, DLC, InU, MBAt, MH, MWiW-C, MiU-C, NHi, NN, RPJCB.

104b.   ———. ⟨Lately published in England.⟩

Norwich: Printed By Robertsons And Trumbull. M,DCC,LXXIV.

[1]-16 p., 8vo, [A]-B⁴.

Evans 13177, Sabin 7896.
Copies: CSmH, MB, MWiW-C, MiU-C, RPJCB.

105a. [CARTWRIGHT, JOHN] 1740-1824.
American Independence The Interest And Glory Of Great Britain;
Or, Arguments to prove, that not only in Taxation, but in Trade, Manu-
factures, and Government, the Colonies are entitled to an entire Inde-
pendence on [*sic*] the British Legislature. . . .
London: Printed for the Author, by H. S. Woodfall. Sold by J. Wilkie.
. . . M.DCC.LXXIV.

[i]-xvi, [i]-iv, [1]-72 p., 8vo, a-b⁴ c² B-K⁴.

> An extract appears in the *Newport Mercury* for January 23, 1775, and
> in the *Virginia Gazette* (Pinkney) for February 16 and 23, 1776.
> This consists of ten letters, dated from March 20 to April 14, 1774,
> that appeared first in a London newspaper. In F. D. Cartwright's
> *The Life and Correspondence of Major Cartwright,* London, 1826,
> vol. II, p. 53, is quoted a letter by the author in which he says "My
> letters on American Independence are now in press."

Sabin 11152.

Copies: BM, CSmH, CtY, DLC, MH, MiU-C, NN, PHi, PPAmP, PPL,
RPJCB, ViU.

105b. [————]. ————. A New Edition. To which is added, A
copious Appendix. . . .
London: Printed for the Author, by H. S. Woodfall. Sold by J. Wilkie.
. . . M.DCC.LXXV.

1 p. l., [i]-xvi, [i]-iv, [1]-72, 1-15, [1]-30, 1-51, [1] p., (last p.
Errata), folding map, 8vo, [-]², a³ b⁴ c² B-K⁴ a-b⁴, A-C⁴ D³, A-F⁴
G².

> This consists of the sheets of 105a with a half-title and new title page
> and all after page 72 added. Pages 1-15, second count, is *Appendix,
> To the Legislature;* 1-30, third count, is *A Letter to Edmund Burke*
> with special title page; 1-51 is a *Postscript.* The Errata on the last page
> corrects errors in all parts of the book. The map is entitled *British
> America, Bounded and Divided as proposed by the Author of American
> Independence. MDCCLXXV. Postscript P. 45,* and measures 7 9/16
> x 9¾.

Sabin 11154.

Copies: BM, CSmH, CtY, DLC, ICN, MB, MH, MiU-C, NN, RPJCB.

105c. [————]. ————.

Philadelphia, Printed and Sold by Robert Bell . . . MDCCLXXVI.

[i]-xxiii, [25]-125 p., 1 l., 8vo, [A]-Q⁴.

Advertised in the *Pennsylvania Gazette* for July 31, 1776. A reprint of no. 105a. Pages 121-125 . . . "Extract From the Monthly Review." Leaf at end "Character of the work From the English Monthly Reviewers."

Evans 14673, Sabin 11153.

Copies: BM, CSmH, CtHWatk, CtY, DLC, ICN, InU, MB, MBAt, MH, MHi, MWA, MiU-C, NHi, NN, PHi, PPL, RPJCB, ViU, WHi.

106a. [CHANDLER, THOMAS BRADBURY] 1726-1790.

The American Querist: Or, Some Questions Proposed Relative To The Present Disputes Between Great-Britain And Her American Colonies. By a North-American. . . .

[New York] Printed [by James Rivington] in the Year 1774.

2 p. l., [1]-31 p., 8vo, [A]² B-E⁴.

At one time attributed to Myles Cooper. For authorship see: C. H. Vance's "Myles Cooper," *Columbia University Quarterly*, vol. XXII (1930), pp. 275-276.

Evans 13220, Sabin 16586, Hewlett 88.

Copies: BM, CSmH, CtY, DLC, InU, MBAt, MH, MHi, MiU-C, PPAmP, PPL, RPJCB, WHi.

106b. [————]. ————. The Tenth Edition.

New-York: Printed by James Rivington, 1774. . . .

2 p. l., [1]-31 p., 8vo, [A]² B-E⁴.

At the bottom of the title page is the following note: "This pamphlet, on the 8th Day of September last, was, in full Conclave of the Sons of Liberty in New York, committed to the Flames. . . ." Printed from substantially the same setting of type as no. 106a with title page reset.

Evans 13221, Sabin 16586, Hewlett 8.

Copies: BM, CtY, MBAt, MH, MWA, MiU-C, NN, PPAmP, RPJCB, ViU.

106c. [————]. ————. The Eleventh edition.

Same imprint with note at bottom.

[1]-32 p., 8vo, [A]-D⁴.

Hewlett 9.
Copies: CSmH, DLC, ICN, MBAt.

106d. [————]. ————.
Boston: Re-printed by Mills and Hicks . . . 1774.
[1]-32 p., 4to, [A]-D⁴.
Advertised in the *Massachusetts Gazette and Boston Weekly News-Letter*
   for September 29, 1774.
Evans 13222, Sabin 16586.
Copies: CtY, MBAt, MH, MHi, MWA, NHi, RPJCB.

106e. [————]. ————.
Printed in North-America, in 1774. London: Reprinted for T. Caddel
[*sic*] . . . M.DCC.LXXV.
   [1]-55 p., 8vo, A-G⁴.
Sabin lists an "Eleventh Edition" printed in London but no copy has
   been located. He probably confused it with no. 106c.
Sabin 16586.
Copies: BM, MiU-C, NHi, PHi, RPJCB.

107a.   [CHANDLER, THOMAS BRADBURY] 1726-1790.
A Friendly Address To All Reasonable Americans, On The Subject
Of Our Political Confusions: In Which The Necessary Consequences
Of Violently Opposing the King's Troops, And Of A General Non-
Importation Are Fairly Stated. . . .
New-York: Printed [by James Rivington] in the Year M,DCC,LXXIV.
   [1]-55, [1] p. (last p. errata), 8vo, A-G⁴.
Advertised in *Rivington's Gazette* for November 17, 1774. At one time
   attributed to Myles Cooper. See: C. H. Vance's article cited in no.
   106a. In the *Adams Papers Microfilms*, reel 344, under the assigned
   date of 1774 is a draft of a reply to this.
Evans 13224, Sabin 16587, Hewlett 89.
Copies: CSmH, CtY, DLC, InU, MB, MBAt, MH, MWA, MWiW-C,
   MiU-C, NHi, NN, PHi, PPAmP, PPRos, PPL, PU, RPJCB, ViU,
   WHi.

107b. [————]. ————.
America: [Boston] Printed for the Purchasers [by Mills & Hicks],
1774. . . .

[1]-55 p., 4to, A-G⁴.

Assigned to Mills & Hicks because of the similarity to the type used by them and because they advertised the pamphlet "In press and speedily will be published . . ." in the *Massachusetts Gazette and Boston Weekly News-Letter* for November 17, 1774. See also: *Proceedings of the Massachusetts Historical Society*, vol. LXI (1927-1928), pp. 302-303.

Evans 13225.

Copies: BM, CtY, DLC, MB, MBAt, MH, MHi, MWA, MiU-C, NN, PPL, RPJCB.

107c. [————]. ————.

New-York, Printed: London, Reprinted for Richardson and Urquhart . . . 1774.

[1]-56 p., 8vo, A-G⁴.

Sabin 16587.

Copies: BM, CtY, DLC, MB, MBAt, MH, MiU-C, NN, NjP, PPL, RPJCB.

107d. [————]. ————.

New-York, Printed: Dublin, Reprinted by Mary Hay, 1775.

[1]-56 p., 8vo, A-G⁴.

Sabin 16587.

Copies: CSmH, ICN, RPJCB.

107e. [————]. ————. Carefully abridged from the Original.

New-York: Printed [by James Rivington] in the Year M,DCC,LXXIV.

[1]-24 p., 8vo, A-C⁴.

Evans 13226, Sabin 16588, Hewlett 90.

Copies: CSmH, DLC, MiU-C, NHi, NN, PPRos, PPL, RPJCB.

108. [CHAUNCY, CHARLES] 1705-1787.

A Letter To A Friend. Giving a concise, but just, representation of the hardships and sufferings the town of Boston is exposed to, and must undergo in consequence of the late Act of the British-Parliament; which, by shutting up its port, has put a fatal bar in the way of that commercial business on which it depended . . . By T. W. A Bostonian.

Boston, N. E. Printed and Sold at Greenleaf's Printing Office . . . M,DCC,LXXIV.

[1]-35 p., 8vo, [A]-D⁴.

Evans 13197, Sabin 12321, Ford-Chauncy 52.

Copies: CSmH, CtY, DLC, InU, MB, MBAt, MH, MWA, MWiW-C, MiU-C, NHi, NN, NcD, RPJCB.

109. [Comment On A Pamphlet by "A Backsettler" In defence of the Rights of America. By a Carolinian.]

[Charlestown, S. C. Peter Timothy, 1774.]

Evans apparently took this from Haven's "Catalogue of Publications in what is now the United States, Prior to the Revolution" in Isaiah Thomas's *The History of Printing in America*, Albany, 1874, vol. II, p. 642. No copy has been located. If it was printed, it was a reply to *Some Fugitive Thoughts on a Letter Signed Freeman*, Charleston, 1774, no. 142, which in turn was a reply to Drayton's *A Letter from Freeman of South Carolina*, Charleston, 1774, no. 111.

Evans 13204.

110a. [DICKINSON, JOHN] 1732-1808.

An Essay On The Constitutional Power Of Great-Britain Over The Colonies In America; With The Resolves Of The Committee For The Province Of Pennsylvania, And Their Instructions To their Representatives In Assembly.

Philadelphia: Printed and Sold, by William and Thomas Bradford . . . M.DCC.LXXIV.

[i]-vii, [1]-127, [1] p. (last p. errata and "Appendix"), 8vo, A⁴ A-Q⁴.

Advertised in the *Pennsylvania Journal* for August 31, 1774, and in the *Maryland Gazette* for May 11, 1775. Two states of signatures K-M noted, may be distinguished by catchwords on page 81, "stature" and "ture." A reply will be found in Thomas Pownall's *The Administration of the Colonies. Fifth Edition*, London, 1774, nos. 5e and f.

Evans 13247, Sabin 20040.

Copies: BM, CSmH, CtHWatk, CtY, DLC, ICN, InU, MB, MBAt, MH, MHi, MWA, MWiW-C, MiU-C, NHi, NN, NjP, PHi, PPAmP, PPL, RPJCB, ViU.

110b. [————]. A New Essay ⟨By the Pennsylvanian Farmer⟩ On The Constitutional Power Of Great-Britain [&c.]. . . .

Philadelphia Printed; and London Re-printed for J. Almon . . . 1774.

[i]-viii, [1]-126 p., 1 l. (last l. advts.), 8vo, [-]⁴ A-Q⁴.

Sabin 20046.

Copies: CSmH, CtY, DLC, ICN, InU, MB, MBAt, MH, MHi, MWiW-C, MiU-C, NN, NjP, PHi, PPAmP, PPL, RPJCB, ViU, WHi.

[DICKINSON, JOHN]. *Letters from a Farmer in Pennsylvania.* London, 1774, see: 54j.

111. [DRAYTON, WILLIAM HENRY] 1742-1779.

A Letter From Freeman [*sic*] Of South-Carolina, To The Deputies Of North-America, Assembled In The High Court of Congress At Philadelphia.

South-Carolina: Charles-Town, Printed By Peter Timothy. M,DCC,LXXIV.

[1]-47 p., 4to, [-]¹ A-E⁴ F³.

Drayton's authorship is established in letter he sent to the Earl of Dartmouth when he sent him a copy of the pamphlet. See: W. M. Dabney and M. Dargan's *William Henry Drayton & the American Revolution,* Albuquerque, 1962, p. 59.

Evans 13256, Sabin 40277.

Copies: CSmH, CtY, DLC, ICN, MBAt, MiU-C, NN, PPRos, PPL, RPJCB.

112. [DRINKER, JOHN] 1733-1800.

Observations On The Late Popular Measures, Offered to the Serious Considerations of the Sober Inhabitants of Pennsylvania, By A. Tradesman of Philadelphia.

Philadelphia: Printed For A Tradesman. MDCCLXXIV.

[1]-24 p., 8vo, [A]-C⁴.

This consists of two essays, one dated August 5th and the other August 20, 1774. The former first appeared in the *Pennsylvania Journal* for August 17, 1774, under the title "Some Observations offered to the serious consideration of the sober Inhabitants of this city and Province." The attribution is from the Library of Congress Catalog. Evans credits the pamphlet to John Brooke. Two states noted, one with and one without errata slip pasted on page 4.

Evans 13179, Sabin 20950 & 56528.

Copies: CSmH, CtY, DLC, MiU-C, PHi, PPAmP, PPL, RPJCB.

113. [FISHER, JABEZ?].

Americanus Examined, And His Principles Compared With Those Of The Approved Advocates For America, By A Pennsylvanian.

Philadelphia: Printed In The Year, MDCCLXXIV.

[1]-24 p., 8vo, [A]-C⁴.

This is a reprint, with commentary, of a letter signed "Americanus" written by Joseph Galloway that first appeared in the *New-York Gazette* for August 15, 1765. It later appeared, paragraphed with Franklin's *Examination,* in both the *Pennsylvania Gazette* and the *Pennsylvania Journal* for September 25, 1766. In the latter newspaper is a letter signed by Galloway in which he acknowledges authorship of the "Americanus" letter. The commentary is in the form of extensive footnotes and a brief essay. It is attributed to Jabez Fisher by Evans. He was probably a member of a Quaker family of Philadelphia, a number of whom were Loyalists.

Evans 13277, Sabin 1275.

Copies: CSmH, CtY, DLC, ICN, PHi, PPAmP, PPL, RPJCB.

114.   FISK, NATHAN, 1733-1799.

The Importance of Righteousness to the Happiness, and the Tendency of Oppression to the Misery of a People; illustrated In Two Discourses Delivered at Brookfield, July 4. 1774. Being a Day observed by general Consent through the Province, (At The Recommendation of the Late House of Representatives) As A Day of Fasting and Prayer. . . .

Boston: Printed by John Kneeland . . . MDCCLXXIV.

[1]-40 p., 8vo, [A]-E⁴.

Evans 13278, Sabin 24553.

Copies: CtHi, MB, MBAt, MHi, MWA, NHi, NN.

115.   [FRANKLIN, BENJAMIN] 1706-1790.

The Causes Of The Present Distractions In America Explained: In Two Letters To A Merchant In London. By F——— B———.

[New York] Printed [by James Rivington] in the Year 1774.

1 p. l., [1]-16 p., 8vo, [A]¹ B-C⁴.

Advertised in *Rivington's Gazette* for November 27, 1774. For authorship, earlier publication in various periodicals, and comment see: Verner W. Crane's "Certain Writings of Benjamin Franklin on the British Empire and the American Colonies," *Papers of the Bibliographical Society of America,* vol. XXVIII (1934), pp. 12-15 and his *Benjamin Franklin's Letters to the Press 1758-1775,* Chapel Hill, 1950, pp. 106-107, 268, 277-278. At one time attributed to Francis Bernard.

Evans 13147, Sabin 4920, Hewlett 91.

Copies: CtY, DLC, ICN, MB, MBAt, MH, MHi, MWA, MiU-C, NHi, NN, PHi, PPAmP, PPL, PU, RPJCB.

116. [HAMILTON, ALEXANDER] 1757-1804.

A Full Vindication Of The Measures of the Congress, From The Calumnies of their Enemies; In Answer to A Letter, Under the Signature of A. W. Farmer. . . .

New-York: Printed by James Rivington. 1774.

[1]-35 p., 8vo, A-D⁴ E².

Advertised in *Rivington's Gazette* for December 15, 1774. A reply to Samuel Seabury's *Free Thoughts on the Proceedings of the Continental Congress*, New York, 1774, no. 136. See also: Clarence H. Vance's edition of *Letters of a Westchester Farmer*, White Plains, New York, 1930, vol. VIII of Publications of the *Westchester County Historical Society* and H. C. Syrett's edition of *The Papers of Alexander Hamilton*, New York, 1961, vol. I, pp. 45-79.

Evans 13313, Sabin 29956, Ford-*Hamilton* 1, Hewlett 10.

Copies: CSmH, CtHi, CtY, DLC, ICN, MB, MH, MHi, MWA, MWiW-C, MiU-C, NHi, NN, PHi, PPAmP, PPL, RPJCB, ViU.

117a. HANCOCK, JOHN, 1737-1793.

An Oration; Delivered March 5, 1774 . . . To Commemorate The Bloody Tragedy of the Fifth of March 1770. . . .

Boston: Printed by Edes and Gill . . . MDCCLXXIV.

[1]-20 p., 4to, [-]² [A]-D².

Advertised in the *Massachusetts Gazette and Boston Weekly News-Letter* for March 24, 1774. W. V. Wells in his *The Life and Public Services of Samuel Adams*, Boston, 1865, vol. II, pp. 138-140, says this was written by Samuel Adams, but he cites no documentary evidence. A. H. Cushing does not include it in *The Writings of Samuel Adams*, Boston, 1904, but he prints a letter from Adams to John Dickinson of April 12, 1774, in which he says he is sending him a copy, but makes no mention of having contributed to it. In his "Autobiography," written between 1802 and 1805, John Adams says that on May 13, 1776, Samuel Adams informed him that Benjamin Church and Joseph Warren composed at least two thirds of this piece. However he was not aware of this at the time he heard it delivered. See *Diary and Autobiography of John Adams* edited by L. H. Butterfield, 1961, vol. II, pp. 89-90, vol. III, p. 384. Philip Davidson in his *Propaganda and the American Revolution*, Chapel Hill, 1941, p. 197, says the speech has been attributed to Samuel Cooper. In all probability a number of Boston radicals had a hand in its composition.

Evans 13314, Sabin 30177.

Copies: BM, CSmH, CtHi, CtY, DLC, MB, MBAt, MH, MHi, MWA, MWiW-C, MiU-C, NN, PHi, PPL, RPJCB, ViU.

117b. ———. ———. The Second Edition.
Same imprint and collation.
Advertised in the *Boston Gazette* for April 4, 1774.
Evans 13315, Sabin 30177.
Copies: CtHi, CtY, DLC, MH, MHi, NN, PPL, PPRos, RPJCB, ViU.

117c. ———. ———.
Newport, Rhode-Island: Reprinted and Sold by S. Southwick ... 1774.
[1]-19 p., 8vo, [A]-B⁴ C².
Advertised in the *Newport Mercury* for April 11, 1774.
Evans 13317, Sabin 30177, Alden 542.
Copies: CSmH, CtHi, CtY, DLC, ICN, NHi, RPJCB.

117d. ———. ———.
New-Haven: Re-Printed by Thomas and Samuel Green. M,DCC,LXXIV.
[1]-15 p., 8vo, [A]-B⁴.
Evans 13316, Sabin 30177.
Copies: CSmH, CtHi, CtY, DLC, MWA, MiU-C, RPJCB.

117e. ———. ———.
Philadelphia: Printed by J. Douglass M'Dougall ... M,DCC,LXXV.
[1]-23 p., 8vo, [A]-C⁴.
Advertised in the *Pennsylvania Ledger* November 11, 1775.
Evans 14097.
Copies: DLC, NN, PHi, PPAmP.

118. HOLLY, ISRAEL, fl. 1763-1784.
God Brings about his holy and wise Purpose or Decree, Concerning many particular Events, by using and improving the wicked Dispositions of Mankind in Order there to . . . Briefly Illustrated In A Sermon, Preached at Suffield, December 27, 1773 the next Sabbath after the report arrived, that the People at Boston had Destroyed a large Quantity of Tea . . . Rather than submit to Parliamentary Acts. . . .
Hartford: Printed by Eben. Watson ... 1774.
[1]-23 p., 4to, [A]-C⁴.

Evans 13333, Sabin 32564.
Copies: CtHi, CtY, NN.

HUTCHINSON, THOMAS. *The Letters of Governor Hutchinson.* London, 1774, see: 96f, 96g, 96h, 96i.

————. ————. Dublin, 1774, see: 96j.

119a. [JEFFERSON, THOMAS] 1743-1826.

A Summary View Of The Rights Of British America. Set Forth In Some Resolutions Intended For The Inspection Of The Present Delegates Of The People Of Virginia. Now In Convention. . . .

Williamsburg: Printed by Clementina Rind [1774].

[1]-23 p., 8vo, [A]-C⁴.

Probably printed in August of 1774. Julian P. Boyd's "Historical and Bibliographical Notes on *A Summary View of the Rights of British America,*" *The Papers of Thomas Jefferson,* Appendix I, vol. I, Princeton, 1950, pp. 669-676, gives a full account of the composition and the circumstances under which the pamphlet was printed in Jefferson's absence and without his knowledge. Following the appearance of the first volume of the *Papers,* in which the DLC copy of this edition with Jefferson's manuscript was used, two more copies with his annotations were found in PPL. None of these alterations found their way into subsequent editions, all of which are reprints of this one.

Evans 13350, Sabin 35918.
Copies: CSmH, DLC, PHi, PPL, RPJCB.

119b. [————]. ————.

Williamsburg: Printed: Philadelphia: Re-Printed by John Dunlap. M,DCC,LXXIV.

[1]-23 p., 8vo, [A]-C⁴.

Advertised in the *Pennsylvania Packet* for September 5, 1774.

Evans 13351, Sabin 35918.
Copies: CtY, DLC, ICN, MB, MBAt, MH, MHi, MWA, MWiW-C, NHi, NN, PHi, PPAmP, PPL, RPJCB, ViU.

119c. [————]. ————.

Williamsburg, Printed by Clementina Rind. London, Re-printed for G. Kearsly . . . 1774.

[i]-xvi, [5]-44 p., 8vo, [A]⁴ a⁴ B-F⁴.

To this edition is added an address "To the King" signed "Tribunus" which is attributed to Arthur Lee. The address was also issued separately, because the *Virginia Gazette* (Dixon & Hunter) for January 14, 1775, prints a news note from London saying that copies of the address are being given away free to Englishmen who have received copies of American editions of the pamphlet. It was also printed in the *Virginia Gazette* (Pinkney) for March 2, 1775.

Sabin 35918.

Copies: CSmH, CtY, DLC, ICN, InU, MBAt, MH, MWA, MiU-C, NN, NcD, NcU, ViU.

119d.   [————].   ————. The Second Edition.

Same imprint and collation.

Boyd, in his discussion cited in 119a, page 673, recapitulates the mentions from time to time of a Norfolk edition (Evans 13352), a Boston, and a New York edition. No copies of any of these editions have been found. They are ghosts derived from advertisements for the London edition in London newspapers.

Sabin 35918.

Copies: BM, CtY, DLC, MH, MiU-C, NN, PHi, PPAmP, RPJCB.

120a.   [Knox, William] 1732-1810.

The Interest of the Merchants And Manufacturers of Great Britain, In The Present Contest With The Colonies, Stated and Considered.

London: Printed for T. Cadell . . . M,DCC,LXXIV.

1 p.l., [1]-50 p., 8vo, [A]¹ B-G⁴ H¹.

The authorship established by the fact that this is one of the pamphlets included in the volume made up by Knox mentioned in the note under no. 17a.

Sabin 34885.

Copies: BM, CSmH, CtY, DLC, ICN, InU, MH, MHi, MiU-C, NN, PHi, PPAmP, PPL, RPJCB, ViU.

120b.   [————].   ————.

Cork: Printed for Mary Edwards . . . by Dennis Donnoghue . . . MDCCLXXV.

[1]-24 p., 8vo, A⁴ [B]⁴ C⁴.

Copies: DLC.

120c. [————]. ————.

Dublin: Printed by the Executors of David Hay . . . MDCCLXXV.

[1]-24 p., 8vo, [A]-C⁴.

Copies: MiU-C, NjP.

120d. [————]. ————.

London: Printed, Boston: Re-printed, and sold by Draper's Printing-Office . . . [1775].

[1]-20 p., 12mo, A⁴ B⁶.

Advertised in the *Massachusetts Gazette and Boston Weekly News-Letter* for March 9, 1775.

Evans 14129, Sabin 34885.

Copies: CSmH, MB, MH, MWA, RPJCB.

121. LATHROP, JOHN, 1740-1816.

A Discourse Preached, December 15th 1774. Being The Day Recommended By the Provincial Congress, To Be Observed In thanksgiving to God. . . .

Boston: Printed by D. Kneeland; and Sold by Samuel Webb . . . 1774.

[1]-39 p., 8vo, [A]-E⁴.

In at least some copies the "i" and "c" in Provincial are corrections in pen and ink, probably made by the printer.

Evans 13370, Sabin 39178.

Copies: BM, CSmH, CtY, DLC, ICN, InU, MB, MBAt, MH, MHi, MWA, MWiW-C, NN, NcD, PPAmP, RPJCB, ViU.

122. LATHROP, JOHN, 1740-1816.

A Sermon Preached To the Ancient and Honorable Artilery-Company In Boston, New-England, June 6th 1774. Being the Anniversary of their Election of Officers. . . .

Boston: Printed by Kneeland and Davis, for Samuel Webb . . . 1774.

[1]-39 p., 8vo, [A]-E⁴.

Evans 13371, Sabin 39186.

Copies: BM, CSmH, CtY, DLC, MB, MBAt, MH, MHi, MWA, NN, NcD, NjP, PPL, RPJCB.

123a. [LEE, ARTHUR] 1740-1792.

An Appeal To The Justice And Interests Of The People Of Great Britain, In The Present Disputes With America. By An Old Member of Parliament.

London: Printed For J. Almon ... MDCCLXXIV.

2 p. l., [1]-63, [4] p. (last 4 pp. advts.), 8vo, [A]² B-H⁴ I² K⁴.

Franklin saw this through the press. See: Verner W. Crane's *Benjamin Franklin's Letters to the Press 1758-1775*, Chapel Hill, 1950, p. li. Reprinted in the *Virginia Gazette* (Purdie) for April 7 to 21, 1775 and *Rivington's Gazette* for September 14 to October 12, 1775. A sequel is Lee's *A Second Appeal To The Justice and Interests of the People, On The Measures Respecting America*, London, 1775, which was not reprinted in pamphlet form in America. However, an extract of it did appear in the *Connecticut Journal* for May 22, 1776.

Sabin 39697.

Copies: BM, CSmH, CtHWatk, CtY, DLC, ICN, InU, MB, MBAt, MH, MiU-C, NHi, NN, PHi, PPAmP, PPL, PU, RPJCB, ViU, WHi.

123b. [————]. ————. The Second Edition, Corrected.

London: Printed for J. Almon ... MDCCLXXV.

[1]-68, [4] p. (last 4 pp. advts.), 8vo, [A]² B-I⁴ [K]².

Sabin 39698.

Copies: BM, CSmH, CtY, DLC, MB, MH, MiU-C, NHi, NN, NcD, PP, PPL, RPJCB.

123c. [————]. ————. The Third Edition, Corrected.

Same imprint.

[1]-32 p., 8vo, A-D⁴.

Sabin 39697.

Copies: BM, CSmH, CtY, DLC, MBAt, MH, MHi, MiU-C, NN, NjP, PPL, RPB, RPJCB.

123d. ————. ————. By Doctor Lee, Of Virginia. The Fourth Edition.

New-York: Printed by James Rivington. MDCCLXXV.

[1]-32 p., 8vo, A-D⁴.

Advertised in *Rivington's Gazette* for September 28, 1775.

Evans 14147, Sabin 39698, Hewlett 34.

Copies: CSmH, MBAt, MiU-C, NHi, PHi, RPJCB.

123e. [————]. ————. The Fourth Edition, Corrected.

London: Printed For J. Almon ... MDCCLXXVI.

[1]-46 p., 1 l. (last l. advts.), 8vo, A-F⁴.

Copies: CSmH, CtY, DLC, InU, MB, MBAt, MH, MHi, MiU-C, NN, PPAmP, PPL, RPJCB, ViU, WHi.

123f. [————]. ————. The Fourth Edition, Corrected.
London Printed: Reprinted at Newcastle Upon Tyne, by Robson, Angus, and Co. . . . MDCCLXXVI.
[1]-72 p., 8vo, A-I⁴.
Copies: BM, CSmH, CtY, MH, MiU-C, RPJCB.

124a. [LEE, ARTHUR] 1740-1792, editor.
A True State Of The Proceedings In the Parliament of Great Britain, And In The Province of Massachusetts Bay, Relative To The Giving and Granting the Money of the People of that Province, and of all America, in the House of Commons, in which they are not represented.
[London: Printed by William Strahan 1774.]
[1]-24 p., folio, A-F².
Caption title.
Compiled by Lee from material furnished by Benjamin Franklin. See: Verner W. Crane's *Benjamin Franklin's Letters to the Press 1758-1775,* Chapel Hill, 1950, pp. li, 236.
Sabin 39706.
Copies: BM, CSmH, CtY, MB, MH, MWA, NN, PPL.

124b. [————]. ————.
London, Printed: Philadelphia: Re-printed by Joseph Crukshank . . . MDCCLXXIV.
[1]-39 p., 8vo, A-E⁴.
Advertised in the *Pennsylvania Packet* for September 18, 1774.
Evans 13282.
Copies: CSmH, CtY, DLC, InU, MB, MH, MHi, MiU-C, PHi, PPAmP, PPL, PU, RPJCB, ViU.

125a. [LEE, CHARLES] 1731-1782.
Strictures On A Pamphlet, Entitled, A "Friendly Address To All Reasonable Americans, On The Subject of our Political Confusions." Addressed To The People Of America. . . .
Philadelphia: Printed and Sold by William and Thomas Bradford . . . M.DCC.LXXIV.
[1]-15 p., 8vo, A-B⁴.

Advertised in the *Pennsylvania Journal* for November 30, 1774, and in the *New-York Journal* for December 15, 1774. Publication was announced in *Rivington's Gazette* in New York in the issue of November 17, 1774 and offered for sale in the issue of December 8, 1774. It was reprinted in a number of newspapers among which were: *South Carolina Gazette* for December 26, 1774, *South Carolina Gazette and Country Journal* for January 10, 1775, *Virginia Gazette* (Pinkney) for January 26, 1775 and (Purdie) for February 3, 1775. Evans 13373 lists an edition with the imprint "America [New York] Printed for the purchasers. 1774. 8vo." It is a ghost. Actually, his 13373 is the same as his 13225, the Boston edition of Chandler's *Friendly Address* (no. 107b), to which this Lee pamphlet is an answer.

Evans 13372, Sabin 39714.

Copies: CSmH, CtHi, CtY, DLC, ICN, MB, MH, MWA, MWiW-C, MiU-C, NHi, NN, NjP, PHi, PPAmP, PPL, RPJCB.

125b. [————]. ————.

America: Boston: Re-Printed and sold at Greenleaf's Printing-Office . . . M,DCC,LXX,V.

[1]-20 p., 8vo, [A]-B⁴ C².

Advertised in the *Massachusetts Gazette and Boston Weekly News-Letter* for January 5, 1775.

Evans 14151, Sabin 39714.

Copies: CtHWatk, CtY, DLC, InU, MB, MBAt, MH, MHi, MWA, MiU-C, NN, PHi, PPL, RPJCB, ViU.

125c. [————]. ————.

New-York, Printed. Boston: Re-printed and sold by I. Thomas . . . MDCCLXXV.

[1]-12 p., 12mo, [A]⁶.

Advertised in the *Massachusetts Gazette and Boston Weekly News-Letter* for January 12, 1775, where the publisher says, "This pamphlet, which has been sold for 6s. OT. is now republished by I. Thomas . . . for the small price of two coppers, in order that every person who is desirous of seeing so well wrote a piece on the subject of our political controversy, may be possessed therewith. N.B. Those who cannot afford to purchase may have it gratis. . . ." The pamphlet was clearly printed at the least possible expense; not only is it a small duodecimo but the type is extremely small and the page is crowded.

It is impossible to give a completely satisfactory explanation for the appearance of New York in the above imprint. There has never been any suggestion in the bibliographies or elsewhere that there was a New York printing before the publication of this edition. It is true that James Rivington, the New York printer, announced the publication of this title in his newspaper, *Rivington's Gazette*, for November 17, 1774. This was two weeks before the appearance of the first edition in Philadelphia (no. 125a) and was worded "In a few days will be published, and sold by the Booksellers. . . ." On December 8, a week after the Philadelphia publication, he advertised it for sale along with nine other political pamphlets. The form of these two advertisements makes it very unlikely that the publication was a Rivington imprint. Had he been offering his own edition he would not have included other booksellers or other pamphlets in the announcements. In all likelihood he was selling the Philadelphia edition.

There still remains the question of where Isaiah Thomas got the text from which he printed this edition and why he assigned it to New York. One explanation could be that he was the victim of the same confusion about the three titles in this series that has plagued later bibliographers and that in his haste to get this edition printed used the imprint of the pamphlet that started it all, Chandler's *Friendly Address*, New York, 1774 (no. 107a). Another explanation could be that he copied from the other Boston edition printed by Greenleaf (no. 125b). This was probably the one he meant when he referred to a high priced edition in his advertisement. Greenleaf did not give the place of origin of the edition from which he copied his edition and Thomas may have assumed it was New York. The explanation may also lie in a combination of these two factors and perhaps some others that we do not know about. It would be a mistake to say that there was never a New York edition printed in 1774 or during the first week or so of 1775. The thirty-odd items in this bibliography reported in a single copy and those few entries for items that may have been printed, but for which we have no copies makes clear the very real possibility that there were pamphlets of which no copies have survived.

Evans 14152, Sabin 39714.

Copies: BM, CtY, DLC, MH, MHi, MWA, RPJCB.

125d. [————————]. ————————.

Philadelphia, Printed: Newport: Reprinted and Sold by S. Southwick . . . 1775.

[1]-15 p., 8vo, [A]-B⁴.

Advertised in the *Newport Mercury* for January 9, 1775.

Evans 14155, Sabin 39714, Alden 606.
Copies: MHi, RPJCB.

125e. [————]. ————.
Philadelphia, Printed: Providence, Reprinted and Sold by John Carter
. . . 1775.
  [1]-15 p., 8vo, [A]-B⁴.
Advertised in the *Providence Gazette* for January 21, 1775.
Sabin 92831, Alden 607.
Copies: NHi, RPJCB.

125f. [————]. ————. The Second Edition. To which is prefixed
An Advertisement, Wrote by a Gentleman in Connecticut.
  Philadelphia, Printed: New-London: Re-printed and sold by T. Green.
MDCCLXXV.
  [1]-16 p., 4to, [A]-B⁴.
  The prefix is attributed to Silas Deane by J. H. Trumbull in his *List of
    Books Printed in Connecticut 1709-1800*, Hartford, 1904, p. 1441.
  Evans 14154, Sabin 39714.
  Copies: CtHi, CtY, MH, NHi, NN, PPL, RPJCB.

[————]. ————.
  [New York] Printed in the Year 1775.
  [13]-25 p.
  This is a part of Rivington's edition of Barry's reply to Lee's pamphlet,
no. 151b. It was not issued separately.

126. A Letter From A Veteran, To The Officers Of The Army En-
camped At Boston.
  [New York] America: Printed [By Hugh Gaine] In The Year, 1774.
  [1]-19, [1] p. (last p. errata), 8vo, A-B⁴ C².
  This has been assigned to Gaine because all but one of the eleven type
    ornaments used in this pamphlet are also found in the *Laws . . . of the
    City of New York* also printed by him in 1774. The authorship of
    this has frequently been attributed to Captain Robert Prescott, 1725-
    1816, who served with the 15th Foot in America.
  Evans 13554, Sabin 40316.
  Copies: CSmH, CtY, DLC, MB, MBAt, MH, MHi, MWA, MiU-C, NHi,
    PHi, RPJCB, ViU.

127a.   A Letter From A Virginian, To The Members of the Congress
To Be Held At Philadelphia. On The first of September, 1774.

[New York] Printed [by Hugh Gaine] In The Year 1774.

1 p. l., [1]-29 p., 4to, [-]¹ [A]-C⁴ D³.

The printing of this pamphlet has been assigned to Gaine because the
manner in which type ornaments are used is similar to that found in
other things printed by him and because three of those ornaments
appear in other Gaine imprints of the same year (Evans nos. 13309,
13471, and 13472). The authorship has sometimes been attributed
to Jonathan Boucher, the Maryland Loyalist. However, there appears to be no direct evidence to support this and Boucher himself
fails to make any mention of it in his *Reminiscences of an American
Loyalist,* Boston, 1925.

Evans 13167, Sabin 40317.

Copies: CSmH, CtHi, CtY, DLC, MB, MH, MiU-C, NN, NjP, PHi,
PPAmP, PPRos, PPL, RPJCB, ViU.

127b.   ———.

Boston: Re-printed and Sold by Mills and Hicks . . . 1774.

[1]-31 p., 4to, [A]-B⁴ D-E⁴.

Advertised in the *Massachusetts Gazette and Boston Weekly News-Letter*
for September 1, 1774.

Evans 13168, Sabin 40317.

Copies: CtY, MB, MBAt, MHi, MWA, MWiW-C, NN, RPJCB, ViU.

127c.   ———.

Boston: Re-printed and Sold by Mills and Hicks . . . and Cox and Berry
. . . M,DDC,LXXIV. [*sic*]

[1]-32 p., 4to, [A]-D⁴.

Evans 13169 lists a 24-page Boston edition in MHi but it is in fact a
defective copy of this. Evans 13170 also lists another Boston 1774
edition of 50 pages. No such printing has been located and it is probably a ghost entry based on no. 127d.

Copies: CSmH, CtY, DLC, MBAt, MH, MWA, PPL.

127d.   ———.

Boston, printed: London, reprinted; for J. Wilkie . . . 1774. . . .

1 p. l., [5]-50 p., 8vo, [A]¹ B-F⁴ G³.

Sabin 40317.

Copies: BM, CSmH, CtY, InU, MBAt, MWiW-C, NcD.

128. [LIVINGSTON, PHILIP] 1716-1778.

The Other Side of the Question: Or, A Defence Of The Liberties of North-America. In Answer To A Late Friendly Address To All Reasonable Americans, On The Subject Of Our Political Confusions. By A Citizen.

New-York: Printed by James Rivington ... M,DCC,LXXIV.

[1]-29, [1] p., 1 l. (last l. advt.), 8vo, A-D⁴.

Advertised in *Rivington's Gazette* for December 8, 1774 and in the *Massachusetts Gazette and Boston Weekly News-Letter* for January 5, 1775. A reply to Thomas Bradbury Chandler's *A Friendly Address to All Reasonable Americans*, New York, 1774, no. 107. Attributed to Livingston by Evans.

Evans 13381, Sabin 41634, Hewlett 16.

Copies: BM, CSmH, CtHi, CtY, DLC, ICN, MB, MBAt, MH, MHi, MWA, MWiW-C, MiU-C, NHi, NN, NjP, PHi, PPRos, PPL, RPJCB, ViU.

129. [NICHOLAS, ROBERT CARTER] 1728-1780?

Considerations On The Present State Of Virginia Examined.

[Williamsburg] Printed in the Year M,DCC,LXXIV.

[1]-43 p., 8vo, [A]-E⁴ F².

Advertised in the *Virginia Gazette* (Purdie & Dixon) for August 25, 1774. A reply to John Randolph's *Considerations*, Williamsburg, 1774, no. 133. For authorship see: Heartman reprint cited in note under that entry.

Evans 13500, Sabin 55170.

Copies: DLC, NN.

POWNALL, THOMAS. *The Administration of the Colonies. The Fifth Edition.* London, 1774, see: 5e.

130. [PRESCOTT, BENJAMIN] 1687-1777.

A Free And Calm Consideration Of The Unhappy Misunderstandings and Debates, Which Have Of late Years arisen, and yet subsist, Between the Parliament of Great-Britain, and These American Colonies. Contained, In Eight Letters ... Formerly printed in the Essex Gazette. ...

Salem: Printed by S. and E. Hall, 1774.

[1]-52 p., 4to, A-F⁴ G².

The letters are dated from August 16, 1768 to July 30, 1770. Attribution from Evans.

Evans 13553, Sabin 65236.

Copies: CSmH, CtHi, CtY, DLC, MB, MBAt, MHi, MWA, MiU-C, RPJCB, ViU.

131a. [PRIESTLEY, JOSEPH] 1733-1804.

An Address To Protestant Dissenters Of All Denominations, On the Approaching Election of Members of Parliament, With respect to the State of Public Liberty in General, And Of American Affairs in Particular.

London: Printed for Joseph Johnson . . . 1774. . . .

[1]-16 p., 8vo, A⁸.

Reprinted in the *Virginia Gazette* (Rind) for December 22, 1774.
Verner W. Crane suggests that Franklin may have had a hand in this in his *Benjamin Franklin's Letters to the Press 1758-1775,* Chapel Hill, 1950, p. li.

Sabin 65500.

Copies: BM, CSmH, CtHWatk, CtY, DLC, ICN, InU, MBAt, MH, MHi, MiU-C, NHi, NN, PPAmP, PPL, RPB, RPJCB, ViU.

131b. [———]. ———.

London, Printed. Philadelphia, Re-Printed: And Sold By James Humphreys . . . MDCCLXXIV.

[1]-24 p., 8vo, [A]-C⁴.

Advertised in the *Pennsylvania Gazette* for October 12, 1774.

Evans 13556, Sabin 65500.

Copies: CSmH, CtHi, CtY, DLC, MB, MWA, PHi, PPAmP, PPL, RPJCB.

131c. [———]. ———.

London, Printed A.D. 1774. Boston, New-England: Re-Printed by Thomas and John Fleet . . . 1774.

[1]-16 p., 8vo, A-B⁴.

Advertised in the *Boston Evening Post* for October 17, 1774.

Evans 13555, Sabin 65500.

Copies: CtHi, CtY, DLC, MB, MBAt, MH, MHi, MWA, NHi, NN, RPJCB.

131d. [———. ———.]

[Wilmington: Printed by James Adams, 1774].

No copy of this printing has been located and it may be a ghost. The

Pennsylvania Packet for September 26, October 17 and 24 carried the following advertisement about the pamphlet, "Wilmington, Sept 23, 1774. Just published and sold by James Adams, at his Printing office in Wilmington, as well as the printer hereof [John Dunlap] and by William Carson, at the Harp and Crown in Third Street, Philadelphia." Normally we would assume that Adams and the others were selling the London edition because the Philadelphia edition (no. 131b) had not yet been printed. However, the fact that two Philadelphia agents were selling the pamphlet for Adams instead of importing it directly raises some doubt about such an assumption. When coupled with the fact that the next year Adams participated in the publication of political pamphlets to the extent of issuing an edition of John Allen's *Oration on the Beauties of Liberty*, no. 91g, of which only two copies have been located for the census, there is the distinct possibility that there was a Wilmington edition. In addition to the above there are two other editions recorded that are most probably ghosts. Evans in a note to no. 131b suggested that there may have been a 12mo Boston edition. No copy has been located nor has any 1775 Boston edition as recorded by Sabin been located.

Evans 13557, Sabin 65500.

132a.   QUINCY, JOSIAH, 1744-1775.

Observations On The Act Of Parliament Commonly Called The Boston Port-Bill; With Thoughts On Civil Society And Standing Armies. . . .

Boston: N. E. Printed For And Sold By Edes And Gill . . . 1774.

1 p. l., [1]-82 p., 8vo, [1]² [A]-K⁴.

Advertised in the *Boston Evening Post* for May 30, 1774, the *Maryland Gazette* for August 25, 1774, and the *Virginia Gazette* (Rind) for August 25, 1774. The first part was published in the *Pennsylvania Journal* for July 4, 1774. No doubt the second part failed to appear because of the publication of no. 132b. The MB copy belonged to the author and has his MS corrections.

Evans 13561, Sabin 67192.

Copies: BM, CSmH, CtHWatk, CtY, DLC, ICN, InU, MB, MBAt, MH, MHi, MWA, MWiW-C, MiU-C, NHi, NN, PHi, RPJCB, ViU.

132b.   ——. ——.

Philadelphia. Printed For John Sparhawk MDCCLXXIV.

[1]-60 p., 8vo, [A]-G⁴ H².

Advertised in the *Pennsylvania Packet* for July 4, 1774.

Evans 13562, Sabin 67192.

Copies: CSmH, CtY, DLC, MB, MBAt, MH, MWA, MiU-C, NN, PHi, PP, PPL, RPJCB.

132c. ———. ———.

Boston, N. E. Printed. London: Re-printed for Edward and Charles Dilly . . . MDCCLXXIV.

4 p. l., [1]-80 p., 8vo, [A]-L⁴.

Sabin 67192.

Copies: BM, CSmH, CtY, DLC, InU, MB, MBAt, MH, MHi, MiU-C, NN, PPL, RPJCB.

133.   [RANDOLPH, JOHN] 1727-1784.

Considerations On The Present State of Virginia.

[Williamsburg] Printed in the Year M.DCC.LXXIV.

[1]-24 p., 8vo, [A]-C⁴.

Published sometime before July 28, 1774, because a poem in answer to it appears in the *Virginia Gazette* (Purdie & Dixon) for that date. For authorship see: the introduction by Earl G. Swem to the reprint issued by Charles F. Heartman, New York, 1919. Robert Carter Nicholas' *Considerations*, Williamsburg, 1774, no. 129, is a reply.

Copies: MWA, NN, NjP, PPAmP.

134a.   [ROKEBY, MATTHEW ROBINSON-MORRIS, 2nd baron] 1713-1800.

Considerations On The Measures Carrying On With Respect To The British Colonies In North America. . . .

London, Sold by R. Baldwin . . . [1774].

2 p. l., [1]-160 p., 8vo, [A]² B-X⁴.

The *South Carolina Gazette* for September 19, 1774 advertised this pamphlet for sale, but it is not possible to tell which edition was involved. States have been noted with a fifteen-line errata slip that is found either as an extra leaf at the end or pasted on the verso of the half-title. There is also a second form of the errata slip with an extra line pasted on the bottom of it. Authorship from the Library of Congress Catalog. Two issues noted, one with and one without "April 1774" at the end.

Sabin 72151.

Copies: BM, CSmH, CtY, DLC, ICN, InU, MB, MBAt, MH, MWiW-C, NHi, NN, NcD, PPAmP, PPL, PU, RPJCB, ViU.

134b. [————]. ————. The Second Edition With Additions and an Appendix. . . .

London, Printed for R. Baldwin . . . E. and C. Dilly . . . J. Johnson . . . Richardson and Co. . . . and J. Almon . . . [1774].

2 p. l., [1]-56, 65-176, 1-45 p., 8vo, [A]² B-D⁸ E⁴ F-M⁸ *A-*B⁸ *C⁷.

The text on pages 49-56 is a shortened version of that appearing in no. 134a. The opening sentence of the Appendix indicates that it was written in November of 1774.

Copies: CSmH, CtY, MB, MBAt, MH, MiU-C, NN, PHi, RPJCB, WHi.

134c. [————]. ————. The Second Edition [&c.]. . . .

Same imprint.

2 p. l., [1]-176, 1-45 p., 8vo, [A]² B-M⁸ *A-*B⁸ C⁷.

A reprint of no. 134b.

Sabin 72152.

Copies: BM, DLC, InU, MBAt, NHi, PPAmP, PPL, RPB, RPJCB, ViU.

134d. [————]. ————. The Third Edition. . . .

Same imprint and collation.

A reprint of no. 134b.

Sabin 72152.

Copies: CtY, RPJCB.

134e. [————]. ————.

London: Printed, And New-York: Re-Printed, By John Holt . . . 1774.

1 p. l., [1]-73 p., 8vo, [-]¹ [A]-I⁴ [K]¹.

Advertised in the *New York Journal* for July 21, 1774, and in the *Connecticut Journal* for August 12, 1774 as "just published in New-York." A reprint of no. 134a.

Evans 13586, Sabin 72151 note.

Copies: CtY, DLC, MWA, MiU-C, NHi, NjP, RPJCB, ViU.

134f. [————]. ————.

London: Printed. Boston, Re-printed And Sold By Edes And Gill . . . M,DCC,LXXIV.

[1]-64 p., 4to, [A]-H⁴.

Advertised in the *Boston Evening Post* for August 1, 1774. A reprint of
no. 134a.

Evans 13582, Sabin 72151 note.

Copies: CSmH, MB, MH, MWA, MiU-C, PPL, RPJCB.

134g. [————]. ————.

Same imprint and collation.

"Fourth Edition" on the half-title. A resetting of no. 134f and may be
distinguished internally by the initial "N" on page 5. In no. 134f
it is plain and in this one it is surrounded by type ornaments. A reprint of no. 134a.

Evans 13583, Sabin 72151 note.

Copies: CSmH, CtY, MH, MWA, NN, RPJCB.

134h. [————]. ————.

Same imprint and collation.

"Fifth Edition" on half-title. Printed from substantially the same setting of type as no. 134g.

Evans 13584, Sabin 72151 note.

Copies: CtY, DLC, MBAt, MWA, NHi, NN, PHi, RPJCB.

134i. [————]. ————.

Philadelphia. Reprinted and Sold by Benjamin Towne ... MDCCLXXIV.
[1]-60 p., 8vo, [A]-G⁴ H².

Advertised in the *Pennsylvania Packet* for August 29, 1774. A reprint
of no. 134a. Two states noted, one with catchword on page 5 "prin-"
and the other with "principles."

Evans 13587, Sabin 72151 note.

Copies: CtHi, CtY, DLC, MB, MBAt, MWA, MiU-C, NHi, NN, PPL,
RPJCB.

134j. [————]. ————.

London: Printed. Hartford: Re-Printed And Sold by Eben. Watson
... M,DCC,LXXIV.

[1]-63 p., 8vo, [A]-H⁴.

Advertised in the *Connecticut Courant* for September 6, 1774. Evans
14438 lists a Norwich edition, but no copy has been located. C. K.
Shipton says that the entry was based on an advertisement in a now
unlocated issue of the *Norwich Packet*. Probably the advertisement
referred to this edition and the entry is a ghost.

Evans 13585, Sabin 72151 note.

Copies: CSmH, CtY, DLC, ICN, InU, MB, MWA, MiU-C, NHi, NN, PHi, PPL, PU, ViU, WHi.

134k.   [————]. Appendix To The Considerations On The Measures Carrying On With Respect To The British Colonies In North America.

     Philadelphia. Reprinted and Sold by Benjamin Towne ... M,DCC,LXXV. [1]-19 p., 8vo, [A]-B⁴ C².

     Advertised in the *Pennsylvania Evening Post* for July 21, 1775. This is a reprint of the Appendix in no. 134b and was issued to supplement no. 134i.

     Evans 14439, Sabin 1794, 72153.

     Copies: CtY, DLC, MWA, NHi, PPL, RPJCB.

135a.   [SEABURY, SAMUEL] 1729-1796.

     The Congress Canvassed: Or, An Examination Into The Conduct of the Delegates, At Their Grand Convention, Held in Philadelphia, Sept. 1, 1774. Addressed, To the Merchants of New-York. By A. W. Farmer. Author of Free Thoughts, &c. ...

     [New-York] Printed [by James Rivington] In The Year M,DCC,LXXIV.

     [1]-27, [1] p. (last p. postscript), 8vo, A-C⁴ D².

     Advertised in *Rivington's Gazette* for December 15, 1774. Dated at end November 28, 1774. Two states noted, one with the first line of text on page 3 ending "you" and the other with it ending "to." It is in the Postscript to this that Seabury first takes note of Alexander Hamilton's *A Full Vindication of the Measures of the Congress*, New York 1774, no. 116, which in turn was an attack on Seabury's earlier pamphlet, *Free Thoughts On the Proceedings of the Continental Congress*, New York, 1774, no. 136. Seabury went on to answer Hamilton more fully in his *A View of the Controversy*, New York, 1774, no. 137. For authorship see: Ford-*Hamilton* 2 note. Also attributed to Isaac Wilkins. See also: Clarence H. Vance's edition of *Letters of a Westchester Farmer*, White Plains, New York, 1930, vol. VIII of *Publications of the Westchester County Historical Society*.

     Evans 13601, Sabin 78562, Ford-*Hamilton* 1 note, Hewlett 94.

     Copies: CSmH, CtHi, CtHWatk, CtY, DLC, ICN, MB, MBAt, MH, MHi, MWA, MWiW-C, MiU-C, NHi, NN, NjP, PHi, PPAmP, PPL, PU, RPJCB, ViU.

135b.　[————].　————.

New-York, Printed: London Reprinted for Richardson and Urquhart
. . . 1775.

　2 p. l., [1]-59 p., 8vo, [A]² B-H⁴ I².

　Sabin 78563.

　Copies: CtY, InU, MBAt, MHi, MiU-C, NN, RPJCB.

136a.　[SEABURY, SAMUEL] 1729-1796.

Free Thoughts, On The Proceedings of The Continental Congress,
Held at Philadelphia Sept. 5, 1774: Wherein Their Errors are exhibited,
Their Reasonings Confuted . . . In A Letter To The Farmers, And Other
Inhabitants Of North America . . . By a Farmer. . . .

　[New-York] Printed [by James Rivington] In The Year
M.DCC.LXXIV.

　[1]-29, [*i.e.* 31] p., 8vo, [A]-D⁴.

　Advertised in *Rivington's Gazette* for November 24, 1774. Signed at
　　end "November 16, 1774. A. W. Farmer." For authorship see:
　　Ford-*Hamilton* 2 note. Also attributed to Isaac Wilkins. See also:
　　Clarence H. Vance's edition of *Letters of a Westchester Farmer*, White
　　Plains, New York, 1930, vol. VIII of *Publications of the Westchester
　　County Historical Society.*

　Copies: CSmH, CtHWatk, DLC, MH, MWA, ViU.

136b.　[————].　————.

　Same imprint.

　[1]-31 p., 8vo, [A]-D⁴.

　Copies: MBAt.

136c.　[————].　————.

　Same imprint.

　[1]-24 p., 8vo, A-C⁴.

　Evans 13602, Sabin 78574, Ford-*Hamilton* 1 note, Hewlett 95.

　Copies: CSmH, CtHi, CtY, DLC, ICN, MB, MBAt, MH, MWA,
　　MWiW-C, MiU-C, NHi, NN, PHi, PPAmP, PPL, PU, RPB, RPJCB.

136d.　[————].　————.

New-York, Printed: London Reprinted for Richardson and Urquhart
. . . 1775.

　2 p. l., [1]-50 p., 8vo, [A]² B-G⁴ H² (H2 blank).

　Sabin 78575.

Copies: CSmH, CtY, DLC, InU, MBAt, MH, MiU-C, NHi, NN, PPAmP, RPJCB, WHi.

137a. [SEABURY, SAMUEL] 1729-1796.

A View Of The Controversy Between Great-Britain and her Colonies: Including A Mode of Determining their present Disputes, Finally and Effecually [*sic*]; And Of Preventing All Future Contentions. In A Letter To the Author of A Full Vindication Of The Measures of the Congress . . . By A. W. Farmer. Author of Free Thoughts, &c.

New-York: Printed by James Rivington, M,DCC,LXXIV.

[1]-37, 8vo, A-E⁴ (E4 blank).

Advertised in *Rivington's Gazette* for January 5, 1775. Signed at the end "A. W. Farmer. December 24, 1774." A reply to Alexander Hamilton's *A Full Vindication of the Measures of the Congress,* New York, 1774, no. 116. For authorship see: Ford-*Hamilton* 2 note. Also attributed to Isaac Wilkins. See also: Clarence H. Vance's edition of *Letters of a Westchester Farmer,* White Plains, New York, 1930, vol. VIII of *Publications of the Westchester County Historical Society.* Two issues noted, the first as above, the second with advertisements on E3 verso and E4 recto.

Evans 13603, Sabin 78581, Ford-*Hamilton* 2, Hewlett 18.

Copies: BM, CSmH, CtHWatk, CtY, DLC, ICN, InU, MB, MH, MHi, MWA, MWiW-C, MiU-C, NHi, NN, PHi, PPAmP, PPL, RPJCB, ViU, WHi.

137b. [————————]. ————————.

New-York, Printed: London Reprinted for Richardson and Urquhart . . . 1775.

1 p. l., [1]-90 p., 8vo, [A]¹ B-M⁴ N¹.

Sabin 78581, Ford-*Hamilton* 2 note.

Copies: BM, CSmH, DLC, ICN, MBAt, MiU-C, NN, PPAmP, RPJCB.

138. A Serious Address To The Inhabitants Of The Colony Of New-York, Containing a full and minute Survey of the Boston-Port Act, calculated to excite our Inhabitants to conspire, with the other Colonies on this Continent, in extricating that unhappy Town from its unparalleled Distresses. . . .

New-York: Printed by John Holt . . . M,DCC,LXXIV.

[1]-14, [1-6] p., 4to, [A]¹ B-D² [E]² [F]¹.

Signed at the end "A Citizen of New-York, May 30th, 1774." The appendices contain the Boston Port Act and Lord Camden's speech on the Declaratory Act. Sabin gives the date at the end as June 11, 1774. No copy with this date has yet been noted.

Evans 13605, Sabin 79246.

Copies: CSmH, DLC, MBAt, MH, MWA, MiU-C, PPL.

139a. SHARP, GRANVILLE, 1735-1813.

A Declaration Of The People's Natural Right To A Share In the Legislature; Which is the Fundamental Principle Of The British Constitution Of State. . . .

London: Printed for B. White . . . M.DCC.LXXIV.

2 p. l., i-xl, 1-32 p., 8vo, [A]² a-e⁴ B-E⁴.

Although this consists of only the first part of no. 139b, it is clear that the pamphlet was first issued in this abbreviated form. Page 32 is an apparent point of termination. The American editions, nos. 139d to g, contain only the text printed here. This is also the version reprinted in the *Virginia Gazette* (Purdie & Dixon) for October 20, 1774.

Sabin 79810.

Copies: DLC, MBAt, NHi, PHi, PPRos, PU.

139b. ———. ———.

Same imprint.

2 p. l., i-xl, 1-244 p., 8vo, [A]² a-e⁴ B-Z⁴ Aa-Hh⁴ Ii² (G4 blank).

Printed from the same setting of type as no. 139a with additional material.

Sabin 79816.

Copies: BM, CSmH, CtY, DLC, ICN, InU, MB, MH, MHi, MWA, MiU-C, NN, NcD, NjP, PHi, PP, PPL, RPB, RPJCB, ViU.

139c. ———. ———. The Second Edition.

London: Printed for B. White . . . M.DCC.LXXV.

Same collation.

Copies: BM, CSmH, CtY, ICN, MiU-C, NN, NjP, PPL, PU, RPJCB.

139d. ———. ———. The Second Edition.

Same imprint.

2 p. l., i-xl, 1-279, [1]-4 p. (last 4 p. advts.), 8vo, [A]² a-e⁴ B-Z⁴ Aa-Hh⁴ Ii² Kk-Oo⁴.

A reprint of no. 139c with an index.

Sabin 79817.

Copies: CtY, DLC, MB, MH, MWA, MiU-C, NHi, RPB, ViU.

139e. ⸻. ⸻.

London, Printed: Philadelphia, Re-Printed And sold by Benjamin Towne ... 1774.

[1]-21 p., 8vo, [A]-C⁴ (C4 blank).

Advertised in the *Pennsylvania Journal* for September 21, 1774. A reprint of no. 139a.

Evans 13612, Sabin 79812.

Copies: DLC, PPAmP, PPL.

139f. ⸻. ⸻.

London, Printed: Philadelphia, Reprinted And sold by John Dunlap ... 1774.

Same collation.

Same setting of type as no. 139e with imprint altered.

Evans 13613, Sabin 79811.

Copies: CSmH, DLC, MHi, NN, PHi, PPAmP, PPL, RPJCB.

139g. ⸻. ⸻. The Third Edition.

London: Printed. Boston: Re Printed and Sold by Edes and Gill ... MDCC.LXXIV.

[1]-22 p., 4to, [A]-B⁴ C³.

A reprint of no. 139a. Evans 13610 lists a 12mo edition in Boston of 1774, but no copy has been located and it is probably a ghost.

Evans 13609, Sabin 79814.

Copies: CSmH, CtHWatk, DLC, MB, MBAt, MH, MHi, MWA, NN, RPJCB.

139h. ⸻. ⸻.

London: Printed. New-York: Re-printed By John Holt ... MDCCLXXIV.

[1]-16 p., 8vo, [A]-B⁴.

Printed in Holt's *New-York Journal* for September 22 and 29, 1774. In that same issue there is the statement that in a few days it will be published as a pamphlet.

Evans 13611, Sabin 79813.

Copies: CtY, MH.

139i. ———. ———. The Third Edition.

Dublin: Printed for T. Armitage, J. Williams, and L. Flin. MDCCLXXVI.

[i]-xliii, 244 p., 12mo, [A]-M¹².
Copies: MiU-C.

140. SHERWOOD, SAMUEL, 1730-1783.

A Sermon, Containing, Scriptural Instructions to Civil Rulers, and all Free-born Subjects. In which the Principles of sound Policy and good Government are established and vindicated; and some Doctrines advanced and zealously propagated by New-England Tories, are considered and refuted. Delivered on the public Fast, August 31, 1774 . . . Also, An Appendix, Stating the heavy Grievances the Colonies labour under from several late Acts of the British Parliament . . . By the Rev. Ebenezer Baldwin, of Danbury. . . .

New-Haven, Printed by T. and S. Green. [1774?].

[i]-x, [11]-81, [1] p. (last p. advts.), 8vo, [A]-K⁴ [L]¹.

Advertised in the *Connecticut Journal* for January 4, 1775, as "just published," but in view of the date of the sermon it is probable that copies were issued before the first of the year.

Evans 13614, Sabin 80456.

Copies: CSmH, CtHi, CtHWatk, CtY, DLC, MB, MHi, MWA, MiU-C, NHi, NN, RPJCB.

SHIPLEY, JONATHAN, bp. of St. Asaph. *A Sermon Preached before the Incorporated Society for the Propagation of the Gospel.* London, 1774, see: 100g.

141a. [SHIPLEY, JONATHAN] bp. of St. Asaph, 1714-1788.

A Speech Intended To Have Been Spoken On The Bill For Altering The Charters Of The Colony of Massachusett's Bay.

London: Printed For T. Cadell . . . MDCCLXXIV.

[i]-vii, [1]-36 p., 8vo, [A]-E⁴ F².

Reprinted in the *Massachusetts Spy* for Sept. 15, 1774, the *Massachusetts Gazette and Boston Weekly News-Letter* for September 22 and 29, 1774, the *Virginia Gazette* (Rind) for September 29, 1774, the *New-York Journal* for September 22, 1774, the *Maryland Gazette* for September 28 and October 6, 1774. Copies were advertised for sale in the *South Carolina Gazette* for October 31, 1774, but it is not possible to tell which edition. Verner W. Crane says there is a hint that Franklin had a hand in the publication of this. See: his *Benjamin Frank-*

lin's Letters to the Press 1758-1775, Chapel Hill, 1950, p. li.
Sabin 80511.

Copies: BM, CSmH, CtHWatk, CtY, DLC, ICN, InU, MBAt, MH, MiU-C, NHi, NN, PHi, PPAmP, PPL, PU, RPJCB, ViU.

141b. [————]. ————. The Second Edition.
Same imprint and collation.
Printed from substantially the same setting of type as no. 141a.
Sabin 80512.

Copies: BM, CSmH, CtY, DLC, InU, MBAt, MH, MiU-C, PHi, PPL, RPB.

141c. [————]. ————. The Third Edition.
Same imprint and collation.
Printed from substantially the same setting of type as no. 141a.
Sabin 80513.

Copies: CSmH, CtY, DLC, MB, MH, MHi, MiU-C, PHi, PP, PPL, RPJCB.

141d. [————]. ————. The Fourth Edition.
Same imprint and collation.
Printed from substantially the same setting of type as no. 141a. Sabin goes on to list a fifth and a sixth London edition. No copies have been located and he probably confused them with the Hartford edition, no. 141j, and the Boston edition, no. 141f.
Sabin 80514.

Copies: CSmH, CtY, DLC, ICN, MB, MH, MHi, MiU-C, NN, NcD, PHi, PPAmP, PPL, RPJCB, WHi.

141e. [————]. ————.
London: To be had of Goadby and Berry ... [1774?].
[1]-16 p., 8vo, A⁸.
Sabin 80515.
Copies: CSmH, CtY, ICN, MB, MH, MiU-C, NN, PPAmP, PPL, RPJCB.

141f. [————]. ————. The Sixth Edition.
London, Printed. Boston: RePrinted, And Sold By Edes And Gill ... MDCCLXXIV.
[i]-vi, [7]-24 p., 4to, [A]-C⁴.

Evans 13616, Sabin 80516.
Copies: CtY, DLC, MB, MBAt, MH, MHi, MWA, MiU-C, PPL, RPJCB.

141g. ————. ————. By The Rev. Jonathan Shipley. . . .
London, Printed . . . Boston, N. E. Re-printed, and sold . . . at Green-
leaf's Printing Office . . . [1774].
[1]-12 p., 12mo, [A]⁴ B².
Advertised in the *Boston Evening Post* for October 10, 1774.
Evans 13615, Sabin 80517.
Copies: MH, NN.

141h. ————. ————.
Salem: N. E. Printed and Sold by E. Russell . . . M,DCC,LXXIV.
[1]-16 p., 8vo, [A]-B⁴.
Evans 13622, Sabin 80518.
Copies: MHi, MWA.

141i. ————. ————.
Salem: Re-printed and sold by S. and E. Hall [1774?].
[1]-16 p., 4to, [A]-B⁴.
Caption title, imprint on p. 16.
Evans 13623, Sabin 80519.
Copies: CSmH, DLC, MB, MH, MHi, MWA, MiU-C, RPJCB.

141j. [————]. ————. The Fifth Edition.
London, Printed; Hartford: Re-printed and Sold by Ebenezer Wat-
son . . . MDCCLXXIV.
[1]-17 p., 12mo, [A]-B⁴ [C]¹.
Evans 13617, Sabin 80520.
Copies: CtHi.

141k. [————]. ————.
London: Printed. New-York: Re-Printed By John Holt . . .
MDCCLXXIV.
2 p. l., [1]-17 p., 8vo, [A]³ B-C⁴.
Advertised in the *New-York Journal* for September 15, 1774. There are
   two states, one without the author's name on the title page and one
   with a slip reading "By the Bishop of St. Asaph" pasted on it.

Evans 13619, Sabin 80521.
Copies: CtY, DLC, MH, NN.

141l. [————]. ————. The Third Edition.
  London, Printed; Philadelphia: Re-printed and Sold by William and
Thomas Bradford . . . M.DCC.LXXIV.
  [i]-vi, [1]-29 p., 8vo, [A]-D⁴ E².
  Advertised in the *Pennsylvania Journal* for September 14, 1774.
  Evans 13620, Sabin 80523.
  Copies: CSmH, CtY, DLC, ICN, MBAt, MH, MWA, NHi, PHi, PPAmP,
    PPL, PU, RPJCB.

141m. [————]. ————.
  London, Printed: Philadelphia, Reprinted and Sold by Benjamin
Towne . . . [1774].
  [i]-v, 7-18 p., 8vo, [A]-B⁴ C¹.
  Advertised in the *Pennsylvania Packet* for September 12, 1774.
  Evans 13621, Sabin 80522.
  Copies: CtY, DLC, MH, PHi, PPL, RPJCB.

141n. ————. ————. The Fifth Edition.
  Lancaster: Printed And Sold By Francis Bailey. MDCCLXXIV.
  [i]-iv, [5]-24 p., 8vo, [A]-C⁴.
  Evans 13618, Sabin 80524.
  Copies: PPL.

141o. [————]. ————.
  Williamsburg: Printed By John Pinkney, For The Benefit Of Clementina Rind's Estate. MDCCLXXIV.
  [1]-15 p., 8vo, [A]-B⁴.
  Copies: CSmH, RPJCB.

141p. ————. The Whole of the celebrated Speech Of The Rev. Dr.
Jonathan Shipley . . . Intended to have been spoken [&c]. . . .
  Printed by S. Southwick . . . Newport, Rhode Island, Sept. 1774.
  [1]-20 p., 8vo, [A]-B⁴ C².
  Evans 13624, Sabin 80526 note, Alden 562.
  Copies: DLC, MBAt, MH, MHi, MWA, MWiW-C, NN, PHi, RPB,
    RPJCB.

142. Some Fugitive Thoughts On A Letter Signed Freeman, Addressed To The Deputies Assembled At The High Court of Congress in Philadelphia. By A. Back Settler.

[Charleston] South Carolina. Printed in the Year MDCCLXXIV.

1 p. l., 1-36 p., 4to, [-]¹ A-D⁴ E².

A reply to William Henry Drayton's *A Letter from Freeman of South Carolina*, Charleston, 1774, no. 111.

Evans 13630, Sabin 86648.

Copies: DLC, NN, PPRos.

143. TENNENT, WILLIAM, 1740-1777.

An Address, Occasioned By The Late Invasion of the Liberties Of The American Colonies By The British Parliament, Delivered in Charlestown, South Carolina. . . .

Philadelphia: Printed and Sold by William and Thomas Bradford . . . MDCCLXXIV.

[i]-iii, [5]-20 p., 8vo, [A]-B⁴ C².

Advertised in the *Pennsylvania Journal* for December 14, 1774, and in the *New-York Journal* for December 15, 1774.

Evans 13649, Sabin 94718.

Copies: CSmH, CtHi, CtY, DLC, ICN, MWA, MiU-C, NN, NjP, PHi, PPL, RPJCB, ViU.

144a. TUCKER, JOSIAH, 1712-1799.

The True Interest of Great-Britain, Set Forth In Regard To The Colonies; And the only Means of Living in Peace and Harmony with Them. . . .

Norfolk [England] Printed in the Year, M.DCC.LXXIV.

[1]-66 p., 8vo, [-]¹ A-H⁴.

This is a reprint of Tract no. IV from his *Four Tracts, Together With Two Sermons, On Political and Commercial Subjects*, Glocester, 1774.

Sabin 97365.

Copies: CtY, MiU-C, PHi, PPL, RPJCB.

144b. ———. ———. To which is Added by the Printer, A few more Words, on the Freedom of the Press in America.

Philadelphia: Printed, and Sold, by Robert Bell . . . MDCCLXXVI.

[1]-66, [1-6] p., 8vo, [-]¹ A-H⁴ I³.

Advertised in the *Pennsylvania Packet* for June 24, 1776. Two states noted, one with Tucker's name alone on the title page and one with three lines that identify him further.

Evans 15119, Sabin 97366.

Copies: BM, CSmH, CtY, DLC, ICN, InU, MB, MBAt, MH, MWA, MiU-C, NN, PHi, PPAmP, PPL, RPJCB, WHi.

145. WEBSTER, SAMUEL, 1719-1796.

The Misery And Duty Of An Oppress'd And Enslav'd People, Represented In A Sermon Delivered at Salisbury, July 14, 1774. On a Day set apart for Fasting and Prayer. . . .

Boston: Printed by Edes and Gill, in Queen-Street. M,DCC,LXXIV.

[1]-31 p., 8vo, [A]-D⁴.

Evans 13758, Sabin 102421.

Copies: BM, CSmH, CtHi, CtY, DLC, ICN, MB, MBAt, MH, MHi, MWA, MiU-C, NHi, NcD, RPJCB.

146. [WELLS, RICHARD].

A Few Political Reflections Submitted To The Consideration Of The British Colonies, By A Citizen of Philadelphia.

Philadelphia: Printed and Sold by John Dunlap. M,DCC,LXXIV.

[1]-86 p., 8vo, A-L⁴ (L4 blank).

Advertised in the *Pennsylvania Packet* for August 29, 1774. This consists of six letters which originally appeared in that newspaper between June 20 and August 8, 1774. Attributed to Wells by the Library of Congress Catalog on the basis of the catalogue of the American Philosophical Society of which Wells was secretary.

Evans 13760, Sabin 102599.

Copies: CSmH, DLC, MB, NHi, NjP, PHi, PPAmP, PPL, RPJCB.

147. WHITNEY, PETER, 1744-1816.

The Transgression of a Land punished by a multitude of Rulers. Considered In Two Discourses, Delivered July 14, 1774 . . . A Day of Fasting and Prayer, On Account of the Dark Aspect of our Public Affairs. . . .

Boston: Printed by John Boyle . . . MDCCLXXIV.

[1]-71 p., 8vo, [A]-I⁴.

Evans 13769, Sabin 103770.

Copies: BM, CSmH, DLC, MH, MHi, MWA, RPJCB, WHi.

148. [WILKINS, ISAAC] 1742-1830.

Short Advice To the Counties of New-York . . . By A Country Gentleman.

New-York: Printed by James Rivington, 1774.

[1]-15 p., 8vo, A-B⁴.

Advertised in *Rivington's Gazette* for December 1, 1774 and in the *Massachusetts Gazette and Boston Weekly News-Letter* for December 22, 1774. For authorship see: his *My Services and Losses in Aid of the King's Cause during the American Revolution*, Brooklyn, 1890, pp. 15-16.

Evans 13772, Sabin 80594, Hewlett 19.

Copies: CSmH, CtY, DLC, ICN, MBAt, MHi, MWA, MWiW-C, MiU-C, NHi, NN, PPL, RPJCB.

149. [WILSON, JAMES] 1742-1798.

Considerations On The Nature And The Extent Of The Legislative Authority Of The British Parliament.

Philadelphia: Printed and Sold, by William and Thomas Bradford . . . M.DCC.LXXIV.

[i]-iv, [1]-35 p., 8vo, A-E⁴.

Advertised in the *Pennsylvania Journal* for September 28, 1774 and in *Rivington's Gazette* for October 13, 1774. For authorship and circumstances of publication see: Charles P. Smith's *James Wilson*, Chapel Hill, 1956, pp. 36-37, 54-58, 89, 391.

Evans 13775, Sabin 104629.

Copies: CSmH, CtHi, CtY, DLC, ICN, MB, MBAt, MWA, MWiW-C, MiU-C, NHi, NN, PHi, PPAmP, PPL, PU, RPJCB.

[ZUBLY, JOHN JOACHIM]. *Great Britain's Right to Tax her Colonies.* [London? 1774?], see: 74b, c.

1775

[ALLEN, JOHN]. *An Oration on the Beauties of Liberty.* Wilmington, 1775, see: 91g.

150. [BARRY, HENRY] 1750-1822.

The Advantages Which America Derives from her Commerce Connexion and Dependance On Britain Address To The People of America. . . .

[Boston] Printed in the Year 1775.

[1]-16 p., 4to, [A]-B⁴.

This probably appeared between January 30 and February 18, 1775. From the correspondence between Eliot and Belknap noted under no. 151a, it is apparent that Eliot had no copy of this pamphlet to send Belknap on the earlier date when he sent a copy of Barry's *The Strictures*, no. 151a. On the later date, he sent a copy of this item to Belknap. This, like no. 151a, has been assigned to Boston because Barry was stationed there.

Evans 13822, Sabin 472.

Copies: BM, CSmH, MH, MHi, MWA, NN.

151a. [BARRY, HENRY] 1750-1822.

The Strictures On The Friendly Address Examined, And A Refutation of its Principles attempted. Addressed To The People Of America. . . .

[Boston] Printed in the Year 1775.

[1]-14 p., 8vo, [A]-B⁴ (B4 blank).

This reply to Charles Lee's *Strictures on a Pamphlet Entitled a "Friendly Address*," Philadelphia, 1774, no. 125a must have been printed during January of 1775. John Eliot sent a copy of the pamphlet with a letter dated January 30th to Jeremy Belknap. It is from the correspondence between these two men that Barry is identified as the author. See: *Collections of the Massachusetts Historical Society* (6th series), vol. IV (1891), pp. 78 and 81. The place of publication is determined from the New York edition, no. 151b, and the fact that Barry was stationed in Boston. Because of the similarity between the title of this and the pamphlet to which it was a reply, a good deal of confusion has arisen about the number of editions. The following Evans numbers can be considered ghosts unless copies are discovered that match his descriptions. Number 13823 "[Boston] Printed by John Howe, 1775, 14 p. 8vo" is credited to MHi which does not have it today. Evans, who assigned this to the wrong author, probably did not realize that the texts of this and the first part of no. 151d were the same and thus was misled by the wording of the imprint of no. 151d. Number 13864 is a duplicate entry of no. 14154 under the wrong author. Number 13865 is also entered under the wrong author with no copy located. Evans probably confused it with this edition. Sabin 3684 also causes confusion by listing what is clearly this pamphlet under a completely wrong title. His listings under the two numbers below are somewhat less inaccurate.

Evans 13863, Sabin 11881, 26867.

Copies: BM, DLC, InU, MBAt, MH, MHi, MWA, MWiW-C, MiU-C, NN, PPL, RPJCB, ViU.

151b. [———]. The General Attacked By a Subaltern: Or The Strictures On The Friendly Address Examined And A Refutation of its Principles attempted [&c.]. . . .

Boston, Printed: New-York, re-printed, by James Rivington. [1775]. [1]-25 p., 8vo, A-C⁴ D¹.

> This consists not only of Barry's pamphlet, but also the one to which it is a reply, Lee's *Strictures,* no. 125, which occupies pages 13-25 at the end. Contrary to Hewlett's suggestion it is unlikely that the two were ever issued separately because the separate title page of Lee's piece comes on leaf B3 which is a comparatively awkward place to separate the two items. His suggestion may have arisen from a misunderstanding of an advertisement in *Rivington's Gazette* on November 17, 1774, discussed in no. 125c.

Evans 13824, Sabin 26867, Hewlett 23.

Copies: CSmH, DLC, MWA, MiU-C, NHi, NN, PHi, PPAmP, PPL, RPJCB.

152. BLAND, WILLIAM.

[A Sermon Preached By The Reverend Mr. Bland, At The Capitol in this City, On the Present Grievances of America.]

[Williamsburg: Printed by John Pinkney? 1775].

> Advertised in the *Virginia Gazette* (Pinkney) for August 30, 1775 as "just published, and to be sold by the printer . . ." No copy has been located.

Evans 13838.

153. BOLTON, THOMAS.

An Oration Delivered March Fifteenth, 1775, At The Request of a Number of the Inhabitants Of The Town Of Boston. . . .

[Boston] Printed in the Year, M,DCC,LXXV.

[1]-9 p., 8vo, [A]-B² C¹.

> This attack on the radical leaders in Boston is a satirical imitation of the Boston Massacre Orations, particularly Warren's of the same year, no. 201.

Evans 13840, Sabin 6249.

Copies: CSmH, MBAt, NHi, PHi, RPJCB.

154. [BRUSH, CREAN] 1725?-1778.

Speech Of A Member Of The General Assembly Of New-York, At Their Session, in 1775.

New-York: Printed in the Year MDCCLXXV.

[1]-12 p., 8vo, [A]⁴ B².

The author of this attack on the Continental Congress identifies himself in the pamphlet.

Evans 13848, Sabin 8771.

Copies: CSmH, MH, MWA.

155a. [BURGOYNE, JOHN] 1722-1792.

The Speech Of A General Officer In The House Of Commons, February 20th, 1775.

[London? 1775?].

1 p. l., [1]-9 p., 4to, [A]⁶.

Reprinted in the *Virginia Gazette* (Dixon & Hunter) for June 3, 1775.

Copies: CSmH, CtHi, CtY, DLC, MWiW-C, MiU-C, NHi, NN, PPL, RPJCB.

155b. [———]. ———.

[Boston? 1775?].

[1]-8 p., 8vo, [A]⁴.

The conjecture that this may have been printed in Boston arises from the following. The *Boston Evening Post* for June 1, 1775, advertised "To be sold at Draper's Printing-Office, in Newbury-Street. Major General Burgoune's Speech." Although this printing attempts to follow the typography of no. 155a, it shows a deterioration in quality that suggests hasty colonial press work. Burgoyne had arrived in Boston on May 25th and put his literary talents to work. He wrote Gage's proclamation of June 12th and generally urged vigorous action. He may have had his speech reprinted as a part of this activity. Abigail Adams mentioned having read the speech in Boston in a letter to John Adams dated July 25, 1775. See: *Familiar Letters*, edited by C. F. Adams, 1876, p. 84.

Sabin 9254.

Copies: MHi, RPJCB.

156a. BURKE, EDMUND, 1729-1797.

Speech of Edmund Burke, Esq. On American Taxation, April 19, 1774.

London: Printed For J. Dodsley ... MDCCLXXV.

[i]-iv, 1-57, [1] p. (last p. errata), 4to, A² B-H⁴ [I]¹.

Reprinted in the *Pennsylvania Journal* for March 22 and 29, 1775.

Sabin 9295 (incorrectly dated 1774).

Copies: BM, CSmH, CtY, DLC, ICN, InU, MiU-C, NHi, NN, NjP, RPJCB, ViU.

156b. ——. ——. The Second Edition.

London: Printed for J. Dodsley ... MDCCLXXV. ....

[i]-iv, 5-96 p., 8vo, A-F⁸.

Two states noted, one with the price at the bottom of the title page in all upper case and one with it in upper and lower case.

Sabin 9295.

Copies: BM, CSmH, CtY, DLC, ICN, MBAt, MH, MiU-C, NHi, NN, NcU, NjP, PHi, PPAmP, PPL, RPJCB, WHi.

156c. ——. ——. The Third Edition.

Same imprint and collation.

Printed from substantially the same setting of type as no. 156b.

Sabin 9295.

Copies: BM, CSmH, CtHWatk, CtY, DLC, MBAt, MH, MHi, MiU-C, NN, PPL, PU, RPJCB.

156d. ——. ——. The Fourth Edition.

Same imprint and collation.

Printed from substantially the same setting of type as no. 156b.

Sabin 9295.

Copies: CSmH, CtY, MH, MiU-C, NHi, NN, PHi, PP, PPL, PU, RPJCB.

156e. ——. ——. The Fourth Edition.

Same imprint and collation.

This is a complete resetting of no. 156d. The two can be distinguished by the fact that on the title page of no. 156d the line "The Fourth Edition" does not have any rules above and below it and in this setting there are rules above and below it.

Copies: CSmH, CtHi, CtY, DLC, MB, MiU-C, NN, PPL, RPJCB.

156f. ——. ——.

Bristol: Re-printed and sold by W. Pine ... Also by all the other Booksellers [1775?].

[1]-51 p., 12mo, A-D⁶ E².

Date of imprint from contemporary manuscript note on the title page of RPJCB copy.

Sabin 9295.

Copies: BM, CtY, ICN, NN, PHi, PPL, RPJCB.

156g. ————. ————. The Third Edition.

New-York: Printed by James Rivington. MDCCLXXV.

[1]-63, [1] p. (last p. advts.), 8vo, A-H⁴.

Advertised in *Rivington's Gazette* for September 21, 1775. This edition also advertised for sale by James Humphreys in the *Pennsylvania Gazette* in October of 1775.

Evans 13853, Sabin 9295, Hewlett 24.

Copies: CSmH, MBAt, MH, NHi, NN, PHi, PPL, RPJCB.

156h. ————. ————. The Third Edition.

London, Printed: Philadelphia, Reprinted and sold by Benjamin Towne ... MDCCLXXV.

[i]-iv, 1-76 p., 8vo, A² B-K⁴ L².

Advertised in the *Pennsylvania Evening Post* for November 28, 1775. See note under no. 157e.

Evans 13852, Sabin 9295.

Copies: DLC, PPAmP, PPL.

157a. BURKE, EDMUND, 1729-1797.

The Speech of Edmund Burke, Esq; On Moving His Resolutions For Conciliation with the Colonies, March 22, 1775.

London: Printed for J. Dodsley. MDCCLXXV.

2 p. l., 1-65 p., 4to, [A]² B-I⁴ [K]².

An extract was published in the *Virginia Gazette* (Pinkney) for August 10, 1775, (Dixon) for March 2, 1776.

Sabin 9296.

Copies: CSmH, CtY, DLC, InU, MBAt, MH, MiU-C, NHi, NN, RPB, RPJCB, ViU, WHi.

157b. ————. ————. The Second Edition.

London: Printed for J. Dodsley ... MDCCLXXV.

2 p. l., 1-107 p., 8vo, [A]² B-H⁸ (H7 & H8 blank).

Sabin 9296.

Copies: BM, CSmH, CtY, DLC, MB, MH, MiU-C, NHi, NN, PHi, PPAmP, PPL, RPB, RPJCB.

157c. ———. ———. The Third Edition.

Same imprint.

[1]-112 p., 8vo, A-G⁸.

Dodsley also issued two other "Third Editions," one dated 1778 and one dated 1785.

Sabin 9296.

Copies: CSmH, DLC, ICN, MH, MiU-C, NN, NcU, NjP, PPAmP, PPL, PU, RPJCB.

157d. ———. ———.

Dublin: Printed for J. Exshaw . . . and R. Moncrieffe . . . M,DCC,LXXV.

2 p. l., 1-88 p., 8vo, [A]² B-M⁴.

Sabin 9296.

Copies: InU, MiU-C, PPL, RPJCB.

157e. ———. ———.

New-York: Printed By James Rivington, 1775.

[i]-v, [7]-71, [1] p. (last p. advts.), 8vo, [A]-I⁴.

Advertised in *Rivington's Gazette* for September 23, 1775. Also offered for sale by James Humphreys in the *Pennsylvania Journal* for September 20, 1775. Evans 13855 lists a Philadelphia edition of this year published by Benjamin Towne. No copy of such an edition has been located and it would appear that he based his entry on the following advertisement that Towne put in the *Pennsylvania Evening Post* for September 16th, "Proposals for printing by subscription Two Speeches By Edmund Burke one delivered April 19, 1774 and the other on the 22nd of March 1775 . . ." It continued to appear until November 28th. If this is the source, then it would be reasonable to suggest that Towne began setting type for his subscribers in September, but by the end of November the competition of the Rivington editions of the two pamphlets sold by Humphreys, no. 156g and this item, made the venture unprofitable so Towne merely issued Burke's speech of April 19th, no. 156h, which he had already in press.

Evans 13854, Sabin 9296, Hewlett 25.

Copies: CSmH, CtHi, DLC, MBAt, MWA, NHi, PHi, PPAmP, PPL, RPJCB.

158a. CARMICHAEL, JOHN, 1728-1785.
A Self-Defensive War Lawful, Proved In A Sermon, Preached at Lancaster, before Captain Ross's Company of Militia . . . June 4th, 1775.
Lancaster: Printed by Francis Bailey . . . [1775].
[1]-25 p., 8vo, [A]² B-D⁴ (D4 blank).
Advertised for sale by Baily in an advertisement dated July 1st, in the *Pennsylvania Packet* for July 8, 1775.
Evans 13861.
Copies: CSmH, MWA, NjP, PHi.

158b. ———. ———.
Philadelphia: Printed for and Sold by John Dean . . . 1775.
[1]-34 p., 8vo, [A]-D⁴ E² (E2 blank).
Advertised for sale in the *Pennsylvania Evening Post* for July 1, 1775. The advertisement in the *Pennsylvania Journal* for July 19, 1775 describes this edition as "corrected [by the author] from the copy printed at Lancaster."
Evans 13862, Sabin 10939.
Copies: DLC, MWA, MiU-C, NHi, NN, NjP, PHi, PP, PPL, RPJCB.

[CARTWRIGHT, JOHN]. *American Independence,* A New Edition. London, 1775, see: 105b.

[CHANDLER, THOMAS BRADBURY]. *A Friendly Address to All Reasonable Americans Carefully Abridged.* New York, 1775, see: 107e.

159a. [CHANDLER, THOMAS BRADBURY] 1726-1790.
What think ye of the Congress Now? Or, An Enquiry, How Far The Americans are Bound To Abide by, and Execute the Decisions of, The Late Congress?
New-York: Printed by James Rivington, M,DCCLXXV.
[1]-48, [1]-4 p., 8vo, A-F⁴ [G]².
Advertised in *Rivington's Gazette* for January 12, 1775. At one time it was attributed to Myles Cooper. The four pages at the end consist of Joseph Galloway's *A Plan of A Proposed Union, Between Great-Britain and the Colonies . . . as Mentioned in the Preceding Work.* Copies may have been issued without the *Plan.* For authorship see: C. H. Vance's "Myles Cooper," *Columbia University Quarterly,* vol. XXII (1930), pp. 275-276, and Julian P. Boyd's *Anglo-American Union,* Philadelphia, 1941.

Evans 13866, Sabin 11882, Hewlett 26.

Copies: BM, CSmH, CtHWatk, CtY, DLC, ICN, InU, MB, MBAt, MH, MWA, MWiW-C, MiU-C, NHi, NN, PHi, PPAmP, PPL, RPJCB, ViU, WHi.

159b. [————]. ————. With A Plan, By Samuel [*sic*] Galloway, Esq; For A Proposed Union . . . To which is added, An Alarm to the Legislature of the Province of New-York. . . .

New-York, Printed . . . London, Reprinted for Richardson and Urquhart . . . 1775.

2 p. l., [1]-90, [1] p. (last p. advts.), 8vo, [A]² B-M⁴ N².

The "Alarm . . ." by Samuel Seabury is a reprint of no. 194.

Sabin 11882.

Copies: BM, CtY, MB, NN, PPL, RPJCB.

160a. DUCHÉ, JACOB, 1737-1798.

The Duty Of Standing Fast In Our Spiritual And Temporal Liberties, A Sermon, Preached In Christ-Church, July 7th, 1775. Before the First Battalion of the City and Liberties of Philadelphia. . . .

Philadelphia. Printed And Sold By James Humphreys, Junior . . . M,DCC,LXXV.

2 p. l., [i]-iv, [1]-25 p., 8vo, [-]¹ [a]⁴ A-C⁴ [D]¹ ([-] 1 blank).

Evans 14013, Sabin 21051.

Copies: CSmH, CtY, DLC, InU, MB, MBAt, MH, MWA, MWiW-C, MiU-C, NHi, NN, PHi, PPAmP, PPL, PU, RPJCB, WHi.

160b. ————. ————.

Philadelphia Printed: London Re-Printed, and sold by T. Evans . . . MDCCLXXV.

2 p. l., [i]-iii, [1]-23 p., 8vo, [-]⁴ A-C⁴.

Copies: BM, CSmH, CtY, DLC, ICN, MBAt, MiU-C, NHi, RPJCB.

161. An Englishman's Answer, To The Address, From The Delegates, To The People of Great-Britain, In A Letter To The Several Colonies . . . .

New-York: Printed by James Rivington, M,DCC,LXXV.

1 p. l., [1]-26 p., 8vo, [-]¹ A-C⁴ D¹.

Although Rivington did not advertise this in his *Gazette*, it probably did not appear after April 27th when he issued his promise not to offend the patriots further (see note under no. 165). This pamphlet was occasioned by "The Address to the People of Great Britain" passed by the First Continental Congress late in October of 1774. Evans and others attribute this to John Lind (1737-1781), the English political writer. However, as the card catalogue in the American Antiquarian Society points out, the pamphlet begins "Though I am at present on a journey of business in America . . ." and the record does not show that Lind was ever in America. From 1773 to 1776, he studied law at Lincoln's Inn. The author shows an extensive knowledge of American affairs, but seems to speak as an Englishman. Lind did write a pamphlet with a similar title, *An Answer to The Declaration of the American Congress*, London, 1776. Until further evidence is brought forward, the Lind attribution seems highly doubtful.

Evans 14159, Sabin 22624, Hewlett 39.

Copies: CSmH, CtY, DLC, ICN, InU, MBAt, MH, MWA, MiU-C, NHi, PPL, RPJCB, WHi.

162. An Essay Upon Government, Adopted By The Americans. Wherein, The lawfulness of Revolutions, are Demonstrated in a Chain of Consequences from the Fundamental, Principles of Society.

Philadelphia: Printed and sold by the Booksellers. MDCCLXXV.

[1]-125 p., 12mo, A-K⁶ L³.

Evans 14023, Sabin 22974.

Copies: CSmH, DLC, MH, MiU-C, PHi, RPJCB.

163. FOSTER, DAN, 1748-1810.

A Short Essay On Civil Government, The Substance of Six Sermons, Preached in Winsor, Second Society, October 1774. . . .

Hartford: Printed by Eben. Watson . . . MDCCLXXV.

[1]-73 p., 8vo, [A]-I⁴ [K]² (K2 blank).

Advertised in the *Connecticut Courant*, April 3, 1775.

Evans 14036.

Copies: CtHi, CtY, DLC, NHi.

164. [GALLOWAY, JOSEPH] 1731-1803.

A Candid Examination Of The Mutual Claims Of Great-Britain, And The Colonies: With A Plan Of Accommodation, On Constitutional Principles.

New-York: Printed by James Rivington, M,DCC,LXXV.

1 p. l., 1-62 p., 8vo, [-]¹ A-G⁴ H³.

Advertised in *Rivington's Gazette* for March 2, 1776. Two states noted, one with "errata" on the verso of the title page and one without. Galloway's statement about his authorship will be found in "Some Letters of Joseph Galloway, 1774-1775," *Pennsylvania Magazine of History and Biography*, vol. XXI (1897), pp. 481-482. Reprinted in London in 1780.

Evans 14059, Sabin 26422, Hewlett 27.

Copies: BM, CSmH, CtHi, CtY, DLC, ICN, InU, MB, MBAt, MH, MHi, MWA, MWiW-C, MiU-C, NHi, NN, NcD, PHi, PPAmP, PPRos, PPL, PU, RPJCB, ViU, WHi.

165. [GALLOWAY, JOSEPH].

A Reply To An Address To the Author of a Pamphlet, entitled, "A Candid Examination of the Mutual Claims of Great Britain and her Colonies," &c. By The Author Of The Candid Examination.

New-York: Printed by James Rivington. M,DCC,LXXV.

[1]-42 p., 8vo, [A]¹ B-F⁴.

Advertised in *Rivington's Gazette* for April 6, 1775. Under the Evans entry there is a note that this was printed in 1775, but not published until 1777. The source of his information has not been determined, but it is reasonable to assume that Rivington did not sell very many copies. On April 27th, he issued a broadside in which he asked pardon of the public for having issued publications that offended patriots and promised to do it no more, Hewlett 43. It is surprising that any copies survived for on the night of May 10th Rivington's shop was wrecked by a mob. The pamphlet was a reply to a letter by John Dickinson and Charles Thomson: "To the Author of a Pamphlet, entitled 'A Candid Examination of the mutual Claims of Great Britain and her colonies' " which had appeared in the *Pennsylvania Journal* for March 8, 1775. For full discussion of this exchange see: Julian P. Boyd's *Anglo-American Union*, Philadelphia, 1941, pp. 45-50. This reply was reprinted in London in 1780 with his *Candid Examination*.

Evans 14060, Hewlett 28.

Copies: CSmH, DLC, MBAt, MiU-C, NN, RPJCB, WHi.

166a. GLOVER, RICHARD, 1712-1785.

The Evidence Delivered on the Petition Presented by the West-India Planters and Merchants To The Hon. House of Commons, As it was introduc'd at the Bar. . . .

[London: printed by H. S. Woodfall, 1775].

1 p. l., [1]-95 [*i.e.* 94] p., 8vo, [A]¹ B-M⁴ N³.

Sabin 27606.

Copies: BM, CSmH, CtHWatk, CtY, DLC, ICN, InU, MB, MBAt, MH, MiU-C, NHi, NN, NcD, NjP, PHi, PPAmP, RPJCB.

166b. ————. The Substance Of The Evidence On The Petition [&c.]. . . .

London: Printed by H. S. Woodfall, For T. Cadell . . . And sold by J. Wilkie . . . [1775].

2 p. l., [1]-47 p., 8vo, [A]² B-G⁴.

Printed from substantially the same setting of type as no. 166a. This abridgment was achieved by removing "The Examination of George Walker and John Ellis," pages 9-56; closing up the forms; and rearranging the pagination. Not to be confused with a pamphlet with a similar title published by J. Wilkie in 1774 relating to merchants trading to Germany and Holland.

Sabin 27610.

Copies: BM, CSmH, CtY, DLC, MBAt, MH, MHi, MWiW-C, NN, NjP, PHi, PPL, RPB, RPJCB, ViU.

166c. ————. ————.

London, Printed: New-York, Re-printed by H. Gaine . . . M,DCC,LXXV.

[1]-75 p., 8vo, [A]-I⁴ K².

A reprint of no. 166b. However, Gaine found the Walker and Ellis evidence that appears in no. 166a and added it at the end.

Evans 14067, Sabin 27610.

Copies: CSmH, CtY, DLC, MB, MBAt, MWA, NN, PHi, RPJCB.

167a. GORDON, WILLIAM, 1728-1807.

A Discourse Preached December 15th 1774. Being The Day Recommended By the Provincial Congress; And Afterwards at the Boston Lecture. . . .

Boston: Printed for, and sold by Thomas Leverett . . . 1775.

[1]-32 p., 1 l., 8vo, [A]-D⁴ [E]¹.

Not to be confused with the *Discourse* delivered by Gordon the morning of the same day with almost the same title. Evans 14071 lists an edition with the date in Roman numerals. No copy has been located and it is probably a ghost. For two replies to this see: Harrison Gray's *Observations*, Boston, 1775, no. 171, and *Remarks upon a discourse* [Boston?], 1775, no. 192.

Evans 14072, Sabin 28005.

Copies: BM, CSmH, CtY, DLC, ICN, MBAt, MH, MHi, MiU-C, NN, NjP, PPAmP, PPL, RPJCB.

167b. ———. ———. The Second Edition.

Same imprint and collation.

Printed from substantially the same setting of type as no. 167a.

Copies: CtHi, DLC, NHi, PPL.

167c. ———. ———.

Boston, Printed: London, Reprinted; and sold by Edward and Charles Dilly ... 1775.

2 p. l., [1]-36 p., 8vo, [A]² B-E⁴ F².

Sabin 28005.

Copies: BM, CSmH, CtY, DLC, InU, MB, MBAt, MH, MiU-C, NHi, PPAmP, RPJCB, ViU.

168. GORDON, WILLIAM, 1728-1807.

A Sermon Preached before the Honorable House of Representatives, On the Day intended for the Choice of Counsellors, Agreeable to the Advice of the Continental Congress. ...

Watertown: Printed and Sold by Benjamin Edes. MDCCLXXV.

[1]-29 p., 4to, [A]-D⁴ (D4 blank).

Half-title reads: "Mr. Gordon's Sermon Preached before the House of Representatives, July 19th, 1775." The House ordered 600 copies for itself—50 for the author and 50 for the Committee for which it paid £12, £1, and £1 respectively on July 28 and 29, 1775. See: Rollo G. Silver's "Government Printing in Massachusetts: 1751-1801," *Studies in Bibliography*, vol. XVI (1963), p. 195.

Evans 14073, Sabin 28010.

Copies: BM, CSmH, CtHWatk, CtY, DLC, ICN, InU, MB, MBAt, MHi, MWA, MiU-C, NHi, NN, NjP, PHi, PPL, RPJCB, ViU, WHi.

169a. GRAHAM, MRS. CATHARINE (Sawbridge) MACAULAY, 1731-1791.

An Address To The People Of England, Scotland, and Ireland, On The Present Important Crisis of Affairs. ...

Printed by R. Cruttwell, in Bath, For Edward and Charles Dilly . . . London. MDCCLXXV.

[1]-29, [1] p. (last p. advts.), 8vo, B⁸ C⁷.

Sabin 42944.

Copies: BM, CSmH, CtY, DLC, ICN, MHi, NN, PHi, PPAmP, RPJCB, ViU.

169b. ———. ———. The Second Edition.

Same imprint and collation.

Printed from substantially the same setting of type as no. 169a. Some of the copies listed under 169c may in fact be this printing.

Copies: MiU-C.

169c. ———. ———. The Second Edition.

London: Printed for Edward and Charles Dilly. M.DCC.LXXV.

[1]-31, [1] p. (last p. advts.), 8vo, A-B⁸.

Sabin 42944.

Copies: BM, CtY, DLC, InU, MB, MiU-C, NN.

169d. ———. ———.

London: Printed For J. Williams . . . [1775?].

[1]-16 p., 8vo, A⁸.

Sabin 42944.

Copies: RPJCB.

169e. ———. ———. The Third Edition.

London: Printed. New-York: Reprinted by John Holt . . . MDCCLXXV.

[1]-15 p., 8vo, [A]-B⁴.

Evans 14173, Sabin 42944.

Copies: CtHi, PHi, PPL.

170a. [GRAY, HARRISON] d. 1794.

A Few Remarks Upon Some Of The Votes and Resolutions Of The Continental Congress, Held at Philadelphia . . . And the Provincial Congress, Held at Cambridge . . . By a Friend to Peace and good Order. . . .

[Boston] Printed for the Purchasers in 1775.

[1]-20 p., 4to, [A]-B⁴ C².

This Tory pamphlet is signed "A friend to peace and good order." Attributed to Gray by Halkett and Laing. See 171 note.

Evans 14074, Sabin 28391.

Copies: BM, CSmH, CtY, DLC, MB, MBAt, MH, MHi, MWA, MiU-C, NHi, NN, PHi, PPL, RPJCB.

170b. [————]. The Two Congresses Cut Up: Or A Few Remarks Upon Some Of The Votes and Resolutions of the Continental Congress [&c.]. . . .

Boston, Printed; New-York, Reprinted, by James Rivington [1775]. [1]-14 p., 8vo, [A]⁴ B³.

Evans 13697 lists a Boston edition with this title and collation. It is a ghost resulting from a misreading of the imprint of this item.

Evans 13698, Sabin 15597, Hewlett 29.

Copies: CSmH, CtY, DLC, NHi, NN, RPJCB.

171. [GRAY, HARRISON?] d. 1794.

Observations On The Reverend Pastor of Roxbury's Thanksgiving Discourse. . . .

Boston: Printed and sold in the Year MDCCLXXV.

[1]-8 p., 4to, [A]⁴.

This is signed "A friend of peace and good order." The catalogue in the American Antiquarian Society points out that Cushing identifies Gray as the user of this pseudonym in *A Few Remarks*, no. 170. As a Loyalist he would have been an appropriate person to reply to William Gordon's *A Discourse Preached December 15th 1774,* Boston, 1775, no. 167. This has also been attributed to Henry Barry.

Evans 14358, Sabin 28007.

Copies: DLC, MB, MHi, MWA, RPJCB.

172. GREAT BRITAIN. PARLIAMENT. HOUSE OF COMMONS.

The Speeches In The Last Session of the present Parliament, Delivered by several of the Principal Advocates In The House Of Commons, In Favour Of The Rights Of America. Viz. Governor Johnstone, Mr. Cruger, The Hon. Capt. Lutterell, Colonel Acland, The Hon. Henry Temple Lutterell, Mr. Hartley, The Marquis of Granby, Son of the late magnanimous Hero, John Manners, Marquis of Granby. With the Speech of Mr. Edmund Burke, in Favour of the Protestant Dissenters, in the second Parliament of George the 3d.

New-York: Printed by James Rivington. MDCCLXXV.

[1]-72 p., 8vo, [A]¹ B-I⁴ K³.

Advertised in *Rivington's Gazette* for September 28, 1775 and in the *Pennsylvania Journal* for September 20th.

Evans 14092, Sabin 89210, Hewlett 30.

Copies: CSmH, DLC, MBAt, NN, PPAmP, PPL, RPJCB.

173. [HAMILTON, ALEXANDER] 1757-1804.

The Farmer Refuted: Or, A more impartial and comprehensive View Of The Dispute between Great-Britain And The Colonies, Intended As A Further Vindication Of The Congress: In Answer To A Letter From A. W. Farmer, Intitled A View of the Controversy. . . .

New-York: Printed by James Rivington, 1775.

[i]-iv, [1]-72, 72-78 p., 8vo, [A]² B-L⁴.

Advertised in *Rivington's Gazette* for March 18, 1775, and in the *Boston Evening Post* for March 27, 1775. Two states noted, one with "Including" standing alone on the third line from the bottom of the title page and one with it beginning the second from last line of the title: "Including A Mode . . ." This is a reply to Samuel Seabury's *A View of the Controversy*, New York, 1774, no. 137. See also: Clarence H. Vance's edition of *Letters of a Westchester Farmer*, White Plains, New York, 1930, vol. VIII of *Publications of the Westchester County Historical Society;* and H. C. Syrett's edition of *The Papers of Alexander Hamilton*, New York, 1961, vol. I, pp. 81-165.

Evans 14096, Sabin 29955, Ford-*Hamilton* 2, Hewlett 32-33.

Copies: CSmH, CtHi, CtHWatk, CtY, DLC, ICN, MBAt, MH, MHi, MWA, MWiW-C, MiU-C, NHi, NN, PHi, PPL, RPJCB, ViU.

HANCOCK, JOHN. *An Oration . . . To Commemorate The Bloody Tragedy of the Fifth of March 1770*. Philadelphia, 1775, see: 117e.

174. HEWES, JOSEPH, 1714-1796.

A Collection of Occurrences and Facts, Known by living Evidences, and also recorded in a public Manner, in printed and written Papers, now in Being, and indisputably true . . . concerning the present Commotions in the Kingdom of Great-Britain.

[Providence?] Printed [by John Carter?] in the Year 1775.

2 p. l., [1]-46 p., 8vo, A-F⁴ G¹.

The printing of this is tentatively attributed to John Carter by Alden on the basis of the typography. Dated (p. [1]) "Providence, April 22, 1775." The author was a prominent Providence physician who was also active in town affairs. His dates were provided by Mr.

Franklin Coyle from the records of the Providence Probate Court. He is not to be confused with the North Carolinian of the same name.

Evans 14115, Alden 605.

Copies: DLC, MB, MBAt, MWA, RPJCB, WHi.

175. HITCHCOCK, GAD, 1718?-1803.

A Sermon Preached At Plymouth December 22d, 1774. Being the Anniversary Thanksgiving, in Commemoration of the first Landing of our New-England Ancestors in that Place, Anno Dom. 1620. . . .

Boston: Printed and Sold by Edes and Gill . . . 1775.

[1]-44 p., 8vo, [A]-E⁸ F².

Evans 14118, Sabin 32261.

Copies: BM, CtHi, DLC, MB, MBAt, MHi, MWA, MiU-C, PHi, RPJCB.

176. HUNT, ISAAC, 1742-1809.

The Political Family: Or A Discourse, Pointing Out The Reciprocal Advantages, Which flow from an uninterrupted Union between Great-Britain and her American Colonies . . . Numb. I.

Philadelphia: Printed, By James Humphreys, Junior. MDCCLXXV.

[1]-32 p., 8vo, [-]² A-C⁴ D².

Advertised in the *Pennsylvania Evening Post* for February 21, 1775. Only this first number was issued.

Evans 14123, Sabin 33866.

Copies: CSmH, CtY, DLC, InU, MBAt, MWA, MiU-C, NHi, PHi, PPAmP, PPL, RPJCB.

177. JONES, DAVID, 1736-1820.

Defensive War in a just cause Sinless. A Sermon, Preached On the Day of the Continental Fast, At Tredyffryn, in Chester County. . . .

Philadelphia: Printed by Henry Miller. 1775.

[1]-27 p., 8vo, A-C⁴ D².

Evans 14133, Sabin 36486.

Copies: CSmH, CtY, DLC, MHi, MWA, MiU-C, NHi, NN, PHi, PPAmP, PPL, RPJCB.

[KNOX, WILLIAM]. *The Interest of the Merchants And Manufacturers of Great Britain.* Cork, 1775, see: 120b.

[———]. ———. Dublin, 1775, see: 120c.

[————]. ————. Boston, [1775], see: 120d.

178. LANGDON, SAMUEL, 1723-1797.

Government corrupted by Vice, and recovered by Righteousness. A Sermon Preached Before The Honorable Congress Of the Colony Of the Massachusetts-Bay In New England, Assembled at Watertown, On Wednesday the 31st Day of May, 1775 ... For the Election of Cousellors. . . .

> Watertown: Printed and Sold by Benjamin Edes, MDCCLXXV.
>
> [1]-29 p., 4to, [A]-D⁴ (D4 blank).
>
> The House ordered 600 copies of this sermon for which they paid £12 on June 20, 1775; see: Rollo G. Silver's "Government Printing in Massachusetts: 1751-1801," *Studies in Bibliography*, vol. XVI (1963), p. 194.
>
> Evans 14145, Sabin 38872.
>
> *Copies:* BM, CSmH, CtHi, CtHWatk, CtY, DLC, MB, MBAt, MH, MHi, MWA, MWiW-C, MiU-C, NN, PPAmP, PPL, RPJCB, ViU.

[LEE, ARTHUR]. *An Appeal to the Justice and Interests of the People of Great Britain.* London, 1775, see: 123b, 123c.

————. ————. New York, 1775, see: 123d.

179a. LEE, CHARLES, 1731-1782.

General Lee's Letter To General Burgoyne, Upon His Arrival in Boston.

> New-York: Printed by J. Anderson ... MDCCLXXV.
>
> [1]-8 p., 8vo, [A]⁴.
>
> This letter was published in numerous newspapers and in various broadside editions. In a sense it belongs with that group of literature, but because of these three pamphlet publications it is included here.
>
> Evans 14148, Sabin 39708.
>
> *Copies:* DLC, MWA, NHi.

179b. ————. A Letter From General Lee, to General Burgoyne, Printed from the New-York Gazetteer, of July 6. To Which Is Added, General Burgoyne's Answer, And a Copy of a Letter from General Lee, declining an Interview proposed by General Burgoyne.

> Boston: Printed and Sold at Draper's . . . MDCCLXXV.
>
> [1]-19 p., 4to, [A]-B⁴ C².

Evans 14149, Sabin 39708.
Copies: RPJCB.

179c. ———. Letters of Major General Lee, To The Right Honourable Earl Percy, And Major General John Burgoyne. With The Answers.

New-York: Printed by J. Rivington . . . M,DCC,LXXV.

[1]-8, [1]-4 p., 8vo, [-]⁴, A².

Advertised in the *Pennsylvania Packet* for September 23, 1775.

Evans 14151, Sabin 39710, Hewlett 35.

Copies: CSmH, DLC, MBAt, NHi, PPL.

[LEE, CHARLES]. *Strictures on A Pamphlet.* Boston, 1775, see: 125b, c.

[———]. ———. Newport, 1775, see: 125d.

[———]. ———. Providence, 1775, see: 125e.

[———]. ———. New-London, 1775, see: 125f.

180a. [LEONARD, DANIEL] 1740-1829.

The Origin Of The American Contest With Great-Britain, Or The
present political State of the Massachusetts-Bay, in general, And The
Town of Boston in particular. Exhibiting the Rise and Progress of the dis-
ordered State of that Country, in a series of weekly Essays, published at
Boston, under the Signature of Massachusettensis. . . .

New-York: Printed by James Rivington, 1775.

1 p. l., [1]-86 p., 8vo, [-]¹ A-K⁴ L³.

Advertised in *Rivington's Gazette* for March 16, 1775. This contains
eight of the seventeen letters that appeared originally in the *Massachusetts Gazette and The Boston Post-Boy and Advertiser* between December 12, 1774 and April 3, 1775. At the bottom of page 86 is a
note that the rest of the letters are in press. They never appeared,
probably because of the promise Rivington made noted in no. 165
note. John Adams undertook an answer in his "Novanglus" series
that began in the *Boston Gazette* on January 23, 1775. For authorship see note at the end of the article on Leonard in the *Dictionary of
American Biography.* Page [1] is a second title page reading *The
Present Political State Of The Province of Massachusetts Bay In General
And The Town Of Boston In Particular. . . .* Some copies have only
this second title page, but we believe with Hewlett that a perfect

copy must contain both. The first title page was probably part of the last signature and thus was part of the original printing of the pamphlet.

Evans 14158, Sabin 40099, Hewlett 36.

Copies: CSmH, CtY, DLC, MB, MBAt, MH, MHi, MiU-C, NHi, NN, PHi, PPL, RPJCB.

180b. [————————]. Massachusettensis.

[Boston: Printed by Mills and Hicks, 1775].

[1]-118 p., 8vo, [A]-P⁴ (P4 blank).

This contains all seventeen of the letters and is the first complete separate edition.

Evans 14157, Sabin 40097.

Copies: BM, DLC, MH, MHi, MWA, MWiW-C, MiU-C, NN, RPJCB.

180c. [————————]. Massachusettensis: Or A Series of Letters, Containing A Faithful State Of Many Important And Striking Facts, Which Laid The Foundation Of The Present Troubles In The Province of the Massachusetts Bay . . . By a Person of Honor upon the Spot. . . .

Boston printed. London reprinted for J. Mathews . . . MDCCLXXVI.

[i]-viii, [1]-118 p., 8vo, [A]-Q⁴ (Q4 blank).

Sabin 40100.

Copies: BM, CSmH, CtY, DLC, InU, MB, MBAt, MWiW-C, MiU-C, NHi, NN, PPL, RPJCB.

180d. [————————]. ————————. The Second Edition.

Same imprint and collation.

Printed from substantially the same setting of type as no. 180c.

Sabin 40100.

Copies: CSmH, CtY, DLC, InU, MBAt, MH, MHi, MiU-C, NN, RPJCB.

180e. [————————]. ————————. The Third Edition.

Same imprint and collation.

Printed from substantially the same setting of type as no. 180c.

Sabin 40100.

Copies: BM, CSmH, CtY, MB, MH, MiU-C, NN, NjP, PPL.

180f. [————————]. ————————. The Fourth Edition.

Same imprint and collation.

Printed from substantially the same setting of type as no. 180c.
Sabin 40100.

Copies: CSmH, CtY, ICN, MH, MiU-C, NN.

180g. [————]. ————. The Fourth Edition.
Boston printed Dublin reprinted for T. Armitage . . . P. Wogan . . .
and W. Gilbert, MDCCLXXVI.

[i]-viii, [1]-103 p., 8vo, [A]-O⁴.

Copies: CtY, InU, MiU-C, RPJCB.

181. MASSACHUSETTS. PROVINCIAL CONGRESS.
A Narrative Of The Excursion and Ravages Of The King's Troops
Under the Command of General Gage, On the nineteenth of April, 1775.
Together With The Depositions Taken by Order of Congress, To sup-
port the Truth of it. . . .

Massachusetts-Bay: Worcester, Printed by Isaiah Thomas, by order
of the Provincial Congress. [1775].

[1]-23 p., 4to, [A]-C⁴.

Evans 14269, Sabin 51804.

A committee was appointed to "transcribe" this narrative on May 8,
1775 and ordered to find a printer for it on May 19th. It is the first
book printed in Worcester. See: Rollo G. Silver's "Government
Printing in Massachusetts: 1751-1801," *Studies in Bibliography,*
vol. XVI (1963), pp. 178-179.

Copies: CSmH, CtY, DLC, MB, MBAt, MH, MWA, MiU-C, NN, NjP,
RPJCB, ViU, WHi.

182. [MATHER, MOSES] 1719-1806.
America's Appeal To The Impartial World. Wherein the Rights of
the Americans . . . are stated and considered. And, The Opposition made
by the Colonies to Acts of Parliament, their resorting to Arms . . . Vindicated. . . .

Hartford: Printed by Ebenezer Watson, 1775.

[1]-72 p., 4to, [A]-I⁴.

Advertised in the *Connecticut Courant* for April 3, 1775. Attributed to
Mather by Evans.

Evans 14253, Sabin 1276 & 46770 note, Holmes 11.

Copies: CSmH, CtHi, CtY, DLC, ICN, InU, MB, MBAt, MWA, MiU-C,
NN, RPJCB, ViU.

183. [Mein, John].

Sagittarius's Letters And Political Speculations. Extracted From the Public Ledger. Humbly Inscribed To the Very Loyal and Truly Pious Doctor Samuel Cooper. . . .

Boston. Printed: By Order of the Select Men and sold at Donation Hall . . . MDCCLXXV.

1 p. l., [1]-127 p., 4to, [-]¹ [A]-Q⁴.

These letters first appeared in the *Public Ledger* in London during 1774. For authorship and discussion see: John E. Alden's "John Mein: Scourge of Patriots," *Publications of the Colonial Society of Massachusetts*, vol. XXXIV (1937-1942), pp. 571-576.

Evans 14255, Sabin 47405.

Copies: CtY, DLC, MB, MH, MHi, MWA, MiU-C, NHi, NN, NcD, PHi, RPJCB.

184. The Middle Line: Or, An Attempt To Furnish Some Hints For Ending the Differences Subsisting Between Great-Britain and the Colonies.

Philadelphia: Printed and Sold by Joseph Crukshank . . . M.DCC.LXXV.

[1]-48 p., 12mo, A-D⁶.

Advertised in the *Pennsylvania Packet* for January 23, 1775. Evans attributes this to Richard Wells.

Evans 14616, Sabin 48823.

Copies: CSmH, DLC, ICN, InU, MB, MBAt, MiU-C, NHi, NN, PPAmP, PPL, RPJCB.

185. Montgomery, Joseph, 1733-1794.

A Sermon Preached At Christiana Bridge And Newcastle, The 20th of July, 1775. Being The Day Appointed By The Continental Congress As a Day of Fasting, Humiliation and Prayer. . . .

Philadelphia: Printed by James Humhreys [*sic*] . . . M,DCC,LXXV.

[1]-30 p., 8vo, A-C⁴ D³.

Evans 14261, Sabin 50153.

Copies: CtHWatk, DLC, NHi, PHi, PPL.

186. No Standing Army In the British Colonies; Or An Address To The Inhabitants Of The Colony Of New-York. Against Unlawful Standing Armies.

New-York: Printed by John Holt . . . MDCCLXXV.

[1]-18 p., 8vo, [A]-B⁴ C² (C2 blank).

Evans 14351, Sabin 55371.

Copies: CtY, DLC, PPL.

187. NOBLE, OLIVER, 1735-1792.

Some Strictures Upon The Sacred Story Recorded In The Book of Esther, Shewing The Power and Oppression of State Ministers . . . In A Discourse, Delivered At Newbury-Port . . . March 8th, 1775. In Commemoration Of The Massacre At Boston, March the Fifth, 1770. . . .

Newbury-Port, New-England: Printed by E. Lunt and H. W. Tinges. MDCCLXXV.

[1]-31, [1] p. (last p. errata), 8vo, [A]-D⁴.

Evans 14352, Sabin 55387.

Copies: BM, CSmH, CtHi, CtY, DLC, ICN, InU, MBAt, MH, MHi, MWA, MWiW-C, MiU-C, NN, PPL, PPRos, RPJCB, ViU.

188. PERRY, JOSEPH, 1733-1783.

A Sermon, Preached Before The General Assembly Of The Colony Of Connecticut . . . On The . . . Election, May 11, 1775. . . .

Hartford: Printed By Eben. Watson . . . M,DCC,LXXV.

[1]-23 p., 4to, [A]-C⁴.

Evans 14383, Sabin 61041.

Copies: CSmH, CtHi, CtY, DLC, ICN, InU, MBAt, MH, MHi, MWA, NHi, NN.

189. Pills For The Delegates: Or The Chairman Chastised. In a Series of Letters, Addressed To Peyton Randolph, Esq: On his Conduct, as President Of The General Congress . . . By Grotius. Originally published in the Massachusetts Gazette. . . .

New-York: Printed by James Rivington, 1775.

[1]-32 p., 8vo, A-D⁴.

Evans 14094, Hewlett 31.

Copies: CSmH, CtY, ICN, NHi, NN, RPJCB.

[PITT, WILLIAM]. *The Celebrated Speech of a Celebrated Commoner.* London, 1775, see: 41e.

190a. PITT, WILLIAM, Earl of Chatham, 1708-1788.

Lord Chatham's Speech On the 20th of January 1775. Taken by a Member.

London: Printed for T. Freeman ... M.DCC.LXXV.

1 p. l., 5-18 p., 4to, [A]¹ B-D² E¹.

This contains Pitt's motion for withdrawing the troops from Boston and his speech in support of that motion. Basil Williams, in his *The Life of William Pitt*, London, 1913, vol. II, pp. 335-337, discusses the unreliable reporting of the privileged Parliamentary debates and tells how contemporary published versions usually bore little relationship to what was actually said. This text undoubtedly falls into that category; see note under 190e for better versions. This version was reprinted in the *Virginia Gazette* (Pinkney) for May 4, 1775 and the *Pennsylvania Evening Post* for April 20, 1775.

Sabin 63075.

Copies: BM, ICN, InU, RPJCB.

190b. ————. The Speech Of The Right Honourable The Earl of Chatham, In The House of Lords, On Friday the 20th of January 1775.

London: Printed for G. Kearsly ... M.DCC.LXXV.

[1]-18 p., 4to, [A]-E² (E2 blank).

The text is printed from substantially the same setting of type as no. 190a.

Copies: BM, CSmH, CtY, NN, PPAmP, RPJCB, ViU.

190c. ————. ————. A New Edition.

Same imprint and collation.

The text is printed from substantially the same setting of type as nos. 190a and b.

Sabin 63076.

Copies: CSmH, CtY, DLC, ICN, InU, MB, MBAt, MH, MiU-C, RPJCB.

190d. ————. ————.

[Newport printed by Solomon Southwick 1775].

[1]-14 p., 8vo, [A]-B⁴ (B4 blank).

Evans did not assign an imprint to this, but it is almost certainly the work of Southwick. The type ornaments used on the title page are the same as the ones he used on each of the nine issues of *The Crisis* attributed to him by Alden nos. 580-589. Also Southwick advertised this pamphlet for sale in the *Newport Mercury* for May 8, 1775, together with two other titles he had published the year before. A reprint of no. 190a.

Evans 14406.
Copies: NN, RPJCB.

190e. ————. ————. On a Motion for an Address to His Majesty, to give immediate orders for removing his Troops from Boston. . . .

Philadelphia: Printed By John Dunlap . . . M,DCC,LXXV.

[1]-16 p., 8vo, [A]-B⁴.

Advertised in the *Pennsylvania Packet* for May 8, 1775 and there described as having been "sent over in manuscript from a Gentleman of Distinction in London to his friend in this city." It is an entirely different text from nos. 190a-d and in all probability is closer to the true version of the speech than they are. Basil Williams, in *The Life of William Pitt*, London, 1913, vol. II, p. 305, states that the best version known to him is to be found in Hugh Boyd's *Genuine Abstracts from Two Speeches of the Late Earl Chatham*, London, 1779. A comparison of this and the Boyd edition shows a close textual similarity. There are a number of differences in detail. The Philadelphia edition has a little more material, particularly on the first two and a quarter pages which are not present in Boyd's version. In his preface Boyd says that his source was a manuscript copy made "by a gentleman whose memory served him sufficiently" to commit the speech to paper, but that the "gentleman" arrived in the House of Lords late and missed the first part of the speech. It is probable that the "gentleman" in question was Boyd himself. He was noted for the extraordinary accuracy of his reports of Parliamentary debates. W. S. Stanhope Taylor and J. H. Pringle stated categorically that it was Boyd's work when they reprinted his version in their *Correspondence of William Pitt*, London, 1840, vol. IV, pp. 377-384 footnote. It would appear, therefore, that this Philadelphia version and the Boyd version came from different sources, but that both are closer to a verbatim report of what was said than any of the other contemporary versions.

The question naturally arises as to the identity of the "Gentleman of Distinction" who sent the manuscript to Philadelphia. Through suggestions offered by Whitfield J. Bell, Jr., it is possible to eliminate certain possibilities. The version is clearly not the one taken down by Josiah Quincy, Jr. and included in the *Memoirs* written by his son. The Quincy version is much shorter. Neither is it like the much longer version in a letter written by Jonathan Williams on January 20th and edited by Bernhard Knollenberg in *Indiana University Library Publications*, no. I (1949). Finally it appears probable that we can eliminate the obvious possibility of Benjamin Franklin. On February 5th, he wrote a letter to Charles Thomson in which he said

"You will see, among the papers herewith sent the motion made by Lord Chatham, as preparatory to his plan, viz: that the Troops should be removed from Boston. I send also a copy of the Plan itself, which you may be assured is genuine. The speeches hitherto published as his, during the Session, are spurious." The Motion was the one offered on the 20th and in support of which this speech was made. The Plan was Pitt's "A Provisional Act for settling the Troubles in America . . ." published in 1775 by John Almon under the title *Plan Offered by the Earl of Chatham*, no. 190Aa. The fact that Franklin mentions the Motion and the Plan but not the Speech indicates that he did not have it when he wrote the letter. He could have obtained a copy of it at a later time and he sent it to Philadelphia, but this is pure conjecture. In any case this version, printed by Dunlap, appears to be just about the best contemporary version.

Evans 14405, Sabin 63077.

Copies: CtHWatk, CtY, DLC, MWA, MiU-C, NHi, NN, PHi, PPAmP, PPL, RPJCB.

190f. ————. Des Hoch-Edlen Grafen von Chatham Rede, gehalten im Hause der Lords, den 20sten Jenner, 1775. . . .

Philadelphia, Gedruckt und haben Henrich Miller . . . 1775.

[1]-16 p., 8vo, A⁸.

Evans 14407.

Copies: PHi.

190Aa. PITT, WILLIAM, EARL OF CHATHAM, 1708-1788.

Plan Offered By The Earl of Chatham, To The House of Lords, Entitled A Provisional Act, for settling the Troubles in America. . . .

London: Printed for J. Almon . . . M.DCC.LXXV.

[1]-14, [1] p. (last p. advts.), 4to, B-E².

Sabin 63071.

Copies: CtY, DLC, ICN, MH, MiU-C, PHi, PPAmP, PPL, RPJCB, ViU.

190Ab. ————. An Authentic Copy of Lord Chatham's Proposed Bill, Entitled A Provisional Act [&c]. . . .

Annapolis: Printed by Frederick Green. MDCCLXXV.

16 p., 8vo, [1]-2⁴.

Copies: ICN.

191a. [RAYNAL, GUILLAUME THOMAS FRANÇOIS].

The Sentiments Of A Foreigner, On The Disputes Of Great-Britain With America. Translated From the French. . . .

Philadelphia: Printed By James Humphreys, Junior . . . M,DCC,LXXV.
[i]-iv, [5]-27, [1] p. (last p. advts.), 8vo, A-C⁴ D².

Advertised in the *Pennsylvania Gazette* for June 21, 1775 and the *Virginia Gazette* (Dixon & Hunter) for July 29th. Reprinted in the *Virginia Gazette* (Pinkney) September 21 to October 5, 1775. Extract reprinted in the *Maryland Gazette* for February 1, 1776. A translation of an extract from his *L'Histoire Philosophique et Politique*, Geneva, 1772.

Evans 14417, Sabin 68105.

Copies: BM, CSmH, CtY, DLC, MBAt, MWA, NHi, PHi, PPAmP, PPL, RPJCB.

191b. [————]. ————.
Belfast: Printed by James Magee . . . MDCCLXXV.
[i]-viii, 3-33 p., 8vo, [A]-E⁴.
Sabin 68105.
Copies: DLC, MiU-C, NN.

192. Remarks Upon A Discourse Preached December 15th 1774. Being the Day Recommended by the Provincial Congress: And afterwards at the Boston Lecture. By William Gordon . . . In a Letter from a Gentleman in the Country to his Friend in Boston.

[Boston?] Printed in the Year MDCCLXXV.
[1]-11 p., 4to, [A]⁴ B².

Evans attributes this reply to Gordon's *Discourse*, Boston, 1774, no. 167, to Henry Barry and it is not impossible that he was the author. However, the piece is dated "Worcester March 10th, 1775" which together with the statement that it was written by "a Gentleman in the Country" does not suggest an army officer serving with his regiment in Boston, which is what Barry was doing. Evans also gives New York as the place of publication. In view of the circumstances surrounding its composition Boston would appear to be a more likely guess.

Evans 13825.
Copies: MWA, RPJCB.

[ROKEBY, MATTHEW ROBINSON-MORRIS, 2nd Baron]. *Considerations on the Measures.* Philadelphia, 1775, see: 134k.

193. SAMPSON, EZRA, 1749-1823.

A Sermon Preached At Roxbury-Camp, Before Col. Cotton's Regiment; On the 20th of July, P. M. 1775. Being A Day set apart for Fasting and Prayer, through-out all the United Colonies in America. By Ezra Samson [*sic*]. . . .

Watertown: Printed and Sold by Benjamin Edes. 1775.

[1]-25 p., 4to, [A]-C⁴ [D]¹.

Evans 14450, Sabin 75928.

Copies: CtHi, DLC, MB, MHi, MWA, NN, RPJCB.

194. [SEABURY, SAMUEL] 1729-1796.

An Alarm to the Legislature Of The Province of New-York, Occasioned By The present Political Disturbances, In North America: Addressed To the Honourable Representatives In General Assembly Convened. . . .

New-York: Printed for James Rivington, M,DCC,LXXV.

[1]-13, [1-2] p. (last 2 p. advts.), 8vo, A⁸.

Advertised in *Rivington's Gazette* for January 19, 1775. Dated at the end: "January 17, 1775." For authorship see: D. William's "The Westchester Farmer," *The Magazine of American History with Notes and Queries*, vol. VIII, part 1 (1882), pp. 117-122. Also printed with the London edition of Chandler's *What Think Ye of the Congress Now?*, no. 159b. See also: Clarence H. Vance's edition of *Letters of a Westchester Farmer*, White Plains, New York, 1930, vol. VIII of *Publications of the Westchester County Historical Society*.

Evans 14453, Sabin 78559, Hewlett 73.

Copies: CSmH, CtHi, CtHWatk, CtY, DLC, ICN, InU, MB, MBAt, MH, MWA, MWiW-C, MiU-C, NHi, NN, PHi, PPAmP, PPL, RPJCB, ViU, WHi.

[SEABURY, SAMUEL]. *The Congress Canvassed.* London, 1775, see: 135b.

[————]. *Free Thoughts on the Proceedings of the Continental Congress.* London, 1775, see: 136c.

195. [SEABURY, SAMUEL] 1729-1796.

[The Republican Dissected: or the Anatomy of an American Whig, in Answer to the Farmer Refuted. Written by A. W. Farmer.]

[New York: Printed by James Rivington, 1775.]

Rivington's Gazette for March 9, 1775 carried the announcement that Seabury was preparing this answer to Hamilton's *The Farmer Refuted*,

New York, 1775, no. 173. The issue of April 13th said that the pamphlet was "In press, and speedily will be published." However, no copy has been found and it is probable that the printing was interrupted or destroyed or both by the raid on Rivington's shop during the last week of April of 1775, described by Hewlett on pages 84-85. See also: Clarence H. Vance's edition of *Letters of a Westchester Farmer*, White Plains, New York, 1930, vol. VIII of *Publications of the Westchester County Historical Society*.

Evans 14626, Hewlett 142.

[SEABURY, SAMUEL]. *A View of the Controversy*. London, 1775, see: 137b.

196a. SMITH, WILLIAM, 1727-1803.

A | Sermon | On The | Present Situation | Of | American Affairs. | Preached in Christ Church, June 23, 1775. |....

Philadelphia. Printed and sold by James Humphreys Junior . . . MDCCLXXV.

2 p. l., [i]-iv, [1]-32 p., 8vo, [-]⁴ A-D⁴.

Advertised in the *Pennsylvania Journal* for July 5, 1775 and in the *Maryland Gazette* for August 17th. The *Pennsylvania Gazette* for July 26th advertised that copies may be had in the following cities: in Lancaster from Matthias Sough and Francis Baily, in New York from Hugh Gaine, and in Charleston, S. C. from Robert Wells. This and no. 197b are entirely different settings and no attempt has been made to determine their priority. This one has been placed first because the line endings of the title page are the same as those in the advertisement and in the *Pennsylvania Journal*. Sabin 84653 lists a New York printing by Rivington based on an advertisement in the *New York Gazetteer*. No copy has been found and it is assumed that the advertisement referred to one of the Philadelphia printings.

Evans 14459, Sabin 84652.

Copies: BM, CSmH, DLC, ICN, MH, MHi, MiU-C, NHi, NN, PHi, PP, PPAmP, PPL, PU, RPJCB, ViU.

196b. ———. A | Sermon | On The Present Situation Of | American Affairs. |....

Same imprint and collation.

Sabin 84651.

Copies: BM, CSmH, CtHi, CtY, InU, MB, MBAt, MWA, MWiW-C, NjP, PP, PPAmP, PU, RPB, RPJCB.

196c. ———. ———.

Wilmington, Printed And Sold By James Adams . . . M,DCC,LXXV.

[i]-iv, 5-17 p., 8vo, [A]-B⁴ C¹.

Evans 14460, Sabin 84654.

Copies: PHi.

196d. ———. ———.

Philadelphia Printed: London Re-Printed, For Edward And Charles Dilly. M,DCC,LXXV.

2 p. l., [i]-iv, [1]-32 p., 8vo, [-]⁴ A⁸ C⁸.

This or no. 196e or g were printed at the expense of the Chamberlain of London who had ten thousand copies prepared. See: Albert F. Gegenheimer's *William Smith Educator and Churchman 1727-1803,* Philadelphia, 1943, p. 169.

Sabin 84655.

Copies: BM, CSmH, CtY, DLC, InU, MBAt, MiU-C, NHi, NN, PHi, PPAmP, PU, RPJCB.

196e. ———. ———.

Philadelphia Printed: London Re-Printed, A Second Time, For Edward And Charles Dilly. M,DCC,LXXV.

2 p. l., [i]-iv, [1]-32 p., 8vo, [A]⁴ B-C⁸.

Printed from substantially the same setting of type as no. 196d with imprint and signature marks altered.

Sabin 84656.

Copies: CSmH, CtY, DLC, ICN, MB, MH, MiU-C, NN, PPAmP, PU, RPJCB.

196f. ———. ———.

Philadelphia Printed: London Re-Printed, a Second Time, For Edward and Charles Dilly. [1775].

Same collation.

A reissue of no. 196e with title page reset and an engraved tail piece added. Smith was probably referring to this when he mentioned an "elegant" edition of the pamphlet in his *Works,* Philadelphia, 1803, vol. II, p. 254.

Copies: CSmH, MiU-C, PHi, PU.

196g. ———. ———.

Philadelphia Printed: London Re-Printed, a Third Time, For Edward and Charles Dilly. M.DCC.LXXV. . . .

[i]-vi, [1]-24 p., 12mo, A¹².

Sabin 85657.

Copies: CSmH, CtHWatk, CtY, DLC, ICN, MH, MHi, MWA, MiU-C, NN, NcD, PHi, PPL, PU, RPJCB.

196h. ———. ———.

Philadelphia: Printed by James Humphreys, Junr. and Re-printed and sold by W. Pine in Bristol, 1775. Price six-penbe [*sic*].

[i]-vii, [1]-32 p., 8vo, A-D⁴.

This edition is made up of the sheets of the Philadelphia edition (either no. 196a or b) and a first signature printed by Pine, and used for no. 196i. Although only the MiU-C copy has been seen in this form, it is believed to be a genuine issue because the stab holes from the sewing indicates that the first signature has always been with the body of the pamphlet.

Sabin 84658.

Copies: MiU-C.

196i. ———. ———.

Same imprint.

[i]-vii, [1]-40 p., 8vo, [A]-E⁴.

Two states noted, one reading "penbe" in the last line of the title page and the other reading "pence."

Sabin 84658A & 84659.

Copies: CtY, DLC, MiU-C, NN, PPL.

196j. ———. ———.

Dublin: Printed by M. Mills . . . M.DCC.LXXV. . . .

[1]-23 p., 8vo, [A]-C⁴.

Sabin 84660.

Copies: DLC.

196k. ———. ———. The Second Edition.

Philadelphia: Printed by James Humphreys, junior. And Dublin: Reprinted by M. Mills . . . M.DCC.LXXV.

[1]-23 p., 8vo, A-C⁴.

Sabin 84661.
Copies: CtY, MiU-C.

196l. ————. ————.
Belfast: Printed by H. and R. Joy . . . M.DCC.LXXV. . . .
[1]-23 p., 8vo, A-C⁴.
Sabin 84662.
Copies: DLC, PPL.

196m. ————. ————.
Philadelphia: Printed by James Humphreys, Jr. And Cork Re-printed
for, and Sold by W. Sargent . . . 1775.
[i]-v, 6-24 p., 12mo, A¹².
Copies: MH.

196n. ————. ————.
Edinburgh. Reprinted and sold by William Schaw . . . MDCCLXXVI.
2 p. l., [i]-iv, [1]-32 p., 4to, [-]⁴ A-D⁴.
Copies: MWA.

196o. ————. Pregeth ar Helynt Bresennol America. A Bregethwyd
yn Christ-Church, Mehefin y 23, 1775. . . .
Brysto: Argraffwyd gan William Pine, 1775.
[i]-iv, 5-23, [1] p., 12mo, A-B⁶.
Sabin 84645.
Copies: MH, MiU-C, RPJCB.

197. Some Seasonable Observations and Remarks Upon The State Of
Our Controversy With Great Britain; And On The Proceedings Of The
Continental Congress . . . By A Moderate Whig.
[Boston?] America: Printed and sold [by Draper] in the Year
MDCCLXXV.
[1]-14 p., 4to, [A]-B⁴ (B4 blank).
Advertised in the *Massachusetts Gazette and Boston Weekly News-Letter*
for May 19, 1775, as "Just published and to be sold at Draper's
office."
Evans 14462, Sabin 86760.
Copies: DLC, MB, MHi, MWA, RPJCB.

198. STEARNS, WILLIAM, d. 1783.

A View of the Controversy subsisting between Great-Britain and the American Colonies. A Sermon, Preached At A Fast In Marlborough in Massachusetts-Bay, On Thursday May 11, 1775. Agreeable to a Recommendation of the Provincial Congress. . . .

Watertown: Printed by Benjamin Edes. 1775.

[i]-vii, [9]-33 p., 4to, [A]-D⁴ [E]¹.

Evans 14474, Sabin 90978.

Copies: CtHWatk, CtY, DLC, MB, MBAt, MH, MHi, MWA, MiU-C, NHi, NN, PPRos, RPJCB.

199. STORY, ISAAC, 1746-1816.

The Love Of Our Country Recommended And Enforced. In A Sermon . . . Delivered On A Day Of Public Thanksgiving, December 15, 1774. . . .

Boston: Printed and Sold by John Boyle . . . MDCCLXXV.

[1]-23 p., 4to, [A]-C⁴.

Evans misdates this 1774.

Evans 13643, Sabin 92275.

Copies: CSmH, DLC, InU, MBAt, MH, NHi, NN, RPJCB.

200. The Triumph Of The Whigs: Or T'Other Congress Convened. . . .

New-York: Printed by James Rivington. M.DCC.LXXV.

[1]-8 p., 8vo, [A]⁴.

This Tory pamphlet has sometimes been attributed to Daniel Leonard, but there seems to be no concrete evidence to support this.

Evans 14523, Sabin 97010, Hewlett 42.

Copies: CSmH, DLC, MB, MiU-C, NN, PHi, PPL, PU, RPJCB.

201a. WARREN, JOSEPH, 1741-1775.

An Oration Delivered March Sixth, 1775. At The Request of the Inhabitants Of The Town of Boston; To Commemorate the Bloody Tragedy Of The Fifth of March, 1770. . . .

Boston: Printed by Messieurs Edes and Gill . . . and by Joseph Greenleaf . . . M,DCC,LXXV.

[1]-23 p., 4to, [A]-C⁴.

Advertised in the *Massachusetts Gazette and Boston Weekly News-Letter* for March 17, 1775. Reprinted in the *Pennsylvania Evening Post* for

March 25, 1775 and the *Virginia Gazette* (Pinkney) for April 13, 1775.

Evans 14608, Sabin 101478.

Copies: BM, CSmH, CtY, DLC, MB, MH, MHi, MWA, MiU-C, NN, PHi, PPL, PPRos, RPB, RPJCB, ViU.

201b. ————. ————.

Newport, Rhode Island: Reprinted and Sold by S. Southwick ... 1775.

[1]-22 p., 8vo, [A]-C⁴ (C4 blank).

Advertised in the *Newport Mercury* for March 20, 1775. Two states noted, one with an "Erratum" on page 22 and one without.

Evans 14610, Sabin 101478, Alden 630.

Copies: CtY, DLC, InU, MB, MH, MWA, NHi, NN, RPB, RPJCB, ViU.

201c. ————. ————.

New-York: Printed by John Anderson ... [1775?].

[1]-16 p., 8vo, [A]⁸.

Evans 14609, Sabin 101478.

Copies: CSmH, MBAt, MHi, MiU-C, NHi, NN.

202. WEBSTER, SAMUEL, 1743-1777.

Rabshakeh's Proposals Considered, In a Sermon, Delivered at Groton February 21, 1775. At the Desire of the Officers of the Companies of Minute Men in that Town. ...

Boston: Printed and Sold by Edes and Gill ... 1775.

[1]-30 p., [A]-C⁴ D³.

Evans 14615, Sabin 102427.

Copies: BM, CSmH, CtY, DLC, MHi, MWA, MWiW-C, MiU-C, NHi, NN, RPJCB.

[WHATELY, THOMAS]. *The Regulations Lately Made ... By ... Geo. Grenville. The Third Edition.* London, 1775, see: 21b.

203. WILLIAMS, SAMUEL, 1743-1817.

A Discourse On The Love of our Country; Delivered On a Day of Thanksgiving, December 15, 1774. ...

Salem, New-England: Printed By Samuel and Ebenezer Hall. 1775.

[1]-29 p., 8vo, [A]-C⁴ C³.

Evans 14627, Sabin 104346.

Copies: BM, CSmH, CtY, DLC, MBAt, MH, MHi, MWA, MiU-C, NHi, RPJCB, WHi.

204a. ZUBLY, JOHN JOACHIM, 1724-1781.

The Law of Liberty. A Sermon On American Affairs, Preached At The Opening Of The Provincial Congress Of Georgia . . . With An Appendix, Giving A Concise Account Of The Struggles Of Swisserland [*sic*] To Recover Their Liberty. . . .

Philadelphia: Printed By Henry Miller. MDCCLXXV.

[i]-xx, [1]-41, [1] p. (last p. advts.), 8vo, [A]-H⁴ (H4 blank).

Advertised in the *Pennsylvania Journal* for October 4, 1775.

Evans 14635, Sabin 106388.

Copies: BM, CtHi, CtY, MB, MBAt, MH, MWA, MiU-C, NHi, NN, NcD, PPL, RPJCB.

204b. ———. ———.

Philadelphia: Printed and Sold by Henry Miller. 1775. Also to be had of Messieurs Bradfords, in Philadelphia; Noel and Hazard, at New-York; William Scott . . . Charles-Town, South-Carolina; and at Mr. Bard's Store, at Savannah, Georgia.

Same collation.

Printed from substantially the same setting of type as no. 204a with the additional section of the imprint added.

Evans 14636, Sabin 106388.

Copies: DLC, MB, MH, NHi, NjP, PHi, PPL.

204c. ———. ———.

Philadelphia Printed; And London Re-printed for J. Almon . . . MDCCLXXV.

1 p. l., 5-73 p., 8vo, [A]¹ B-I⁴ K³.

Sabin 106338.

Copies: CSmH, CtHWatk, CtY, DLC, ICN, InU, MHi, MiU-C, NHi, NN, PU, RPJCB.

1776

205a. [ADAMS, JOHN] 1735-1826.

Thoughts On Government: Applicable To The Present State Of The American Colonies. . . .

Philadelphia, Printed By John Dunlap. M,DCC,LXXVI.

[1]-28 p., 8vo, A-C⁴ D².

Advertised in the *Pennsylvania Packet* for April 22, 1776. It is in part a reply to the proposals for an American government in Thomas Paine's *Common Sense*, Philadelphia, 1776, no. 222. For the circumstances of composition see: L. H. Butterfield's edition of the *Diary and Autobiography of John Adams*, 1961, vol. 3, pp. 331-333. Adams sent a copy to Joseph Warren on April 20th, two days before it was first advertised in the newspaper.

Evans 14639, Sabin 251.

Copies: CSmH, DLC, ICN, MWA, MiU-C, NHi, NN, NjP, PHi, PPAmP, PPL, RPJCB.

205b. [————]. ————.

Philadelphia, Printed. Boston: Re-Printed by John Gill . . . M,DCC,LXXVI.

[1]-16 p., 4to, [A]-B⁴.

Sabin is incorrect in describing this as an abridgement.

Evans 14640, Sabin 251.

Copies: MB, MHi, MWA, NN.

206. BALDWIN, SAMUEL, d. 1784.

A Sermon, Preached At Plymouth, December 22, 1775. Being the Anniversary Thanksgiving, in commemoration of the first landing of the Fathers of New-England, there; anno domini, 1620. . . .

America, Massachusetts-Bay: Boston, Printed by Powars and Willis . . . MDCCLXXVI.

[1]-39 p., 4to, [A]-E⁴.

Evans 14657, Sabin 2909.

Copies: CSmH, DLC, MB, MHi, MWA, MiU-C, RPJCB.

207. [BRAXTON, CARTER] 1736-1797.

An Address To The Convention Of The Colony And Ancient Dominion Of Virginia; On The Subject of Government in general, and recommending a particular Form to their Consideration. . . .

Philadelphia: Printed By John Dunlap . . . M,DCC,LXXVI.

[1]-25 p., 8vo, A-C⁴ [D]² (D2 blank).

This was printed in the *Virginia Gazette* (Dixon & Hunter) for June 8, 15, 1776. In part it was stimulated by John Adams's *Thoughts on Government*, Philadelphia, 1776, no. 205. Attributed to Braxton in the Library of Congress Catalog.

Evans 14669, Sabin 7466.

Copies: CSmH, DLC, NN, PHi, PPL, RPJCB.

[CARTWRIGHT, JOHN]. *American Independence.* Philadelphia, 1776, see: 105c.

208a. [CHALMERS, JAMES] d. 1806.

Plain Truth; Addressed To The Inhabitants Of America, Containing Remarks On A Late Pamphlet, entitled Common Sense . . . By Candidus. . . .

Philadelphia: Printed, and Sold, by R. Bell . . . MDCCLXXVI.

4 p. l., 1-84 p., 8vo, [A]-K⁴ L³ M⁴.

Advertised in the *Pennsylvania Gazette* for March 13, 1776. A full account of the American publication of this pamphlet will be found in my "The Authorship and Printing of Plain Truth by 'Candidus,'" *Papers of the Bibliographical Society of America,* vol. XLIX (1955), pp. 230-248. The listing here is a summary of that information. At the end is an extract of a reply to *Common Sense,* signed "Cato," by Provost William Smith which was published in the *Pennsylvania Gazette* on the 13th. At various times the pamphlet has been attributed to Smith, George Chalmers, Charles Inglis, Richard Wells, Joseph Galloway, and Alexander Hamilton.

Evans 15088, Sabin 84642 and note.

Copies: BM, CSmH, DLC, MBAt, MH, MHi, MWA, MiU-C, NHi, NN, NjP, PPRos, PPL, PU.

208b. [―――]. ―――.

Same imprint.

[1]-84, [*i.e.* 94], [2] p. (last 2 p. advts.), 8vo, [A]-K⁴ L³ M⁴.

There are a number of incorrectly paged variants of this issue resulting from the addition of the complete Smith letter and another attack on Paine signed "Rationalis."

Copies: CtHWatk, DLC, MH, MHi, PHi, PPAmP, PPL, PU.

208c. [―――]. ―――.

Same imprint.

[1]-96 p., 4 l., [97]-136 p., 8vo, [A]-M⁴ [-]⁴ N-P⁴ [Q-R]⁴.

This contains the *Additions to Plain Truth,* also by Chalmers, which was issued separately on April 17th. However, it was also issued with the original pamphlet. See no. 209.

Sabin 84642 note.

Copies: CSmH, CtY, DLC, ICN, MB, MBAt, MH, MWA, MiU-C, NN, PHi, PPL, PU, RPJCB.

208d.   [————].   ————. The Second Edition.

Same imprint and collation.

Advertised in the *Pennsylvania Gazette* for May 8, 1776.

Evans 15089, Sabin 84642 note.

Copies: CtY, DLC, MHi, NcD, PHi, WHi.

208e.   [————].   ————.

Philadelphia, Printed: London, Reprinted for J. Almon . . . M.DCC.LXXVI.

2 p. l., [1]-47, [1] p. (last p. advts.), 8vo, [-]² A-F⁴.

This was also issued with the four Almon editions of *Common Sense*. For full discussion see: Richard Gimbel's *Thomas Paine: Bibliographical Check List of Common Sense*, New Haven, 1956, nos. CS 24-CS 39 and CS 206a-CS 212. A reprint of no. 208a.

Sabin 84642 note.

Copies: BM, CSmH, CtY, DLC, InU, MB, MBAt, MH, MWA, MiU-C, NN, NjP, PPL, PU, WHi.

208f.   [————].   ————. The Second Edition.

Same imprint and collation.

Printed from substantially the same setting of type as no. 208e.

Sabin 84642 note.

Copies: CSmH, CtY, MBAt, MH, MHi, MiU-C, NHi, NN, PPL, PU, RPB, RPJCB, ViU.

208g.   [————].   ————.

Philadelphia, Printed: Dublin, Reprinted by M. Mills . . . MDCCLXXVI.

2 p. l., [1]-44 p., 8vo, [-]² A-B⁸ C⁶.

A reprint of no. 208a.

Sabin 84642 note.

Copies: DLC, MiU-C, NN, PPL, PU, RPJCB.

209. [CHALMERS, JAMES] d. 1806.

Additions To Plain Truth; Addressed To The Inhabitants Of America, Containing, further Remarks On A Late Pamphlet, entitled Common Sense . . . Written By The Author Of Plain Truth. . . .

Philadelphia: Printed, and Sold, by R. Bell ... MDCCLXXVI.

4 p. l., [97]-136 p., 8vo, [-]⁴ N-P⁴ [Q-R]⁴.

Advertised in the *Pennsylvania Gazette* for April 17, 1776. For the various issues and states see the article cited in no. 208a. Also issued with nos. 208c and d.

Evans 15089 (2nd title), Sabin 84642 note.

Copies: CSmH, CtHWatk, CtY, DLC, MB, MBAt, MHi, MWA, MiU-C, NN, PHi, PPAmP, PPL, PU.

210. CHAMPION, JUDAH, 1729-1810.

Christian And Civil Liberty And Freedom Considered And Recommended: A Sermon, Delivered Before The General Assembly ... On the Day of Their Anniversary Election, May 9th, 1776. . . .

Hartford: Printed by E. Watson ... 1776.

[1]-31 p., 8vo, [A]-D⁴.

Evans 14675, Sabin 11828.

Copies: CSmH, CtHi, CtY, DLC, ICN, MB, MH, MWA, NHi, NN, PHi, RPJCB.

211. Civil Prudence, Recommended To The Thirteen United Colonies Of North-America. A Discourse, Shewing That it is in the Power of Civil Prudence to prevent or cure State Distempers, and to make an industrious, wealthy, and flourishing People. . . .

Norwich: Printed and sold by Judah P. Spooner. 1776.

[i]-vi, [7]-55 p., 8vo, [A]-G⁴.

In his long dedication to "Common Sense" (*i.e.* Thomas Paine), the author states that this was written not long after the repeal of the Stamp Act. He felt that in view of the independence proposed by Paine his proposals for trade might still be useful. Evans gives the imprint incorrectly.

Evans 14677, Sabin 13163.

Copies: CtHi, CtY, DLC, ICN, MHi, MWA, PPL, RPB, RPJCB.

212. CLARK, JONAS, 1730-1805.

The Fate of Blood-thirsty Oppressors, and God's tender Care of his distressed People. A Sermon, Preached At Lexington, April 19, 1776. To commemorate the Murder, Bloodshed and Commencement of Hostilities, between Great-Britain and America ... To Which Is Added, A Brief Narrative of the principal Transactions of that Day. . . .

Massachusetts-State: Boston, Printed By Powars And Willis. M,DCC,LXXVI.

[1]-31, 1-8 p., 8vo, [A]-D⁴ [E]².

Evans 14679, Sabin 13316.

Copies: BM, CtY, DLC, MB, MBAt, MHi, MWA, MiU-C, NN, RPB, RPJCB.

213. [DAVIS, TIMOTHY].

A Letter From A Friend To Some Of His Intimate Friends, On the Subject of paying Taxes, &c.

Watertown: Printed and Sold by B. Edes ... 1776.

[1]-8 p., 8vo, [A]⁴.

Attributed to Davis in Arthur J. Mekeel's "Free Quakers Movement In New England During the American Revolution," *Bulletin of Friends Historical Association*, vol. XXVII (1938), p. 74. Evans incorrectly dates this 1775.

Evans 14003, Sabin 40279.

Copies: MB, MWA, PPL.

214a. A Discourse On The Times.

Norwich: Printed by Judah P. Spooner, for the Author, 1776.

[1]-16 p., 4to, [A]-B⁴.

The Library of Congress Catalog quotes a note in a George D. Smith catalogue which says of this "The authorship of the tract is credited by a former owner to Jabez Huntington."

Evans 14737, Sabin 20224.

Copies: CtHi, RPJCB.

214b. ———. The Second Edition.

Norwich Printed by Judah P. Spooner, for the Author. M,DCC,LXXVI.

Same collation.

This edition has a number of revisions. A third edition was printed in Norwich in 1777. A copy is to be found in MH.

Evans 14738, Sabin 20244.

Copies: CtHi, CtY, DLC, MB, MH, MWA, NN, PPL, RPJCB.

215. Four Letters On Interesting Subjects.

Philadelphia: Printed by Styner and Cist ... MDCCLXXVI.

1 p. l., 1-24 p., 8vo, [-]¹ A-C⁴.

This was advertised in the *Pennsylvania Evening Journal* for July 17, 1776. Ordinarily it would not have been included; however, the following words "To the Reader" on the verso of the title page make it a useful addition: "The rapid turn which Politics have taken within the course of a few days, makes it almost impossible for the Press to keep pace therewith; which will account for some remarks in the first and second of the following letters. . . ." Those letters were written before the Declaration of Independence and in all probability the printers had them in type before that time. The fact that the title page was printed separately from the rest of the signature suggests that it was done last and perhaps later than the body of the pamphlet.

Evans 14759, Sabin 25285.

Copies: CSmH, DLC, ICN, InU, MWA, MiU-C, NHi, NN, PHi, PPAmP, PPL, RPJCB.

216a. [GREEN, JACOB] 1722-1790.

Observations On The Reconciliation Of Great-Britain, And The Colonies, In Which Are Exhibited Arguments For, And Against, That Measure. . . .

Philadelphia; Printed, by Robert Bell . . . MDCCLXXVI.

[1]-40 p., 8vo, [A]-E⁴ (E4 advts.).

Advertised in the *Philadelphia Evening Post* for April 20, 1776. Two states noted, one with a comma and one with a colon after "Observations" on the title page. Pages 33-40 contain "The Plan Of An American Compact, With Great-Britain. First Published at New York." For authorship see: Ashbel Green's *Life of Jacob Green*, New York, 1849, p. 46.

Evans 14791, Sabin 56558.

Copies: CSmH, CtY, DLC, ICN, InU, MB, MH, MHi, MWA, NHi, NN, PHi, PP, PPL, ViU, WHi.

216b. [————]. ————.

New-York: Printed by John Holt . . . MDCCLXXVI.

[1]-16 p., 8vo, [A]-B⁴.

Advertised in the *New-York Journal*, April 25, 1776.

Evans 14790.

Copies: DLC, NHi.

217.   GRIFFITH, DAVID, 1742-1789.

Passive Obedience Considered: In A Sermon Preached At Williamsburg, December 31st 1775 . . . Published At The Request Of The General Convention.

Williamsburg: Printed by Alexander Purdie [1776].

[1]-26 p., 4to, [A]-C⁴ D¹.

Advertised in the *Virginia Gazette* (Purdie) for March 29, 1776.

Evans 14793, Sabin 28823.

Copies: CSmH, DLC, NjP, PPL.

218. HUNTINGTON, ENOCH, 1739-1809.

The Happy Effects Of Union, And The Fatal Tendency Of Diversions. Shewn In A Sermon Preached Before The Freemen Of The Town Of Middletown ... April 8, 1776. ...

Hartford: Printed By Eben. Watson ... MDCCLXXVI.

[1]-28 p., 8vo, [A]⁸ B⁴ C².

Evans 14805, Sabin 33958.

Copies: CtHi, CtY, DLC, MH, MHi, MiU-C, NHi.

219a. [INGLIS, CHARLES] 1734-1816.

The Deceiver Unmasked; Or, Loyalty And Interest United: In Answer To A Pamphlet Entitled Common Sense. By A Loyal American. ...

New-York: Printed By Samuel Loudon. M.DCC.LXXVI.

[i]-viii, [9]-87 p., 12mo, A-G⁶ H².

Advertised in the *New-York Gazette & Weekly Mercury* for March 18, 1776. The existence of this reply to Thomas Paine's *Common Sense,* Philadelphia, 1776, no. 222, was first noted by A. J. Wall in "The Burning of the Pamphlet 'The Deceiver Unmasked' in 1776," *The American Book Collector,* vol. III (1926), pp. 106-111. There he tells of the destruction of the entire edition by a mob on the night of March 19th. In confirmation of this there is bound in the John Carter Brown copy of the second Philadelphia edition, no. 219c, a leaf of manuscript headed "For His Excellency William Eden Esq From The Author." It reads in part, "This Pamphlet was first printed at New York, in March 1776; & when advertised for Sale, the whole impression seized & burned by the *Sons of Liberty.* The Author, with much Trouble & no less Hazard, conveyed a Copy to Philadelphia, after expunging some Passages that gave greatest offence, softening others, inserting a few adapted to the Spirit of the Times, & altering the Title Page" had it printed. For authorship see: John W. Lydekker's *The Life and Letters of Charles Inglis,* London, 1936, p. 152.

Copies: NHi, PPAmP.

219b. [————]. The True Interest Of America Impartially Stated, In Certain Strictures On A Pamphlet Intitled Common Sense. By An American. . . .

Philadelphia. Printed And Sold By James Humphreys, Junr., . . . M,DCC,LXXVI.

[i]-viii, [9]-71 p., 8vo, A-I⁴.

Advertised in the *Pennsylvania Gazette* for May 29, 1776.

Evans 14809, Sabin 97119.

Copies: CSmH, CtY, DLC, MBAt, MWA, MiU-C, NHi, NcD, PHi, PPAmP, PPL, RPJCB, ViU.

219c. [————]. ————. The Second Edition.

Same imprint and collation.

Advertised in the *Pennsylvania Packet* for July 1, 1776. Printed from substantially the same type as no. 219b.

Evans 14810, Sabin 97119.

Copies: BM, CSmH, CtY, DLC, ICN, InU, MB, MBAt, MHi, MWA, MiU-C, NN, PHi, PPL, PU, RPJCB.

[LEE, ARTHUR]. *An Appeal to the Justice and Interests of the People of Great Britain.* London, 1776, see: 123e.

[————]. ————. Newcastle Upon Tyne, 1776, see: 123f.

[LEONARD, DANIEL]. *Massachusettensis.* London, 1776, see: 180c, 180d, 180e, 180f.

[————]. ————. Dublin, 1776, see: 180g.

220a. [MACPHERSON, JAMES] 1736-1796.

The Rights Of Great Britain Asserted Against The Claims Of America: Being An Answer To The Declaration Of The General Congress.

London: Printed for T. Cadell . . . MDCCLXXVI.

2 p. l., [1]-92 p., fold. table, 8vo, [A]² B-L⁴ M² N⁴.

This is a reply to the Continental Congress's "Declaration . . . Setting Forth The Causes and Necessity of their Taking up Arms" adopted July 6, 1775, and here reprinted on pp. 85-92. The *Monthly Review* for February, 1776 states that "This celebrated performance is said to have been written, printed and liberally distributed both in Great Britain and America, at the instance and expense of government . . ."

The authorship has been the subject of dispute. The Macpherson claim seems to be the strongest. Beginning in 1776, Lord North employed him as a political writer. In the "Advertisement" at the front the author says that he ". . . had access to original papers, accurate estimates, and authentic dispatches" and ". . . the records of both Houses of Parliament . . ." The RPJCB copy of the eighth edition, no. 220k, was in the library of Sir John Mackintosh, 1765-1832. In it he made a note on September 13, 1809 as follows, "This pamphlet was written by James Macpherson the translator of *Ossian*." He later changed his mind because there is another note reading "Now owned to be by Sir John Dalrymple." However, this second note must have been made many, many years after the event and neither of the two Sir John Dalrymples to whom he might have been referring is as likely a candidate as Macpherson. Sir John Dalrymple, fifth earl of Stair, 1720-1789, was active in politics, but in 1774 he presented a petition on behalf of Massachusetts to the House of Commons and is known to have opposed the measures that led to the Revolution, while Sir John Dalrymple, fourth baronet of Cranstoun, 1726-1810, became baron of the exchequer in 1776, but is not known to have had any direct interest in American affairs before that time. The attributions to Henry Mackenzie and Lord George Germain apparently have no really strong support.

Sabin 18347.

Copies: BM, CSmH, CtY, DLC, ICN, InU, MB, MH, MiU-C, NHi, NN, PPAmP, RPJCB.

220b. [————]. ————. The Second Edition.

Same imprint and collation.

Printed from substantially the same setting of type as no. 220a.

Sabin 18347.

Copies: CSmH, CtY, DLC, MH, MHi, MWA, MiU-C, NN, RPJCB.

220c. [————]. ————. The Second Edition.

[London] Printed [for T. Cadell] in the Year MDCCLXXVI.

2 p. l., [1]-92 p., fold. table, 8vo, [A]² B-D⁸ E-H⁴ K² I⁴.

This may be the printing designed for America mentioned in the note under 220a.

Copies: CSmH, CtY, MB, MBAt, MHi, MiU-C, PU, ViU.

220d. [————]. ————. The Third Edition, With Additions.

London: Printed for T. Cadell . . . MDCCLXXVI.

2 p. l., [1]-96 p., fold. table, 8vo, [A]² B-N⁴.

Sabin 18347.

Copies: BM, CSmH, DLC, MiU-C, RPJCB.

220e. [————]. ————. The Third Edition, With Additions.

Same imprint.

3 p. l., [1]-96 p., fold. table, 8vo, [A]³ B-N⁴.

Same sheets as no. 220d with an "Advertisement" on one leaf describing how the pamphlet was written inserted in the first signature.

Copies: CtY, ICN, MH, MiU-C, NN.

220f. [————]. ————. The Third Edition, With Additions.

Same imprint.

3 p. l., [1]-101 p., fold. table, 8vo, [A]³ B-N⁴ O³.

Same sheets as no. 220e with the "Articles of Confederation," on pp. 97-101, added at the end. The Articles were adopted November 15, 1777, which means that this and all subsequent editions like it were not printed in 1776. However, they are included because they are so dated.

Copies: MiU-C.

220g. [————]. ————. The Fourth Edition, With Additions.

Same imprint.

2 p. l., [1]-103 p., fold. table, 12mo, [A]² B-I⁶ K⁴.

A reprint of no. 220f.

Sabin 18347.

Copies: BM, CSmH, CtY, DLC, ICN, MiU-C, NHi, NN.

220h. [————]. ————. The Fifth Edition, With Additions.

Same imprint.

2 p. l., [1]-115 p., fold. table, 8vo, [A]² B-P⁴ Q².

A reprint of no. 220f.

Sabin 18347.

Copies: CSmH, CtY, MB, MH, MiU-C, NHi, NcD, PPAmP, PPL, RPJCB.

220i. [————]. ————. The Sixth Edition To Which Is Now Added A Refutation Of Dr. Price's State of the National Debt.

Same imprint.

2 p. l., [1]-123 p., fold. table, 8vo, [A]² B-P⁴ Q² R⁴.

Printed from substantially the same setting of type as no. 220h with the answer to Price added on pp. 116-123 at the end.

Copies: CSmH, CtY, InU, MH, MiU-C.

220j. [————]. ————. The Seventh Edition To Which Is Now Added A Refutation Of Dr. Price's State of the National Debt.

Same imprint.

2 p. l., [1]-84 p., fold. table, 12 mo, [A]² B-H⁶.

Sabin 18347.

Copies: CSmH, CtY, MiU-C, NHi, PPAmP, PPL, ViU.

220k. [————]. ————. The Eighth Edition To Which Is Now Added A Refutation of Dr. Price's State of the National Debt.

Same imprint.

2 p. l., [1]-123 p., fold. table, 8vo, [A]² B-P⁴ Q² R⁴.

Printed from substantially the same setting of type as no. 220i.

Sabin 18347.

Copies: CSmH, CtY, DLC, InU, MH, MiU-C, NN, PPAmP, RPJCB.

220l. [————]. ————. The Ninth Edition. To Which Is Now Added, A Further Refutation Of Dr. Price's State of the National Debt.

Same imprint.

2 p. l., [1]-131 p., fold. table, 8vo, [A]² B-P⁴ Q² R-S⁴.

Printed from substantially the same setting of type as no. 220i with new material on pp. 123-131.

Sabin 18347.

Copies: CSmH, CtY, DLC, InU, MH, MBAt, MiU-C, NHi, NN, PPL.

220m. [————]. ————. The Tenth Edition. To Which Is Now Added, A Refutation Of Dr. Price's State of the National Debt.

Same imprint.

2 p. l., [1]-131, [1] p., fold. table (last p. advts.), 8vo, [A]² B-P⁴ Q² R-S⁴.

Printed from substantially the same setting of type as no. 220l with advertisements added on the verso of the last leaf.

Copies: BM, CSmH, CtY, DLC, MB, MH, MiU-C, RPJCB.

220n. [————]. ————. The Third Edition.
Dublin: Printed by Caleb Jenkins ... MDCCLXXVI.
2 p. l., [1]-60 p., fold. table, 8vo, [A]² B-G⁴ H⁶.
A reprint of no. 220a.
Copies: CtY, ICN, MiU-C, NN, RPJCB.

220o. [————]. ————. The Third Edition.
Same imprint.
3 p. l., [1]-66 p., fold. table, 8vo, [A]³ B-G⁴ H⁶ I³.
Same printing as no. 220n with the additions made to no. 220e to form
    no. 220f.
Copies: MiU-C.

220p. [————]. ————.
Glasgow: Printed From The Fourth London Edition. MDCCLXXVI.
[1]-78 p., fold. table, 8vo, [-]² A-I⁴ K².
Copies: CtHWatk, CtY, DLC, MB, MH, MWA, MiU-C.

220q. [————]. ————. The Sixth Edition With Additions.
Edinburgh: Printed for Charles Elliot. M,DCC,LXXVI.
2 p. l., [1]-98 [2] p., fold. table (last 2 p. advts.), 12mo, [A]² B-I⁶
    K².
A reprint of no. 220f.
Sabin 18347.
Copies: BM, CSmH, CtY, DLC, MB, NN, PHi, PPL.

220r. [————]. ————. The Seventh Edition With Additions.
Aberdeen: Printed by J. Chalmers and Co. MDCCLXXVI.
[1]-72 p., 12mo, A-F⁶.
A reprint of no. 220f.
Copies: CtY, MiU-C.

220s. [————]. ————. Said to be Written by Lord George Ger-
maine [*sic*].
London Printed: Philadelphia Re-Printed, and Sold by R. Bell ...
MDCCLXXVI.
[1]-92, [1-4] p., fold. table, 8vo, [A]⁸ B-K⁴ M⁴.
A reprint of no. 220a. Evans 14728 lists a second Philadelphia edition,
    but no copy has been located.

Evans 14727, Sabin 18347.

Copies: CSmH, CtHWatk, CtY, DLC, MB, MBAt, MH, MHi, MWA, MiU-C, PHi, PPL, PU, RPJCB, ViU.

220t. [————]. Les Droits De La Grande Bretagne, Etablis contre les prétentions des Américains, Pour servir de Réponse à la Déclaration Du Congrès Général. Ouvrage traduit de l'Anglois, sur la seconde Edition. Par Mr. Fréville.

A La Haye, Chez Pierre-Frederic Gosse . . . MDCCLXXVI.

1 p. l., [1]-98 p., fold. table, 8vo, [-]¹ A-F⁸ G³ (G2 & G3 blank).

Sabin 18348.

Copies: CSmH, CtY, MB, MiU-C, NHi, NN, PU.

221a. MORTON, PEREZ, 1751-1837.

An Oration; Delivered At the King's-Chapel In Boston, April 8, 1776, On the Re-Interment of the Remains of the late Most Worshipful Grand-Master Joseph Warren . . . Who was Slain in the Battle of Bunker's-Hill, June 17, 1775. . . .

Boston: Printed, And To Be Sold By J. Gill . . . 1776.

[1]-13 p., 4to, [A]⁴ B³.

Evans 14892, Sabin 51021.

Copies: BM, CSmH, CtY, DLC, MB, MHi, MWA, MiU-C, NHi, PHi, RPJCB.

221b. ————. ————. ⟨The Second Edition.⟩

Same imprint and collation.

The edition statement appears at the bottom of the title page outside the mourning border. Printed from substantially the same setting of type as no. 221a.

Evans 14893, Sabin 51021.

Copies: MB, MH, MHi, MWA, RPJCB.

221c. ————. ————.

Boston: Printed, New-York: Re-printed, by John Holt. MDCCLXXVI.

[1]-11 p., 8vo, [A]² [B]⁴.

Advertised in the *New-York Journal* for May 30, 1776.

Evans 14894, Sabin 51021.

Copies: MBAt, NN.

221d. ———. ———.

Boston, Printed: Philadelphia, Re-Printed By John Dunlap . . .
MDCCLXXVI.

[1]-16 p., 4to, [A]-D².

Evans 14895, Sabin 51021.

Copies: MiU-C, PHi, PPL.

222a. [Paine, Thomas] 1736-1809.

Common Sense: Addressed To The Inhabitants Of America. . . .

Philadelphia; Printed, and Sold, by R. Bell . . . MDCCLXXVI.

2 p. l., [1]-79, [1] p. (last p. advts.), 8vo, [A]² B-L⁴.

Advertised in the *Pennsylvania Evening Post* for January 9, 1776. No
   attempt has been made here to provide a complete analysis of the
   many editions, issues, and states of this pamphlet. Those problems
   have been solved by Richard Gimbel in his *Thomas Paine A Bibliographical Check List of Common Sense With An Account of its Publication,*
   New Haven, 1956. The listing here is primarily a summary of that
   work. Two issues of this edition exist. The first has line one of Subject IV on the title page ending "mis-" and the second ends "some."

Evans 14954, Gimbel CS 1 & 2.

Copies: CSmH, CtY, DLC, InU, MBAt, MH, MHi, MWA, MiU-C,
   NN, PHi, PP, PPL, PU, RPJCB.

222b. [———]. ———. The Second Edition.

Same imprint and collation.

Advertised in the *Pennsylvania Evening Post* for January 27, 1776.

Evans 19464, Gimbel CS 3.

Copies: CtHi, CtY, MB, MBAt, MH, MHi, MiU-C, PHi, PPL, PU.

222c. [———]. ———. The Third Edition.

Same imprint and collation.

This edition is also found with the *Large Additions* bound at the end, no.
   222a to form no. 222f.

Evans 14966 (2nd title), Gimbel CS 4.

Copies: CtHWatk, ICN, MBAt, MH, MWA, NN, PU.

222d. [———]. ———.

Philadelphia, Printed. And Sold by R. Bell . . . 1776.

2 p. l., 1-77 p., 4to, [A]-K⁴.

This consists of *Common Sense*, pp. 1-44, and the *Large Additions*, pp. 45-77. Gimbel suggests that this edition was issued late in February of 1776.

Gimbel CS 8.

Copies: CSmH, CtY, MWA, NHi, NN, PU, RPJCB.

222e. [————]. Common Sense; With The Whole Appendix: The Address To The Quakers: Also, The Large Additions, And A Dialogue between the Ghost of General Montgomery . . . and an American Delegate . . . On the Grand Subject of American Independancy.

Philadelphia: Printed, and Sold by R. Bell . . . MDCCLXXVI.

3 p.l., [1]-79, [3], [81]-147, [3] p., 1 l., [5]-16 p., 8vo, [A]³ B-L⁴ [a]-[b]² [c]¹ N-U⁴ [d]² A⁴ [B]².

Gimbel says that there is a newspaper advertisement of March 19, 1776, referring to this that reads "Lately printed, published and now selling." There is also an advertisement for February 20th for the *Large Additions* which has a note saying "The large edition of *Common Sense*, with all the Additions and Appendix, may be had at said Bell's . . ." The latter may have been referring to this edition or to no. 222d. The "Appendix" was taken from no. 222f. The "Additions" were taken from various Philadelphia newspapers. The sixteen pages at the end consists of *A Dialogue between The Ghost of General Montgomery . . . and an American Delegate* with a special title page. For details see Gimbel.

Evans 14966, Gimbel CS 9.

Copies: DLC, ICN, MH, NN, PHi, PPL, PU, RPJCB, WHi.

222f. [————]. Common Sense; Addressed To The Inhabitants Of America . . . A New Edition, with several Additions . . . To which is added an Appendix; together with an Address to the People called Quakers. . . .

Philadelphia Printed. And Sold by W. and T. Bradford. [1776].

3 p.l., [1]-50 p., 8vo, [A]³ B-G⁴ H¹.

Advertised in the *Pennsylvania Journal* for February 14, 1776. Bradford had two separate printings prepared for him by two different printers. For details see Gimbel.

Evans 14959, Gimbel CS 10, 11, 12, 13.

Copies: BM, CSmH, CtHWatk, CtY, DLC, MB, MWA, MWiW-C, MiU-C, NHi, NN, PHi, PPAmP, PPL, PU, RPJCB.

222g. [————]. ————. A New Edition. . . .

Philadelphia: Printed and Sold by W. and T. Bradford. M,DCC,LXXVI.

[1]-99 p., 8vo, [A]-M⁴ N².

Gimbel asks whether this might have been printed in Dublin, or perhaps London. There are certain hiatuses in the text which suggest a British printing. When one recalls the frequency with which Irish printers reprinted American political pamphlets of this period it seems odd to find that there is no edition of *Common Sense* with an Irish imprint. Gimbel notes two states. A reprint of no. 222f.

Gimbel CS 14 & 15.

Copies: BM, CSmH, CtY, DLC, InU, MWA, MiU-C, NN, PHi, PU, RPJCB.

222h. [————]. ————. A New Edition. . . .

Philadelphia Printed: Newbury-Port, Reprinted, for Samuel Phillips, jun. of Andover. [1776].

[1]-61, [1] p., 8vo, [A]-H⁴ (H4 blank).

A reprint of no. 222f. See also no. 222p.

Gimbel CS 17.

Copies: CtY, MH, NN, RPJCB.

222i. [————]. ————.

Philadelphia, Printed. Boston, Re-Printed And Sold by Edes & Gill and T. & J. Fleet. MDCCLXXVI.

2 p. l., [1]-44 p., 4to, [A]-F⁴.

A reprint of no. 222a. See also no. 223b.

Evans 14955, Gimbel CS 18.

Copies: CtY, DLC, MB, MH, MHi, MWA, NN, PU, RPJCB, ViU.

222j. [————]. ————.

Philadelphia: Printed and Sold by R. Bell . . . And Re printed and Sold in Charlestown, South Carolina, By David Bruce . . . MDCCLXXVI.

2 p. l., [1]-68 p., 8vo, [A]² B-I⁴.

A reprint of no. 222a.

Gimbel CS 20.

Copies: Bodl.

222k. [————]. ————. A New Edition. . . .

Hartford: Re-Printed, and Sold by Eben. Watson. [1776].

[1]-59 p., 12mo, [A]⁴ B-E⁶ [F]².

Half-title wanting from only located copy, but assumed from the sequence of signatures and pagination.

Gimbel CS 22.
Copies: MWA.

222l. [————]. ————. A New Edition ... The Fourth Edition.
Lancaster: Printed by Francis Bailey ... [1776].
[1]-63 p., 8vo, [A]-H⁴.
A reprint of no. 222f.
Evans 14960, Gimbel CS 23.
Copies: DLC, MiU-C.

222m. [————]. ————.
Philadelphia Printed: New-York, Reprinted and Sold, by John Ander-
son ... [1776].
2 p. l., [1]-56 p., 8vo, [A]-G⁴ H².
Advertised in a New York newspaper for February 15, 1776. A re-
print of no. 222a.
Evans 14956, Gimbel CS 40.
Copies: CSmH, CtHi, CtHWatk, MWA, NN, PHi, RPJCB.

222n. [————]. ————. The Second Edition.
Same imprint and collation.
The last part of this is from substantially the same setting of type as
no. 222m. A reprint of no. 222a.
Gimbel CS 41.
Copies: CtY, NN.

222o. [————]. ————. A New Edition. ...
Philadelphia Printed: Newbury Port, Reprinted, by John Mycall ...
[1776].
[1]-61, [1] p., 8vo, [A]-H⁴ (H4 blank).
Printed from substantially the same setting of type as no. 222h. A re-
print of no. 222f.
Evans 14961, Gimbel CS 42.
Copies: CSmH, CtY, DLC, MBAt, MH, MWA, MiU-C, NHi, NN, PHi,
PU, RPJCB.

222p. [————]. Common Sense [&c.]. ...
Newport: Printed and Sold by Solomon Southwick. M,DCC,LXX,VI.
2 p. l., [1]-16 p., [1]-31 p., 8vo, [A]-B⁴ C² [A]³ B-D⁴.

Advertised in the *Newport Mercury* for April 8, 1776. This consists of the sheets of no. 222bb with the title page removed and the first half of the text added in the first sixteen pages. Undoubtedly this first section was also sold or given away separately to those who had already acquired no. 222bb. A reprint of no. 222a.

Alden 639, Gimbel CS 46.

Copies: BM, DLC, MB, MHi, MWA, NHi, RPB.

222q. [————]. ————.

Philadelphia: Printed. Norwich: Re-printed and Sold by Judah P. Spooner, and by T. Green, in New London, MDCCLXXVI.

[1]-56 p., 4to, [A]-G⁴.

A reprint of no. 222a.

Evans 14957, Gimbel CS 49.

Copies: BM, CtHWatk, CtY, DLC, MH, MWA, NN, PU.

222r. [————]. ————. A New Edition. . . .

Philadelphia: Printed. Norwich: Re-printed and Sold by Judah P. Spooner, and by T. Green, in New-London [1776].

[1]-64 p., 4to, [A]-H⁴.

A reprint of no. 222f.

Gimbel CS 50.

Copies: MWA, MiU-C, RPJCB.

222s. [————]. ————. The Sixth Edition.

Philadelphia, Printed: Providence, Re-printed and Sold by John Carter . . . M,DCC,LXXVI.

[1]-33 p., 4to, [A]-D⁴ [E]¹.

Advertised in the *Providence Gazette* for February 24, 1776. A reprint of no. 222a.

Evans 14958, Alden 636, Gimbel CS 51.

Copies: CtY, DLC, MH, MHi, MWA, NHi, NN, PHi, PPL, PU, RPJCB.

222t. [————]. ————. The Sixth Edition.

Same imprint.

[1]-45, [1] p., 4to, [A]-D⁴ [-]¹ E-G².

This consists of the sheets of no. 222s plus *Appendix to Common Sense: The Necessity of Independency* on pp. [35]-45. The last section was advertised for sale separately in the *Providence Gazette* for March 2,

1776, but it was also issued with no. 222s. A reprint of no. 222f.

Alden 637, Gimbel CS 51 & 52.

Copies: DLC, PU, RPB.

222u. [————]. ————. The Tenth Edition.

Same imprint.

[1]-33 p., 4to, [A]-D⁴ E¹.

A reprint of no. 222a. Some copies may be found with the *Appendix* described in no. 222t.

Alden 638, Gimbel CS 53.

Copies: CtY, DLC, MWA, RPJCB.

222v. [————]. ————. The Third Edition.

Philadelphia Printed: Salem: Re-Printed and sold by E. Russell . . . MDCCLXXVI.

[1]-28 p., 4to, [A]-C⁴ D².

A reprint of no. 222a.

Evans 14962, Gimbel CS 55.

Copies: DLC, MHi, MWA, PU.

222w. [————]. ————. A New Edition. . . .

Printed, For the Perusal of the Inhabitants of the Thirteen United Colonies. MDCCLXXVI.

[i]-viii, 9-44 p., 8vo, [A]-E⁴ F².

A reprint of no. 222f.

Gimbel CS 56.

Copies: PPL.

222x. [————]. ————. A New Edition. . . .

Philadelphia, Printed . . . Edinburgh, reprinted . . . Sold by Charles Elliot, Edinburgh; and William Anderson, Stirling, MDCCLXXVI.

1 p. l., [1]-99 p., 12mo, [-]¹ A-H⁶ I².

A reprint of no. 222f.

Gimbel CS 21.

Copies: BM, CtY, InU, MBAt, MiU-C, PHi, PPL.

222y. [————]. ————. A New Edition. . . .

Philadelphia, Printed, London, Reprinted, For J. Almon . . . 1776.

2 p. l., [1]-54 p., 8vo, [A]² B-G⁴ H² I¹.

This was also issued with a collective half-title, in four editions with James Chalmers's *Plain Truth*, no. 208e and f. There are a number of states. See Gimbel for details. A reprint of no. 222f.

Gimbel CS 26, 27, 30, 31, 34, 35, 38, 39.

Copies: BM, CSmH, CtY, DLC, InU, MBAt, MH, MWiW-C, MiU-C, NHi, NN, NjP, PHi, PPAmP, PPL, PU, RPB, RPJCB, ViU, WHi.

222z. [————]. ————. A New Edition. . . .
Philadelphia, Printed, Newcastle Upon Tyne, Re-printed: By T. Robson and Co. for the Newcastle Weekly Magazine. MDCCLXXVI.
[1]-56 p., 8vo, [-]⁴ C-H⁴.
A reprint of no. 222f.
Gimbel CS 43.
Copies: PU.

222aa. [————]. ————. A New Edition. . . .
Same imprint.
[1]-94 p., 8vo, [-]⁴ C-M⁴ N³.
Same sheets as no. 223a with the *Additions* added at the end. These *Additions* are a reprint of the edition printed in London, no. 223d.
Gimbel CS 44.
Copies: CSmH, MH, NN, RPJCB.

222bb. [————]. Thoughts of the present state of American Affairs: Extracted from a Pamphlet, Lately published in Philadelphia, entitled Common Sense. . . .
Newport: Printed and Sold by Solomon Southwick. MDCCLXXVI.
[1]-31 p., 8vo, [A]-D⁴.
This consists of only the second half of *Common Sense*. Southwick later combined it with the first part, see no. 222p.
Evans 14965, Gimbel CS 45, Alden 641.
Copies: NN.

222cc. [————]. Gesunde Vernunft an die Einwohner von America . . . Nebst Einem Anhang. . . .
Philadelphia, Gedruckt bey Melchior Steiner und Carl Cist . . . 1776.
[i]-viii, 1-70 p., 8vo, [-]⁴ A-J⁴ (J4 blank).
A translation of no. 222f.
Evans 14963, Gimbel CS 16.
Copies: CtY, MiU-C, NN, PHi, PPL.

222dd. [———]. Le Sens Commun, Addressé Aux Habitants De L'Amérique . . . Nouvelle Edition, Avec plusieurs additions dans le carpo de l'ouvrage, aquel on a ajouté un Appendix, Et une Lettre au peuple Appelle Quakers . . . Traduit De L'Anglois. Sur la nouvelle édition, imprimée à Philadelphie & réimprimée à Londres.

A Rotterdam [*i.e.* Paris?], Chez J. Hofhout et E. Wolfsbergen, Libraires . . . 1776.

[1]-80 p., 8vo, A-E⁸.

A translation of no. 222f.

Gimbel CS 54.

Copies: DLC, MH, MiU-C, PPL, PU.

223a. [Paine, Thomas] 1736-1809.

Large Additions to Common Sense. . . .

Philadelphia: Printed, and Sold, by R. Bell . . . MDCCLXXVI.

1 p. l., [81]-147, [2] p., 8vo, [M]⁴ [-]¹ N-T² U³.

Advertised in the *Pennsylvania Evening Post* for February 17, 1776 to appear on the 19th. This is primarily made up of the "Additions," pages 81-119, which are not by Paine, but which had appeared in various Philadelphia newspapers, and of the "Appendix," which was by Paine and first appeared in no. 222f. Although the contents are the same, Gimbel notes three different editions and issues. The first has five subjects listed and the line following the subjects reads "To which is added. . . ." The second has six subjects and the line reads as above. The third has six subjects and the line reads "To which are added. . . ." Although issued alone, this was also issued with no. 222c to make up no. 222e. It also appeared in no. 222d.

Evans 14966 (3rd title), Gimbel CS 5, 6, 7.

Copies: BM, CtHi, CtHWatk, DLC, MBAt, MHi, MWA, NN, PHi, PPL, PU.

223b. [———]. ———.

Boston: Printed and Sold [by Edes & Gill] at the Printing-Office in Queen-Street. 1776.

[1]-43, [1] p., 8vo, [A]-E⁴ F².

Issued to accompany no. 222i with which it is sometimes bound.

Gimbel CS 19.

Copies: MB, MH, MHi, MWA, MiU-C, NN, RPJCB.

223c. [———]. ———.

Philadelphia, Printed: Newport, Re-printed and Sold by S. Southwick, 1776.

1 p. l., [33]-70 p., 1 l., 8vo, [A]-E⁴ [F]¹.

Advertised in the *Newport Mercury* for March 18, 1776. Also issued with no. 222p.

Evans 14965 (2nd title), Alden 640, Gimbel CS 48.

Copies: CtHWatk, InU, RPJCB.

223d. [————]. Additions to Common Sense Addressed to The In-habitants of America.

Philadelphia, Printed: London, Reprinted for J. Almon . . . 1776.

[1]-47, [1] p. (last p. advts.), 8vo, [A]² B-F⁴ G².

Properly this should not be listed under Paine. It consists of five of the six things in 222a drawn from the Philadelphia newspapers which Paine did not write plus four other things from other sources.

Gimbel CS 203.

Copies: BM, CSmH, CtY, DLC, ICN, InU, MHi, MWA, MiU-C, NcD, PHi, PPAmP, PPL, PU, RPJCB, ViU.

224a.   PRICE, RICHARD, 1723-1791.

Observations On The Nature Of Civil Liberty, The Principles Of Government, And The Justice And Policy Of The War With America. . . .

London: Printed for T. Cadell . . . M.DCC.LXXVI.

4 p. l., [1]-128 p., 8vo, [A]⁴ B-I⁸.

Sabin 65452.

Copies: BM, CSmH, CtHWatk, CtY, DLC, ICN, InU, MH, MWA, MWiW-C, MiU-C, NHi, NN, NcD, NjP, PPAmP, PPL, RPJCB, ViU, WHi.

224b.   ————.   ————. The Second Edition.

Same imprint and collation.

Printed from substantially the same setting of type as no. 224a.

Sabin 65452.

Copies: BM, CSmH, CtY, DLC, InU, MB, MH, MHi, MiU-C, NN, PPL, RPB, RPJCB.

224c.   ————.   ————. The Third Edition.

Same imprint and collation.

Printed from substantially the same setting of type as no. 224a.

Sabin 65452.

Copies: BM, CSmH, CtY, DLC, InU, MH, MHi, MiU-C, NN, PHi, PPAmP, PPL, RPJCB, WHi.

224d. ———. ———. The Fourth Edition.

Same imprint and collation.

Printed from substantially the same setting of type as no. 224a.

Copies: BM, CSmH, CtY, DLC, MB, MBAt, MH, MHi, MiU-C, NHi, NN, PP, PPAmP, PPL, PU, RPJCB.

224e. ———. ———. The Fifth Edition.

Same imprint.

4 p. l., [1]-132 p., 8vo, [A]⁴ B-I⁸ K².

Printed from substantially the same setting of type as no. 224a except that "Preface to The Fifth Edition" dated March 16, 1776, has been placed in signature A in place of the half title and a "Post-script" (pp. 129-132) has been added at the end.

Sabin 65452.

Copies: BM, CSmH, CtY, DLC, ICN, InU, MBAt, MH, MHi, MiU-C, NN, PPAmP, PPL, RPJCB, ViU.

224f. ———. ———. The Sixth Edition.

Same imprint and collation.

Printed from substantially the same setting of type as no. 224e.

Sabin 65452.

Copies: BM, CSmH, CtY, MH, MHi, MiU-C, NN, PHi, PPAmP, PU, RPJCB.

224g. ———. ———.

London: Printed in the Year M.DCC.LXXVI.

[1]-48 p., 8vo, A-C⁸.

No edition statement on the title page.

Copies: CSmH, CtY, MH, MiU-C, PPL, RPJCB.

224h. ———. ———. The Sixth Edition.

London: Printed for E. and C. Dilly . . . and T. Cadell . . . MDCCLXXVI.

Same collation.

Printed from substantially the same setting of type as no. 224g.

Copies: BM, CSmH, CtY, DLC, MH, MiU-C, NHi, NN, PPAmP, PPL, PU, RPJCB.

224i. ———. ———. The Seventh Edition, With Corrections and Additions.

London: Printed for T. Cadell . . . M.DCC.LXXVI. . . .

4 p. l., [1]-134 p., 8vo, [A]⁴ B-I⁸ K⁴ (K4 blank).

Printed from substantially the same setting of type as no. 224e through page 111.

Sabin 65452.

Copies: CtY, MWA, MiU-C, NHi, NN, NjP, PPAmP, RPJCB, ViU.

224j. ———. ———. The Seventh Edition.

London: Printed for E. and C. Dilly . . . and T. Cadell . . . M.DCC.LXXVI.

[1]-48 p., 8vo, [A]-C⁸.

Printed from substantially the same setting of type as no. 224g.

Copies: BM, CtY, DLC, MH, MWA, MiU-C, PHi, PPL, RPJCB.

———. ———. The Eighth Edition. With Corrections and Additions.

London: Printed for T. Cadell . . . MDCCLXXVI. . . .

3 p. l., [1]-112 p., 8vo, [a6-a8] B-H⁴.

This is not a separate publication, but was issued as a part of his *Two Tracts On Civil Liberty*, London, 1778. Obviously this and later Cadell editions and probably some of the earlier ones were not issued in 1776. They are included here, however, because they are so dated.

224k. ———. ———. The Ninth Edition.

London: Printed For Edward And Charles Dilly, And Thomas Cadell. M.DCC.LXXVI.

[1]-48 p., 8vo, A-C⁸.

Sabin 65452.

Copies: BM, CSmH, CtY, DLC, MB, MBAt, MHi, MiU-C, NHi, NN, NjP, PPAmP, PPL, RPJCB.

224l. [———. ———. The Tenth Edition].

[London, 1776].

No copy located. Included here to complete the numerical sequence.

Sabin 65452.

224m. ———. ———. The Eleventh Edition, with Additions; corrected by the Author.

London: Printed for T. Cadell . . . E. and C. Dilly . . . and J. Johnson . . . M.DCC.LXXVI.

[1]-71 p., 12mo, A-C¹².

Sabin 65452.

Copies: BM, MB, MHi, PPAmP, RPJCB.

224n. [————. ———— The Twelfth Edition].

[London, 1776].

No copy located. Included here to complete the numerical sequence.

Sabin 65452.

224o. ————. ————. The Thirteenth Edition, with Additions; corrected by the Author.

London: Printed for T. Cadell . . . E. and C. Dilly . . . and J. Johnson . . . M.DCC.LXXVI. . . .

[1]-72 p., 12mo, A-C¹².

Printed from substantially the same setting of type as no. 224m through
page 60.

Copies: MH, MWA, RPJCB.

224p. ————. ————. A New Edition corrected by the Author.

London: Printed for T. Cadell . . . and J. Johnson . . . M.DCC.LXXVI.
. . .

1 p. l., [1]-76 p., 12mo, [-]¹ A-B¹² C-D⁶ E².

Sabin 65452.

Copies: BM, CSmH, CtY, MHi, MWA, MiU-C, NN, NjP, PPL, RPJCB,
ViU.

224q. ————. ————. The Eighth Edition, newly corrected by the
Author.

Edinburgh . . . Printed for J. Wood and J. Dickson. M,DCC,LXXVI.

4 p. l., [1]-94 p., 12mo, [-]⁴ A-H⁶ (H6 blank).

A reprint of no. 224e.

Sabin 65452.

Copies: BM, CtY, DLC, InU, MBAt, MiU-C, PHi, RPJCB.

224r. ————. ————.

Dublin: Printed for J. Exshaw, S. Price, W. Whitestone, W. Sleater
. . . [and sixteen others] M,DCC,LXXVI.

4 p. l., [1]-180 p., fold. table, 12mo, [A]⁴ B-H¹² I⁶.

A reprint of no. 224a.

Copies: BM, CSmH, CtY, ICN, MH, MiU-C, RPJCB.

224s. ————. ————. The Eighth Edition.

Dublin: Printed By W. Kidd, For J. Exshaw, S. Price, W. White-stone, W. Sleater ... [and sixteen others] 1776.

   [i]-xii, [1]-179 p., 12mo, [A]⁶ B-H¹² I⁶.

A reprint of no. 224a.

Sabin 65452.

Copies: CSmH, CtY, DLC, MH, MWA, NN, PP, PPL.

224t. ————. ————.

London Printed, 1776. Philadelphia: Re-printed and Sold by John Dunlap ... [1776].

   [1]-61 [*i.e.* 71] p., 8vo, [A]-I⁴.

Advertised in the *Pennsylvania Packet* for July 1, 1776. A reprint of no.
   224a.

Evans 15030, Sabin 65452.

Copies: CtY, DLC, MHi, MWA, MiU-C, NHi, NN, PPAmP, PPL,
   RPJCB.

224u. ————. ————.

London Printed, 1776. Philadelphia: Re-printed and Sold by John Dunlap ... MDCCLXXVI.

   [1]-71 p., 8vo, [A]-I⁴.

Printed from substantially the same setting of type as no. 224t. A reprint of no. 224a.

Evans 15031, Sabin 65452.

Copies: BM, CtY, DLC, MBAt, MH, MWA, MiU-C, NHi, NN, NcD,
   NjP, PHi, PU, RPJCB, ViU, WHi.

224v. ————. ————.

London, Printed: New-York, Re-printed by S. Loudon ... 1776.

   [1]-107 p., 12mo, A-I⁶.

A reprint of no. 224a.

Evans 15033, Sabin 65452.

Copies: CSmH, CtHWatk, CtY, DLC, ICN, MBAt, MH, MWA, NHi,
   NN, PHi, PPL, RPJCB, ViU.

224w. ——————. ——————.

London Printed 1776. Boston, Re-printed and Sold by T. and J. Fleet [1776?].

[1]-71 p., 4to, [A]-I⁴.

A reprint of no. 224a.

Evans 15032, Sabin 65452.

Copies: BM, CSmH, CtHi, CtY, DLC, ICN, MB, MBAt, MH, MHi, MWA, MWiW-C, MiU-C, NN, PHi, PPAmP, PPL, RPJCB, ViU.

224x. ——————. ——————.

London: Printed for T. Cadell . . . and Reprinted And Sold By David Bruce In Charlestown, South-Carolina. MDCCLXXVI.

4 p. l., [1]-104 p., 8vo, [A]-M⁴ N⁸.

A reprint of no. 224e.

Evans 15034, Sabin 65452.

Copies: DLC, RPJCB.

224y. ——————. Aanmerkingen Over Den Aart Der Burgerlyke Vryheid, Over De Gronden Der Regeering, En Over De Regtveerdigheid En Staatkunde Van Den Oorlog Met Amerika . . . Naar den Elfden door den Schryver Vermeerderden en Verbeeterden Druk uit het Engelsch vertaald. Door Johan Derk Baron Van Der Capellen. . . .

Te Leyden By L. Herding, 1776.

[1]-18, [1-2], 1-116, 1-25, 1-2 p. (last 2 p. advts.), 8vo, *⁸ **² A-G⁸ H² A-B⁸.

Translated from no. 224e.

Sabin 65455.

Copies: CSmH, CtY, MBAt, MH, NN, RPJCB.

224z. ——————. Observations Sur La Nature De La Liberté Civile, Sur Les Principes Du Gouvernement, Sur La Justice Et La Politique De La Guerre Avec L'Amérique. auxquelles on a ajouté un Appendix & un Postscriptum . . . Traduit de l'Anglois, Sur la onzième Édition. . . .

A Rotterdam [*i.e.* Paris?], Chez Hofhout & Wolfsbergen . . . MDCCLXXVI.

3 p. l., 1-148 p., 8vo, *² [-]¹ A-I⁸ K².

Sabin 65453.

Copies: CtY, ICN, MB, MH, PPL, RPJCB.

225.   Remarks On A Late Pamphlet Entitled Plain Truth. By Rusticus.

Philadelphia: Printed By John Dunlap . . . M,DCC,LXXVI.

[1]-31 p., 8vo, B⁴ B-D⁴.

This is a reply to James Chalmers's *Plain Truth,* Philadelphia, 1776, no. 208. It has frequently been attributed to John Dickinson. This attribution is most unlikely. The author who signed the pamphlet "New-Jersey, May 8th, 1776" apparently had been living in New Jersey for some time because he says "I have a friend in the city who furnishes me with all political publications . . . but by some miscarriage the pamphlet entitled Plain Truth did not get to hand till within these few days." He then goes on to castigate Chalmers for his effrontery in dedicating *Plain Truth* to Dickinson. During these spring months of 1776, Dickinson was at his home in Philadelphia, a member of the Congress. Furthermore, the sentiments expressed by this pamphlet are decidedly different from those known to have been held by Dickinson as early as January, 1776 and expressed in his "Speech of John Dickinson Opposing the Declaration of Independence, 1 July, 1776," edited by J. H. Powell in *The Pennsylvania Magazine of History and Biography,* vol. LXV (1941), pp. 458-481. Also Dickinson did not include it in his *Political Writings,* Wilmington, 1801, 2v.

Evans 14735.

Copies: CSmH, DLC, MB, MWA, NHi, PHi, PPAmP, PPL, RPJCB.

226.   Ross, Robert, 1726-1799.

A Sermon, In Which The Union Of The Colonies Is Considered And Recommended; And The Bad Consequences Of Divisions Are Represented. Delivered On The Public Thanksgiving. November sixteenth, 1775. . . .

New-York: Printed by John Holt . . . MDCCLXXVI.

[1]-28 p., 8vo, [A]-C⁴ D².

Evans 15070, Sabin 73407. The death date of 1782 that Evans gives for the author actually applies to Aeneas Ross who died in New Castle, Delaware, in that year.

Copies: CSmH, CtY, MHi, MWA, NHi, NN, PHi, WHi.

Sharp, Granville. *A Declaration of the People's Natural Right.* Dublin, 1776, see: 139h.

227. SHERWOOD, SAMUEL, 1730-1783.

The Church's Flight Into The Wilderness: An Address On The Times. Containing Some very interesting and important Observations on Scripture Prophecies: Shewing, that sundry of them plainly relate to Great-Britain, and the American Colonies; and are fulfilling in the present day. Delivered on a Public Occasion, January 17, 1776. . . .

New-York: Printed by S. Loudon. M.DCC.LXXVI.

[1]-54 p., 8vo, [A]-G⁴ (G4 blank).

Evans 15082, Sabin 80455.

Copies: CSmH, CtY, DLC, ICN, MBAt, MH, MHi, MWA, MiU-C, NN, PHi, PPAmP, RPJCB.

228a. SMITH, WILLIAM, 1727-1803.

An Oration In Memory Of General Montgomery, And Of The Officers And Soldiers Who Fell With Him, December 31, 1775 Before Quebec . . . (. . . Delivered February 19th, 1776.) At The Desire Of The Honorable Continental Congress. . . .

Philadelphia: Printed by John Dunlap . . . M,DCC,LXXVI.

2 p. l., [1]-44 p., 8vo, [-]² A-E⁴ [F]².

Advertised in the *Pennsylvania Packet* for March 4, 1776. Two states noted, one with "errata" on page 44 and one without. The Library of Congress Catalog describes this as having 3 p. l. However, investigation proved their collation to be incorrect. The Congress was so annoyed with some of the things Smith said in this Oration that it refused to vote him their thanks. He had it printed himself after omitting some of the more offensive passages. See: letter from John Adams to Abigail Adams April 28th, 1776, *Familiar Letters,* edited by C. F. Adams, 1876, p. 167.

Evans 15084, Sabin 84633.

Copies: CSmH, CtY, DLC, ICN, MB, MBAt, MH, MHi, MWA, MiU-C, NHi, NN, NjP, PHi, PPAmP, PPRos, PPL, PU, RPJCB.

228b. ———. ———.

Philadelphia Printed: New-York Re-printed by John Anderson . . . MDCCLXXVI.

[1]-36 p., 8vo, [A]-D⁴ E².

Sabin 84632 lists a second New York edition printed by Hugh Gaine from an advertisement in his *New-York Gazette and Weekly Mercury* for March 25, 1776. No copy has been located and it probably is a ghost. There is no evidence other than this that Gaine ever put his name on pamphlets of this kind. He was probably selling Dunlap's Philadelphia edition, no. 228a, or this edition.

Evans 15085, Sabin 84634.

Copies: MBAt, MWA, NN.

228c. ———. ———.

Philadelphia, Printed: Newport: Re-Printed By Solomon Southwick. M,DCC,LXXVI.

1 p. l., [1]-30 p., 8vo, [A]-D⁴.

Advertised in the *Newport Mercury* for April 8, 1776.

Evans 15086, Sabin 84635, Alden 669.

Copies: DLC, MHi, MiU-C, NHi, NN, PHi, PU, RPJCB.

228d. ———. ———.

Philadelphia Printed: Norwich: Re-printed, by Robertsons and Trumbull, 1776.

[1]-22 p., 8vo, [A]-C⁴ (C4 blank).

Evans 15087, Sabin 84636.

Copies: CSmH, CtHi, CtY, DLC, MH, MWA, NHi, PU, RPJCB.

228e. ———. ———.

Philadelphia, Printed; London, Reprinted for J. Almon . . . MDCCLXXVI.

[i]-iv, [1]-36 p., 8vo, [-]² A-D⁴ E².

Sabin 84637.

Copies: BM, CtY, InU, MB, MH, MWiW-C, MiU-C, NHi, NN, PHi, PU, RPJCB.

228f. ———. ———. The Second Edition.

Same imprint and collation.

Sabin 84638.

Copies: CtY, MB, MH, MHi, MWA, MiU-C, NN, PU, WHi.

228g. ———. ———.

Philadelphia, printed: New Castle, Reprinted by T. Robson and Co. . . . [1776?].

[1]-35 p., 4to, A-C⁴ D⁶.
Sabin 84639.
Copies: CtY, NN.

228h. ———. ———.
Philadelphia: Printed . . . and Belfast: Reprinted, by James Magee . . .
MDCCLXXVI.
    [1]-48 p., 8vo, A-F⁴.
Sabin 84640.
Copies: MiU-C, PPL.

SMITH, WILLIAM. *A Sermon on the Present Situation of American Affairs.*
Edinburgh, 1776, see: 196n.

229. THACHER, PETER, 1752-1802.
An Oration Delivered At Watertown, March 5, 1776. To Commem-
orate The Bloody Massacre At Boston: Perpetrated March 5, 1770. . . .
Watertown: Printed and Sold by Benjamin Edes . . . M,DCC,LXXVI.
    [1]-15 p., 8vo, [A]-D².
Evans 15101, Sabin 95172.
Copies: BM, CSmH, CtHi, CtY, DLC, InU, MB, MH, MHi, MWA,
MiU-C, NN, PHi, PPRos, RPJCB, ViU.

TUCKER, JOSIAH. *The True Interest of Great Britain.* Philadelphia, 1776,
see: 144b.

230. WEST, SAMUEL, 1731-1807.
A Sermon Preached Before The Honorable Council, And The Hon-
orable House of Representatives Of The Colony of the Massachusetts-
Bay, In New-England. May 29th, 1776. Being The Anniversary For
The Election Of The Honorable Council For The Colony. . . .
Boston: Printed By John Gill, In Queen-Street. 1776.
    [1]-70 p., 8vo, [A]-I⁴ (I4 blank).
Evans 15217, Sabin 102744.
Copies: BM, CSmH, CtHi, CtHWatk, CtY, DLC, ICN, MB, MH, MHi,
MWA, MiU-C, NHi, NN, NcD, PHi, PPL.

231. WITHERSPOON, JOHN, 1722-1794.
The Dominion of Providence over the Passions of Men. A Sermon

Preached At Princeton, On the 17th of May, 1776. Being The General Fast appointed by the Congress through the United Colonies. To Which Is Added, An Address to the Natives of Scotland residing in America. . . .

Philadelphia: Printed And Sold By R. Aitken . . . M.DCC.LXXVI.

2 p. l., [1]-78 p., 1 l. (last l. "erratum"), 8vo, [-]² A-K⁴.

Evans 15224, Sabin 104934.

Copies: BM, CSmH, CtHi, CtY, DLC, MB, MBAt, MH, MHi, MWA, MiU-C, NN, NjP, PHi, PPL, RPJCB.

Index to Pamphlet Exchanges

THIS short-title index lists in chronological order by the date of the first publication the nineteen groups of pamphlet exchanges that took place between 1764 and 1776 in the area covered by this bibliography. Within each group the pamphlets are arranged in their proper sequence. In general the name assigned to each series is based on the author, or when not known, the title of the first publication. The numbering within each series reflects the relationship of each of the pamphlets to the others. Thus, 2b is the second reply to the first pamphlet, 3 is the first and only reply to the second pamphlet, and 2c1 is the first reply to the third reply to the first pamphlet, see Paine series.

1764

Pownall Series

1.   [Pownall, Thomas]. *The Administration of the Colonies*. London, 1764, no. 5a.
1b. [Knox, William]. *The Claim of the Colonies*, London, 1765, no. 17a-b.
1c. [Jenyns, Soame]. *The Objections to the Taxation of our American Colonies*, London, 1765, no. 16Aa-b.
2.   [Dulany, Daniel]. *Considerations on the Propriety of Imposing Taxes*. [Annapolis], 1765, nos. 11a-g.

1765

Hopkins Series

1.   [Hopkins, Stephen]. *The Rights of Colonies Examined*. Providence, 1765, nos. 14a-b.
2.   [Howard, Martin]. *A Letter from a Gentleman at Halifax*. Newport, 1765, no. 16.
3a. [Hopkins, Stephen]. "A Vindication of a Late Pamphlet entitled, The Rights of Colonies Examined. . . ." *Providence Gazette*, Feb. 23, March 2, 9, and April 8, 1765, no. 15, note.
3b. [Otis, James]. *A Vindication of the British Colonies*. Boston, 1765, nos. 20a-c.
4.   [Howard, Martin]. *A Defense of the Letter from a Gentleman at Halifax*. Newport, 1765, no. 15.
5a. [Hopkins, Stephen]. *A Letter to the Author of the Halifax Letter*. [Newport] 1765, no. 13.
5b. [Otis, James]. *Brief Remarks on the Defense of the Halifax Libel*. Boston, 1765, no. 19.

Whatley Series

1.   [Whatley, Thomas]. *The Regulations Lately Made*. London, 1765, nos. 21a-b.

2.   [Bland, Richard]. *An Inquiry into the Rights of the British Colonies.* Williamsburg, 1766, nos. 22Aa-Ab.

First Knox Series

1.   [Knox, William]. *The Claim of the Colonies.* London, 1765, nos. 17a-b.
2a. [Dulany, Daniel]. *Considerations on the Propriety of Imposing Taxes in the British Colonies.* [Annapolis] 1766, nos. 11a-g.
2b. [Devotion, Ebenezer]. *The Examiner Examined.* New London, 1766, nos. 26a-b.

1766

Dickinson Series

1.   [Dickinson, John]. *An Address to the Committee of Correspondence in Barbados.* Philadelphia, 1766, no. 27.
2a. *A Letter to the North American, on Occasion of his Address to the Committee of Correspondence in Barbados.* Barbados, 1766, no. 34.
2b. [Morrison, Kenneth]. *An Essay Towards the Vindication of the Committee of Correspondence in Barbados.* Barbados, 1766, no. 36.
3.   *Candid Observations on two Pamphlets Lately Published, viz. "An Address to the Committee of Correspondence in Barbados. . . ." And "An Essay towards the Vindication of the Committee. . . ."* Barbados, 1766, no. 23.

Pitt Series

1.   [Pitt, William]. *Political Debates.* London, 1766, nos. 41a-b.
2.   [Hicks, William]. *The Nature and Extent of Parliamentary Power.* Philadelphia, 1768, nos. 56a-b.

1767

A Representation of Facts Series

1.   Charleston, S. C. Merchants. *A Representation of Facts, Relative to the Conduct of Daniel Moore.* Charleston, S. C., 1767, no. 47.
2.   [Laurens, Henry]. *Extracts from the Proceedings of the Court of Vice-Admiralty.* [Philadelphia] 1768, nos. 57a-c.
3.   Leigh, Sir Egerton. *The Man Unmasked.* Charleston, S. C., 1769, no. 66.
4.   [Laurens, Henry]. *An Appendix to the Extracts from the Proceedings of the High Court of Vice-Admiralty.* Charleston, S. C., 1769, no. 57c note.

1768

The Constitutional Right Series

1.   *The Constitutional Right of the Legislature of Great Britain to Tax the British Colonies.* London, 1768, no. 53.
2.   *A Letter to the Right Honourable the Earl of Hillsborough.* London, 1769 and Boston reprinted, 1769, nos. 67a-b.

1769
Bernard Series

1a. Massachusetts. Governor. *Copies of Letters from Governor Bernard &c.* [Boston, 1769] nos. 68a-e.
1b. Massachusetts. Governor. *Letters to the Ministry from Governor Bernard, General Gage, and Commodore Hood.* Boston, 1769, nos. 69a-c.
1c. Massachusetts. Governor. *A Third Extraordinary Budget of Epistles and Memorials.* [Boston, 1769] no. 70.
2. Boston. *An Appeal to the World.* Boston, 1769, nos. 62a-d.
3. Massachusetts, General Court. *Copy of the Complaint of the House of Representatives . . . against Sir Francis Bernard.* [London, 1770] nos. 81a-c.

Second Knox Series

1. [Knox, William]. *The Controversy Between Great-Britain and her Colonies Reviewed.* London, 1769, nos. 65a-c.
2. [Bancroft, Edward]. *Remarks on the Review of the Controversy.* London, 1769, New-London reprinted, 1771, nos. 61a-b.

1770
Boston Massacre Series

1. Boston. *A Short Narrative of the Horrid Massacre in Boston.* Boston, 1770, nos. 75a-i.
2. *A Fair Account of the Late Unhappy Disturbance at Boston.* London, 1770, no. 77.
3. Massachusetts. Council. *Proceedings of His Majesty's Council of the Province of Massachusetts-Bay, Relative to the Deposition of Andrew Oliver.* Boston, 1770, no. 80.

1773
Mather Series

1. [Mather, Samuel]. *An Attempt to Shew, that America must be known to the Ancients.* Boston, 1773, no. 98.
2. [Prout, Timothy]. *Diana's Shrines Turned into Ready Money.* New York, 1773, no. 99.

1774
Randolph Series

1. [Randolph, John]. *Considerations on the Present State of Virginia.* [Williamsburg] 1774, no. 133.
2. [Nicholas, Robert Carter]. *Considerations on the Present State of Virginia Examined.* [Williamsburg] 1774, no. 129.

Chandler Series

1. [Chandler, Thomas Bradbury]. *A Friendly Address to All Reasonable Americans*. New York, 1774, nos. 107a-e.
2a. [Livingston, Philip]. *The Other Side of the Question*. New York, 1774, no. 128.
2b. [Lee, Charles]. *Strictures On a Pamphlet, entitled A "Friendly Address to all Reasonable Americans*. Philadelphia, 1774, nos. 125a-f.
3. [Barry, Henry]. *The Strictures on the Friendly Address Examined*. [Boston] 1775, nos. 151a-b.

Seabury Series

1. [Seabury, Samuel]. *Free Thoughts on the Proceedings of the Continental Congress*. New York, 1774, nos. 136a-c.
2. [Hamilton, Alexander]. *A Full Vindication of the Measures of the Congress*. New York, 1774, no. 116.
3a. [Seabury, Samuel]. *The Congress Canvassed*. New York, 1774, nos. 135a-b.
3b. [Seabury, Samuel]. *A View of the Controversy*. New York, 1774, nos. 137a-b.
4. [Hamilton, Alexander]. *The Farmer Refuted*. New York, 1775, no. 173.
5. [Seabury, Samuel. *The Republican Dissected*. New York, 1775.] Intended as an answer to Hamilton's pamphlet, but apparently was never published, no. 195.

Drayton Series

1. [Drayton, William Henry]. *A Letter from Freeman [sic] of South-Carolina*. Charleston, S. C., 1774, no. 111.
2. *Some Fugitive Thoughts on a Letter Signed Freeman . . . by a Back Settler*. [Charleston, S. C.] 1774, no. 142.
3. [*Comment on a Pamphlet by "A Backsettler"* . . . . Charleston, S. C., 1774.] No copy located, may be a ghost, no. 109.

1775

Gordon Series

1. Gordon, William. *A Discourse Preached December 15th, 1774*. Boston, 1775, nos. 167a-c.
2a. [Gray, Harrison]. *Observations on the Reverend Pastor of Roxbury's Thanksgiving Discourse*. Boston, 1775, no. 171.
2b. *Remarks upon a Discourse Preached December 15th*. [Boston?] 1775, no. 192.

Galloway Series

1. [Galloway, Joseph]. *A Candid Examination of the Mutual Claims of Great-Britain and the Colonies*. New York, 1775, no. 164.
2. [Dickinson, John and Charles Thomson]. "To the Author of a Pamphlet entitled 'A Candid Examination,' " *Pennsylvania Journal*, March 8, 1775, no. 165 note.

3. [Galloway, Joseph]. *A Reply to an Address to the Author of a Pamphlet, entitled "A Candid Examination. . . ."* New York, 1775, no. 165.

1776

Paine Series

1. [Paine, Thomas]. *Common Sense.* Philadelphia, 1776, no. 222.
2a. [Chalmers, James]. *Plain Truth.* Philadelphia, 1776, no. 208.
2a1. *Remarks on a Late Pamphlet Entitled Plain Truth.* Philadelphia, 1770, no. 225.
2b. [Inglis, Charles]. *The Deceiver Unmasked.* New York, 1776, no. 219.
2c. [Adams, John]. *Thoughts on Government.* Philadelphia, 1776, no. 205.
2c1. [Braxton, Carter]. *An Address to the Convention of the Colony and Ancient Dominion of Virginia.* Philadelphia, 1776, no. 207.
2d. *Civil Prudence, Recommended to the Thirteen United Colonies.* Norwich, 1776, no. 211.

Index

Numbers refer to entries.